'What a valuable goldmine of ideas, innovations and connections for Solution Focused practitioners across Asia and indeed around the world. The chapters are short, the contexts specific, the examples telling, the skill evident – and the passion of all these SF workers is infectious. This book will be both a key piece in the developing SF jigsaw and also an inspiration to those in other parts of the world to write about their work and experiences.'

Dr Mark McKergow, *Centre for Solutions Focus at Work*
Edinburgh, Scotland

'This remarkable book offers fascinating examples of skillful, culturally respectful implementation of the Solution Focused coaching approach in a wide range of contemporary Asian settings. Readers will be inspired and uplifted by fresh, creative ideas for implementing SF coaching in a manner that simultaneously appreciates, embraces and productively incorporates clients' unique individual contexts and cultural traditions. This book is a "must-read" for anyone seeking to enhance their skills and competence in SF coaching in diverse settings ranging from the emerging field of relationship coaching to education and business.'

Yvonne Dolan, *Founding Director of the*
Institute for Solution-Focused Therapy, USA
Co-founder of Solution Focused Brief Therapy
Association (SFBTA) and the International Alliance of
Solution-Focused Training Institute (IASTI)

'This essential book is on the application of Solution Focused approach within the Asian context. A must read for any practitioners doing work in this region or wanting to better understand the systemic implications for people from this region. We live in a globalised society where we are more interconnected than ever before. As such, anyone in the helping profession has an ethical responsibility to both understand and examine how philosophies originating from the west apply in various parts of the world. This book is the first of its kind for Asia and a valuable read for all practitioners.'

Dr Saba Hasanie, *Managing Director and Senior Partner,*
OSC Leadership Development, Singapore

"It's so Western! It won't work in a culture that doesn't share these individualistic values." "Coaching is just to bring poor performers up to speed." I have often heard this kind of comment about Solution Focused coaching and this book proves both of them wrong. Spanning a huge range of applications, including business and management, health, and everyday

conversations, this book is a rich collection showing how SF coaching is taking root throughout Asia.'

Jenny Clarke, *Partner, sfwork, Edinburgh, Scotland*

'This is an invaluable resource for solution focused methodology in action. It is a wealth of knowhow from practitioners who have taught, instilled and implemented positive change in individuals, leaders and organisations across various vocational settings. A must-read for those seeking to build thriving organisations and in everyday life.'

Koh Juat Muay, *Chief at Nano-E, Singapore*

'This extraordinary collection offers valuable SF perspectives of how to be present with a client coming from an Asian heart.'

Peter Szabo, *MCC, Switzerland*

'This is a must read book! The editors have provided an extraordinary range of applications of Solution Focus (SF) Coaching in Asia. The cases include examples of how SF Coaching is applied to leadership develop-ment, organisational development, and team coaching as well as career, health and wellness, family and faith based coaching. The applications across so many contexts gives testament to the range of issues that the SF approach can successfully be applied. However, this book should not be of interest to only SF coaches. It should also be read by anyone interested in learning more about coaching applications in Asia written by professionals who have extensive experience in the region.'

Hermann Ditzig, *Founder and CEO of LeAD*
Consulting Group, Past President of ICF Singapore

Solution Focused Coaching in Asia

Through inspiring stories illustrating the diverse application of coaching within Asian contexts, this data-rich volume dives into the theory and practice of Solution Focused coaching offering numerous tools and techniques that can be used immediately.

With the rising demand for coaching across Asia, there is a need for coaches to have access to up-to-date practice-based evidence of its effectiveness. The Solution Focused approach, as a social-constructionist approach, privileges the clients' experience, resources, and preferred future over an 'analytic' or deficit-oriented stance. Contributors analyse real case examples from many countries across Asia including Singapore, Malaysia, Indonesia, China, Taiwan, Hong Kong, Japan, Cambodia, and Sri Lanka. Practical in its approach, this book offers new insights into established areas of coaching and also highlights innovations in coaching in areas where Solution Focused coaching and other models have not reached until recently. These areas include health and wellness coaching for medical compliance needs, faith-based coaching, and coaching incarcerated fathers.

This is an essential and comprehensive resource that is written for both beginner and experienced coaches and addresses the need for effective and culturally sensitive coaching models in Asia. It will also be beneficial for managers and health care professionals looking to enhance their work through coaching skills.

Debbie Hogan is an accredited coach, psychotherapist, accredited supervisor, trainer, and author. Having learned Solution Focused practice from the developers, Insoo Kim Berg and Steve de Shazer, she became inspired and has been training others since 2004, when she founded the Academy of Solution Focused Training in Singapore.

Jane Tuomola is an accredited coach, clinical psychologist, coaching supervisor, trainer, and author. She has been using Solution Focused coaching for 15 years and been based in Asia for over 10 years. She is keen to make sure her work is both culturally sensitive and evidence based, and aims to inspire others to do the same.

Sukanya Wignaraja is an accredited coach, psychotherapist, trainer, and author. She was drawn to Solution Focused practice by its powerful and transformative qualities, and has been practicing SF coaching and therapy for 15 years. She has lived in Asia for over two decades and is now in private practice in Colombo, Sri Lanka.

Solution Focused Coaching in Asia

History, Key Concepts, Development, and Applications

Edited by Debbie Hogan, Jane Tuomola, and Sukanya Wignaraja

Routledge
Taylor & Francis Group

LONDON AND NEW YORK

Designed cover image: Keisuke Taketani

First published 2025
by Routledge
4 Park Square, Milton Park, Abingdon, Oxon OX14 4RN

and by Routledge
605 Third Avenue, New York, NY 10158

Routledge is an imprint of the Taylor & Francis Group, an informa business

British Library Cataloguing-in-Publication Data
A catalogue record for this book is available from the British Library

ISBN: 978-1-032-55636-9 (hbk)
ISBN: 978-1-032-55635-2 (pbk)
ISBN: 978-1-003-43148-0 (ebk)

DOI: 10.4324/9781003431480

Typeset in Times New Roman
by MPS Limited, Dehradun

Contents

Acknowledgments

To all our associates, graduates, attendees of our training, and to the authors of this book. We share the excitement and sense of deep gratitude for your contribution and for making this book a reality.

Debbie Hogan

To Dave, my husband and partner in life, work and play. To my precious daughter, Breda who brings me great joy every day. Thank you both for cheering me on and encouraging me through the rough times. To Jane and Sukanya, whom I adore, and with whom I have found great pleasure in working on this project. Without their diligence and persistence, it would not have been completed. And to Yvonne and Insoo, my mentors and friends who have inspired me, every step of the way.

Jane Tuomola

To my husband Petri for supporting me through the highs and lows of the writing and editing process for the second time. I have promised to take a break from writing for a while! To my children Alexandra and Oliver for bringing so much joy into our lives. To Debbie for introducing me to the SF approach 15 years ago and being my teacher, mentor, colleague, and above all dear friend. To Debbie and Sukanya for having fun on this journey together – what a great team to be part of. And thanks to all of my clients for inspiring me with their stories.

Sukanya Wignaraja

To my husband Ganeshan and my daughter Leela who always cheer me on from the sidelines and believe in me; to my guru, mentor and friend Debbie Hogan who has taught me everything I know about SF.

Foreword

This book is a welcome and valuable addition to the growing library of Solution Focused (SF) coaching experience. The SF approach is unusual; it seems to work equally well not only for many kinds of problem but also across many fields of endeavour, social classes, income levels – and national cultures. The many cases assembled by Debbie Hogan, Jane Tuomola, and Sukanya Wignaraja are testament to the ways that SF is being used in many Asian settings.

Some of the authors here are explicit in pondering how this American-developed, European-inflected way of working can sit so well within the more hierarchical, relationship-based and multi-faceted world of business and organisation in Asia. And they find, again and again, that it not only sits well but is taken up with enthusiasm, produces results and inspires people across the continent.

Having been involved with the SF scene for over thirty years, I have come to think it works so well because it fundamentally taps into the way we operate as people, finding and negotiating our way through a complex, subtle and emerging world. When executed with skill, SF has a way of flexing to suit the context and bringing about rapid, effective and lasting change. This latest collection is a valuable goldmine of ideas, innovations, and connections for SF practitioners across Asia and indeed around the world.

Dr Mark McKergow, The Centre for Solutions
Focus at Work, Edinburgh, Scotland – January 2024

Biographies of the Editors

Debbie Hogan

Debbie Hogan is the founder and Managing Director of the Academy of Solution Focused Training Pte Ltd. She and her team of associates have been involved in the quality development of training Solution Focused practitioners across the globe since 2004. She has been in Private Practice since 1993 as a psychotherapist, having worked with a wide spectrum of clinical issues, as an Executive and Leadership Coach with teams and individuals, and as a Supervisor and Mentor Coach. She is a Master Clinical Member and Clinical Supervisor with the Singapore Association for Counseling and a founding member of International Alliance of Solution Focused Teaching Institutes (IASTI). Debbie is a Master Solution Focused Coach with IASTI, Master Certified Coach with the ICF, Master Practitioner and Accredited Coach Supervisor and Mentor with the European Mentoring and Coaching Council. Her coach training is accredited with the International Coaching Federation as a Level 1 ACC, Level 2 PCC, and Level 3 MCC. Debbie has contributed to four books and is co-editor of *Solution Focused Practice in Asia* with Dave Hogan, Jane Tuomola, and *Solution Focused Practice Around the World* with Kirsten Dierolf, Sukanya Wignaraja, and Svea van der Hoorn. From the US, Debbie has lived in Korea, Japan, Okinawa, New Guinea, and Singapore, where she has lived and worked for the past 37 years. As a Third Culture Kid, she has experienced the unique flavour of living and working abroad.

Jane Tuomola

Dr Jane Tuomola has her own company in Singapore where she has worked for 11 years. She works as both a Clinical Psychologist (specialising in adult mental health) and as a Life and Executive Coach, and Coaching Supervisor. She is an Associate Fellow of the British Psychological Society; Master Solution Focused Practitioner with the International Alliance of Solution Focused Teaching Institutes; a Professional Certified Coach with the International Coaching Federation; and a Senior Practitioner and an Accredited Coach Supervisor with the European Mentoring and Coaching Council. She is an Associate Trainer and Supervisor with the Academy of

Solution Focused Training in Singapore, offering training in Solution Focused Brief Therapy, coaching and coaching supervision. One area of expertise is cross-cultural adjustment – having lived and worked in four countries across three continents she uses her personal and professional experience to help people thrive in new surroundings. She is passionate about cross-cultural psychology and culturally sensitive work – hence the passion for writing on this topic to help other practitioners. She is a co-editor of *Solution Focused Practice in Asia* with Dave Hogan, Debbie Hogan, and Alan Yeo, as well as having written research articles and other book chapters.

Sukanya Wignaraja

Sukanya Wignaraja has a Masters in Social Work from Oxford University, UK. She is a Master Solution Focused Practitioner with the International Alliance of Solution Focused Teaching Institutes and a Professional Certified Coach with the International Coach Federation. Sukanya worked in the mental health field in the UK for many years across a range of settings, including community teams, hospitals, and the prison service. She was a Specialist Advisor in Social Work to the UK Foreign & Commonwealth Office. Sukanya was an Executive Coach and Senior Psychotherapist in mental health NGOs in Manila and Tokyo, where she also conducted training programmes for counsellors. Since 2017, Sukanya has been in private practice in Colombo, Sri Lanka where she works with individuals and couples and as an Executive Coach. Sukanya is a Mentor Coach and Associate Coach Trainer with the Academy of Solution Focused Training. She is a Clinical Supervisor, and is Co-Director of the Academy's Peer Supervision Programme. Sukanya was co-editor of *Solution Focused Practice Around the World* with Kirsten Dierolf, Debbie Hogan, and Svea van der Hoorn.

Contributors

Kapila Ahuja, BTech, Coach – ICF-ACC, Singapore

Helen Banwell, B App Sc Pod, M Hlth Sc Pod, PhD, Senior Lecturer in Podiatry, University of South Australia, Adelaide, Australia

Jesse Cai, BSc, Bchiro, Founder and Chiropractor, Square One Active Recovery, Singapore

Chee Seng Cha, MIT, MFA, Coach – ICF-PCC, consultant and trainer, Co-Identity, Singapore

Ru-Ya Chang, MS, ICF-MCC Executive Coach, Supervisor and Psychotherapist, Taiwan and China, Vice President, Blooming Light Coaching Academy, Taiwan

Sam Chia, MBA, FCCA, FCA Singapore, Coach – ICF-PCC, Managing Director, SC Coaching Asia Pte Ltd, Singapore

Edwin Choy, MSc, ICF-PCC, Co-founder, Centre for Fathering, Singapore

Kirsten Dierolf, MA, Director, SolutionsAcademy, Germany

Kristin Graham, PhD, BPscyhSc (Hons), DipAppSc (Podiatry), Academic, University of South Australia, Adelaide, Australia

Dian Handayani, MA, MSc, Certified Sex Coach, Sex Therapist, Art psychotherapist, Nambani Pte Ltd, Singapore

Marabelle Heng, BSc, BPod, MSc, Adjunct Lecturer and PhD candidate, University of South Australia, Adelaide, Australia

Dave Hogan, BA, MTh, Coach – ICF-MCC, EMCC-SP, ESIA, Consultant and Trainer, Director of the Academy of Solution Focused Training, Singapore

Debbie Hogan, BS, MS, ICF-MCC, EMCC-MP, ESIA (EMCC), Psychotherapist, Coach, Supervisor, Trainer, Managing Director, Academy of Solution Focused Training Pte Ltd, Singapore

Chris Iveson, BSc, Therapist, Coach, Trainer, Founder of BRIEF, London, UK

Sandeep Joshi, MSc, Executive Enterprise Coach, Standard Chartered Bank, Managing Director, MASSIVUE Pte Ltd, Singapore

Karen Leong, BAcc, Founding Director, Influence Solutions Pte Ltd, Singapore

Cheng-Tseng Lin, PhD, Psychotherapist, Supervisor, and Trainer, Assistant Professor, National Open University, Taiwan

Juan Pablo Lisdero, BA, ICF-ACC, ASFP, OELP, Head of HR External Markets, Dubai, UAE

Lawrence Luo, PhD, Professor, Psychiatrist, Coach, Supervisor, Trainer of Affiliated Mental Health Centre, ZheJiang University, School of Medicine (HangZhou Seventh People's Hospital), President of Hangzhou Solution Focused Institute, Hangzhou, China

David Macdonald, BA, MSc, Coach – ICF-ACC, Founder and CEO, DJMAC GK, Japan

Abhishek Mehta, MBA, Head of Transformation, Client Coverage Technology, Standard Chartered Bank, Singapore

Steven Nicaud, BMiss, Senior Pastor, Antioch Centre for the Nations, Singapore and President, Moved with Compassion, USA

Yee Lin Ng, BA, Coach – ICF-PCC, Consultant, Community Business, Hong Kong

Jaime Ong-Yeoh, Master of Managerial Psychology, Coach, Change management consultant, Intercultural and organisational culture consultant, Kuala Lumpur, Malaysia

Julie Samuel, MBA, MSFP, Career Coach – ICF-PCC, Facilitator, Mentor Coach, Singapore

Keisuke Taketani, MA, Certified SF Coach, Graphic Facilitator, Freelancer, Ashiya, Japan

Alex Tan, BA, Executive Coach (ICF-PCC, EMCC-SP, IASTI-MSFC) and Consultant, Founder and Managing Director of Avidity International, Malaysia and Singapore

Benny Tan, Founder and CEO, Dealxpert Sales System, Singapore

Jane Tuomola, BA, MA, DClinPsy, Coach (ICF-PCC, EMCC-SP), Coaching Supervisor (ESIA), Clinical Psychologist, Director of Pebble Psychology Pte. Ltd, Associate Academy of Solution Focused Training, Singapore

Joseph Wang, HDip, BA, Counsellor (Advanced SF Practitioner) and Coach, Ling Yue Psychological Studio, Hangzhou, China

Keran Wei, Undergraduate Student BPod, University of South Australia, Adelaide, Australia

Dennis Welch, BBS, ICF-PCC, MSFC, CSFC, Certified Coach, Trainer, Mentor, Assessor, Cambodia Director of the Academy of Solution Focused Training, Singapore, Kampot, Cambodia

Sukanya Wignaraja, MA Edin, MSc Oxon, Solution Focused Coach, Therapist and Trainer, Professional Certified Coach – ICF-PCC, EMCC-SP, ESIA, CSFT, Private practice in Colombo, Sri Lanka

Huajing Yang, BA, Positive Discipline Trainer, Encouragement Consultant Master, Parenting Coach, Counsellor, Hangzhou, China

Confidentiality

Throughout the preparation of this book, protecting client confidentiality has been of the utmost importance to the authors and editors. The majority of the clients in this book (whether individual, couples, groups, or teams) are based on actual coaching clients seen by the authors. These clients' details have been anonymised by changing names and key details of their stories. All clients have read the chapter in which their story appears and given written consent for their story to be included. All organisations mentioned by name have also given written consent for the name of their organisation to be included in the chapter. Some authors have chosen to further deidentify their work by creating composite cases drawn from several real coaching experiences. As such any resemblance to real clients is purely coincidental.

A Note about Naming

Asian names with a Chinese origin are normally written in the format Family Name First Name Middle Name. Due to publishing requirements, all names have to appear in the book in the order first name, middle name, family name.

Section 1

History and Philosophy of the Solution Focused Approach

1 Introduction to Solution Focused Coaching in Asia

Debbie Hogan

Overview of the Introduction

This introduction chapter of the book will provide an overview of the mindset, key assumptions, and processes involved in Solution Focused (SF) practice.

I will also share a basic framework in SF coaching, highlighting the significance of the mindset and philosophy that underpins this unique approach. I also hope to clarify some common misunderstandings about what SF coaching is, in order to provide clarity around what makes this approach unique.

Finally, I will give a summary of the 35 chapters from 35 authors represented in this book. Each of the ten sections represents a theme or common topic in coaching and provides rich case scenarios, personal experiences, and practical 'how-to-do' examples that the reader can adapt to their setting.

What Is the Solution Focused Approach?

Based on a Mindset and Philosophy

The SF approach is not a technique, but rather a mindset and philosophy of how we engage with an individual, team, or organisations. Since it is not technique driven, it is more about how we engage in the change mechanism and invite the person to consider a different perspective, emotion, behaviour, or approach in managing their situation. Insoo Kim Berg says we invite the other to shift their perspective with questions that evoke a different pathway of thinking with 'a tap on the shoulder.' She suggests we might stand 'one step behind' and view the situation from the clients' point of view. And then we give a little 'tap on the shoulder' and explore with the client to consider different points of view (Berg & de Shazer, 1993). It engages imagination and creativity versus the linear, cause and effect methodology that often leads to the blame frame. If something is wrong, then there must be a cause, and once we find the causality, we fix, solve, and remove it. Chances are people have tried everything they know and hence go around in circles.

DOI: 10.4324/9781003431480-2

Early Developers

Steve de Shazer, Insoo Kim Berg, and their colleagues were pivotal in the development of SF practice at the Brief Family Therapy Center (BFTC) in Milwaukee, Wisconsin, USA. They wanted to distinguish themselves as different from the problem-focused paradigm of the Mental Research Institute (Haley, 1991) and instead, explore the solution narrative, hence their approach became known as Solution Focused.

As a longtime collaborator with the original developers of the SF approach, Steve de Shazer and Insoo Kim Berg, Yvonne Dolan is a co-developer of the original evidence-based version of the SF approach, and describes the essence of SF. She shares:

> Solution Focused therapy is a future-focused, goal-directed, evidence-based approach that helps people and organisations achieve change by creating solutions, rather than focusing on problems and the events that led to them. This approach motivates and empowers people to develop lasting solutions by focusing directly on desired changes instead of dwelling on the problem. (Dolan, 2024, p. 2)

Cross-over from Therapy to Coaching

As this approach became more widely accepted and successful, other practitioners outside of the therapy space started to apply this practical and effective approach in coaching, business, organisations, education, and many other areas. Jackson and McKergow (2007) developed the OSKAR model and Szabo (Berg & Szabo, 2005) developed Brief Coaching and subsequently, many more books have emerged about SF coaching. The common features presented in these books represent the key ideas based on SF therapy. Most coaching approaches come from the human development movement and psychological theories (Brock, 2012). So, it comes as no surprise that a successful and pragmatic therapeutic approach was adapted to other areas. One of the unique features of SF practice is its isomorphic quality, and over time, practitioners have experienced the ease and natural adaptation of this approach into coaching.

Development of Solution Focused Coaching in Asia

I had discussions with many people across Asia, Europe, and the US to gain an understanding of SF coaching in Asia. Almost every conversation I had circled back to the same individuals who were pivotal in bringing SF coaching to Asia. There were a few that studied SF therapy in the US or Canada and subsequently developed SF coaching in their area. Others had been trained by Insoo Kim Berg in SF therapy, but not in coaching. It is my impression, therefore, that the key people involved in the development of SF coaching in Asia include Mark McKergow, Peter Szabo, Kirsten Dierolf, and the Academy of Solution Focused Training (ASFT; Dave & Debbie Hogan).

The ASFT, founded by Debbie Hogan in 2004, was the first to bring SF coaching and professional certification in SF coaching to Singapore, which then spread across the region. The ASFT was accredited by the Canadian Council of Professional Certification (CCPC) in 2004 and was instrumental in the CCPC adding SF Coaching Certification to its list of accreditations. In 2010, Debbie and Dave, as founding members of the International Alliance of Solution Focused Teaching Institutes (IASTI), were part of the team to create certification in therapy and coaching. In 2016, the ASFT was accredited by the International Coaching Federation (ICF) to offer Level 1 ACC and Level 2 PCC credentials. In 2023, the ASFT was accredited by ICF to offer Level 3 MCC credentials. Mark McKergow and Jenny Clarke were invited to Singapore in 2004 to help the ASFT launch the SF coaching programme and in 2007 Peter Szabo joined the team and in 2014 Kirsten joined the team. The ASFT has continued to train, mentor, and supervise graduates of their programme, which is now a global community. 2024 is the 20th Anniversary of the ASFT.

Keys in Solution Focused Coaching

A bedrock of SF coaching is the mindset, philosophy, and assumptions that practitioners share. Kirsten Dierolf highlights these important keys in Chapter 2. While there might be 'techniques' involved in coaching, the stance of the coach rests on these keys.

Common techniques or a basic coaching framework involves the use of 'elegant tools' in the form of questions (Jackson & McKergow, 2007). The structure of these questions is intentionally phrased, using presuppositional language, and reflects a co-constructive process based on collaborative mutual respect and the stance of the coach, based on the key assumptions below (Solution-Focused Brief Therapy Association, 2013):

- Clients are the ultimate experts on their own lives and what is needed in order for their lives to get better.
- SF practitioners are the experts on which questions to ask in order to co-construct practical, sustainable real-life solutions with their clients.
- No problem happens all the time; there are always exceptions that can be utilised.
- Small steps can lead to larger changes.
- The future is both created and negotiable.
- Clients have a good reason for the ways that they think and behave.

Solution Focused Coaching in a Nutshell

First Session Process

> *If you don't know exactly where you're going, how will you know when you get there?*
>
> – Steve Maraboli

In addition to developing a comfortable connection between the coach and client as a start, the first session establishes clarity around the desired outcome and direction of the coaching. This is of paramount importance. The client not only wants something different or better but also is ready to do something about it and sees themselves as part of the process. The coach asks about the client's best hopes from the coaching session and enquires about clues or indicators that the client has got what they wanted. A useful SF question is: 'What might be the first small clue you were on the right track?'

In exploring the importance or meaning of working on something, the client often gets in touch with deeper motives or values. Coaching is about meaning-making and invites the client to explore the significance, within their context. Often it leads to a stronger sense of purpose when connected to personal values.

Through our elegant questions, we discover capabilities, experiences, knowledge, and skills about the client, which can be utilised in helping them achieve what they want. Often unknown, forgotten, or not considered significant, with our expert ears, we unleash a reservoir of client's existing capabilities and past successes. Questions include:

- You mentioned that as a manager, you make hundreds of decisions every day. What do you know already about good decision-making?
- How have you approached similar situations in the past?

Miracle Question

The miracle question is another unique feature of SF coaching and can be utilised in different ways. There are subtleties in maximising its impact and effectiveness. The intent is to engage imagination and create a different pathway of creative thinking, versus the linear, cause and effect method. We partner with the client, seeking a willingness to engage 'in a strange question,' 'requiring imagination,' and 'are they willing?' This helps to set the stage for maximum effect. We slow down, giving them time to think and reflect.

The coach explores rich details of the client's narrative – life with the problem gone – with the client as part of the picture. We explore how they are feeling, thinking, reacting differently and how they would notice being 'at their best' in spite of everything.

The coach explores insights, learnings, applications, reflections from this process, and the contribution it has made to the client's situation. This can be followed up with a scale or exploring what has emerged from the process.

Scaling Tool to Chart Progress

Scaling is very versatile and enables the client to view their own progress in a situation. Most people are familiar with scaling. In SF, we use the scale within the context of the conversation. The parameters are based on 1–10, with '10' representing the presence of something and '1' as the lowest. For instance, if a client presented their coaching topic as having anxiety related to public speaking, we would want to explore what they wanted instead. It's hard to work on the absence of something ('I don't want to be anxious when …'). We would co-construct what the client wants instead of anxiety, which might lead to having more confidence. So, we would scale 'confidence' and not anxiety. This is a unique feature of SF scaling. We can scale many things such as progress, willingness to change, hope, project completion, or decision-making. The nature of the scale emerges during the context of the coaching conversation.

Coping

When relevant, asking how a client managed a situation or is coping with a situation can add value to the perception of the client. When the client shares the problem narrative, it can provide validation and acknowledgement. SF is like a resilience model, in that we are curious to explore the client's capabilities and self-efficacy, and how they have managed in spite of the difficulty. This can serve as reminder that the client has managed thus far.

Outside Perspective

Since things happen interactionally and in the context of the client's life, an added dimension is the outside perspective. The coach asks questions about what the client's colleagues, team, family, or friends might notice that's different. Sometimes clients struggle with imagining themselves a certain way, so engaging the outside perspective provides a full panoramic view of internal awareness from the client and external awareness from others.

Exploring Exceptions

Exceptions are described as times in the client's life when a problem is not happening, happening less, or is somehow less troublesome (Dolan, 2024). Clients tend to think in dichotomies, as either all or none. Asking questions around times when exceptions occurred can be useful as it evokes awareness of shades of grey. It serves to remind them that if they did it once, they can do it again: 'When was a recent time you could have felt anxious and you didn't give in to that?'

Offering Evidence-Based Affirms

The SF coaching approach often uses compliments as a way of affirming a client. In the Asian culture, however, people often feel shy about receiving compliments and can discount them. How they are offered and how they are received is a delicate process. Giving compliments needs to be done in a culturally sensitive way and the coach uses their understanding of the client to offer a compliment that fits the client. Making sure it is evidence based using something we hear, see, or observe something the client says or does is important. One subtle, yet powerful way is to offer an indirect compliment: 'You mentioned you gave your monthly report to your team and they all clapped. How did you do that?'

Wrapping up the Session

Ending the session involves connecting the thread of what the client wants from the session and their progress and satisfaction of where they are. We can offer a summary or invite the client to give a summary of what they learned, what is different as a result, and any action steps to keep things moving in the right direction. We also partner with the client to get a sense of how far along they are in the topic and when it is time to end the sessions.

Second Session Process – EARS

The coach uses the EARS (Elicit, Amplify, Reinforce, Start Again) process (Berg & De Jong, 2013) to review the client's progress towards the desired outcome established during the first session and explore change in the right direction and the differences it made.

• Elicit

By exploring 'What is better?' the intention is to explore change in the desired direction. The SF coach is curious about any small, even unnoticed change, which can jar the client's memory and often results in acknowledging some things are different in a positive way, which can lead to more noticeable changes. We encourage the client to be an observer of their own life, to draw out important elements of change in the right direction. Sample questions include: I'm curious about what's been better or different, even just a little bit? What have you noticed? What do you suppose your boss noticed?

• Amplify

We amplify what we hear to support the changes the client wants. The coach explores the behaviours, actions, and specifics of what led to the change, which often leads to the client's heightened awareness in making these important connections. For example asking: How did you manage that? What difference has this made?

• Reinforce

In exploring the client's capability and noticing these changes, the coach reinforces what they hear, which often surfaces the client's sense of self-efficacy and their ability to move in the direction of desired change, even if a very small step occurred.

• Start Again

The coach continues to the explore desired change and the impact it has had on the client and their situation by exploring what else is better, and then amplifying and reinforcing each change.

End of Session Review

The coach engages the client in a review of what was discussed, learnings, and reflections and if appropriate, explores how they want to continue with the current coaching topic. While the questions the SF coach asks sound simple, it takes practice and expertise to stay in the 'not knowing' stance (Anderson & Goolishian, 1992) and remain curious, to support the desired outcome. It is important to stay focused on the solution narrative. The quality of our questions should be focused on stretching the client's awareness and not to satisfy our need for information (McKergow, 2023).

Overview of the Chapters

The 35 chapters in this book represent ten sections: History and Philosophy of the Solution Focused Approach; Coaching in Organisations; Executive and Leadership Coaching; Team Coaching; Life Coaching; Coaching with Youth, Family, and Schools; Health and Wellness Coaching; Faith-Based Coaching; Career Coaching; and Novel Applications of SF Coaching. The final Chapter 35 includes the editors' thoughts and reflections on this book. The chapters in each section are summarised below.

Section 1: History and Philosophy of the Solution Focused Approach

The inclusion of Kirsten Dierolf's 'History and Philosophy of the Solution Focused Approach' in Chapter 2 is pivotal to this book. Hopefully, it orients the reader with a solid background into the origins of this unique approach. Additionally, it provides a background to the theory development and the subsequent phases of its development with the founders, Steve de Shazer and Insoo Kim Berg. There is also an exploration of possible ways in which the SF approach fits well within Asian philosophies, such as Buddhism and Taoism, which advocate for mindfulness and being fully present in the moment and in cultivating awareness of the present without attachment to the past or concern for the future.

Section 2: Solution Focused Coaching in Organisations

Four authors present their work with large-scale organisations and how SF coaching made a positive impact.

Juan Lisdero, in Chapter 3, describes an initial SF coaching pilot project that involved 500 people in a large-scale change management process with a multinational company in Asia. It was so successful, it was escalated to more than 5,000 people across different Asian countries.

In Chapter 4, Kapila Ahuja was part of a Diversity, Equity, and Inclusion initiative at a large organisation in Singapore to promote more women into senior leadership positions and to create a more inclusive and diverse workplace. A large pool of SF coaches were trained to make coaching more widely accessible for women leaders. The impact of this initiative led to enhanced leadership capabilities as well as organisational shifts in culture, promoting learning, open communication, and improved retention rates.

In Chapter 5, Karen Leong describes how to transcend common biases against coaching encountered in working with leaders in Asia and how these conversations increased trust, empowerment, and accountability, and increased talent development within an organisation. Through facilitating everyday coaching conversations, leaders were able to experience the power and the important differences that coaching conversations can make.

In Chapter 6, Abhishek Mehta and Sandeep Joshi offer an interesting and compelling chapter on how they facilitated positive micro change by utilising SF coaching. As a result, they rolled out this initiative at a macro level to create a coaching culture at Standard Chartered Bank in Singapore. They describe how they overcame challenges, such as resistance to change, and how navigating through the traditional Asian hierarchical organisational culture led to benefits in the complex business landscape.

Section 3: Executive and Leadership Coaching

Six chapters offer insights, experiences, and reflections in this field.

In Chapter 7, Sam Chia emphasises important considerations when coaching Asian leaders. He highlights the distinctive features of Asian leadership and the importance of focusing on cultural and historical factors that shape expectations for leaders. He strongly advocates the use of SF coaching in developing and improving leadership effectiveness in Asia.

In Chapter 8, Yee Lin Ng designs and coaches C-suites and organisations on their Diversity and Inclusion journey in Hong Kong. She reviews a powerful case example from her work, in engaging the client using the power of imagination, and shares the significant results experienced by the client.

In Chapter 9, Jane Tuomola interviews Alex Tan on a case example of working with two founders of a company, utilising a combination of individual and team coaching to strengthen their partnership and business. He shares his insights, experiences, and reflections on working in the Asian cultural context as well as highlighting the differences between entrepreneurial culture and corporate settings.

In Chapter 10, Cheng-Tseng Lin and Ru-Ya Chang showcase 'Solution Focused Executive Coaching in Taiwan.' They illustrate this using a case study with a transcript so the reader can understand and appreciate the powerful conversations that SF coaching can evoke. Through this experience, the executive was able to enhance motivation and engagement of his team, which led to new initiatives and sustainable growth for the company.

In Chapter 11, David MacDonald highlights the business differences that need to be understood when working in Japan and how an SF coaching framework can be used to support Japanese business leaders for better performance.

In Chapter 12, Jaime Ong-Yeoh describes her journey as a change manager and cultural consultant using SF coaching. She shares her reflections on both the cultural challenges faced by her clients as well as her own learnings from coaching.

Section 4: Team Coaching

Three chapters share their case examples and the positive impact SF team coaching had on the teams and the organisations.

In Chapter 13, Dave Hogan shares case examples of team coaching across Asia who were struggling and on the brink of despair. Through the use of 'What else' questions, he demonstrates how teams were able to move forwards and find hope in spite of challenges.

Chapter 14, Debbie Hogan and Jane Tuomola present the power of team coaching on the team as a unit and how it enhanced the team's performance, raised moral, and increased productivity for the organisation.

In Chapter 15, Cheng-Tseng Lin and Ru-Ya Chang describe the Taiwanese business context and the specific cultural challenges that can affect the role of the team coach. They share a Taiwanese enterprise case study using an SF team coaching process and the positive impact it had on the team.

Section 5: Life Coaching

Five chapters describe various applications of life coaching in Asia.

Jane Tuomola in Chapter 16 explores the impact of culture in the challenges of 'Thriving Through Transitions Using Solution Focused Coaching' and how to listen to a client's story with an SF mindset using the Chinese character 'tīng' (to listen).

In Chapter 17, Sukanya Wignaraja examines how SF coaching can be used to help clients work through difficult decision-making situations and dilemmas where cultural norms and expectations are involved.

Joseph Wang, in Chapter 18, shares the power of SF Coaching with female clients in China who are looking for effective ways to handle the challenges of growing up in a patriarchal culture, from being passive to proactive, in finding their self-worth and creating new meanings in their lives.

In Chapter 19, Chris Iveson and Jane Tuomola highlight examples of when performance coaching makes a significant impact during critical points in the life of a client when exploring 'being at your best.'

In Chapter 20, Dian Handayani discusses how emotions and shame are addressed with sex coaching within Southeast Asia and how an SF approach facilitates empowerment for the client to achieve their desired outcomes.

Section 6: Coaching with Youth, Families, and Schools

Three chapters cover different aspects of coaching with youth, families, and schools.

In Chapter 21, Debbie Hogan highlights the use of SF coaching in three areas of relationship coaching: with couples, youth, and parents; and discusses the interactional nature of change, how the coach facilitates alternative views for the client on themselves and their context, which leads to a sense of self-efficacy.

In Chapter 22, Lawrence Luo and Huajing Yang explore SF coaching in addressing the common response of 'I don't know' with youth. They describe how a 'game-like' approach in inviting the youth to 'make a guess' facilitates rapport, opening up an alternate pathway of communication.

In Chapter 23, Edwin Choy shares how SF coaching is applied in four areas within schools. He shares examples and reflections from the clients and the impact on the educational setting.

Section 7: Health and Wellness Coaching

Three chapters highlight different areas of health and wellness coaching.

Lawrence Luo and Huajing Yang in Chapter 24 discuss how the SF approach fits well with Chinese cultural values, by focusing on strengths and resources to minimise the sense of shame or loss of face for not following medical advice. The coach acknowledges and validates the challenges and co-creates a more self-empowered view of taking ownership for their own treatment.

In Chapter 25, Marabelle Heng, Helen Banwell, Keran Wei, and Kristin Graham present considerations and recommendations for facilitating client compliance with diabetic treatment. Instead of the usual practice of telling, giving, and educating, the clinicians share how co-designing treatment strategies make a positive difference in treatment compliance.

Jesse Cai, in Chapter 26, shares how SF coaching conversations aided his practice in Singapore by helping pain sufferers cultivate a positive mindset and increased their sense of self-efficacy and control.

Section 8: Faith-Based Coaching

Two chapters highlight coaching in spiritual contexts.

In Chapter 27, Steven Nicaud, a pastor, describes spontaneous moments in which coachable opportunities surfaced and how this led to impactful and meaningful conversations.

In Chapter 28, Dennis Welch discusses how SF coaching can be a catalyst for change in Asian Christian ministry settings and shares a case example.

Section 9: Career Coaching

Two chapters focus on two different aspects of career coaching as an internal and external career coach.

In Chapter 29, Joyce Wing Tung Tse, in her role as an HR professional, describes the impressive development of the OMRON APAC Development Centre, to help their talent work towards their future career aspirations. With the success of the programme, the company aims to expand this further.

In Chapter 30, Julie Samuel highlights the usefulness of SF coaching in career coaching. She describes step by step, using the OSKAR coaching framework, how this approach facilitated clients resolving challenges and experiencing 'aha' moments.

Section 10: Novel Applications of SF Coaching

Five chapters highlight novel applications of SF coaching, which include using visual language with SF coaching, graphic coaching, sales coaching, and group coaching within prisons.

In Chapter 31, Chee Seng Cha shares a case study demonstrating the transformative power of SF coaching with Chinese idioms and proverbs using BIKABLO visualisation techniques. The case study demonstrates how visual notes and SF coaching intertwine to enable profound personal growth.

In Chapter 32, Keisuke Taketani highlights the transformative opportunity for individuals to 'see' situations from different perspectives and how the integration of visual thinking in coaching can unlock even greater potential.

In Chapter 33, Benny Tan discusses the differences and synergies between selling and coaching, and uses a case example to illustrate the specific application and the positive impact.

In Chapter 34, Edwin Choy shares a moving example of utilising SF coaching with a group of incarcerated fathers in Changi Prison in Singapore who had become estranged from their families and struggling with the impact of shame. Through the 'I CAN CHANGE' programme, these fathers were able to rebuild and reconnect with their families and regain their self-worth, not only for themselves but also in the eyes of their families.

In the concluding Chapter 35, the editors share their reflections, thoughts, and themes that have emerged across the book related to SF coaching in Asia. The editors reflect across time how SF coaching has expanded and grown in Asia. Interesting reflections emerge around culture and context and the significance of these themes for this book. The book ends with reflective guided exercises to invite the reader to consider their desired future as the coach they aspire to be.

Conclusion

Through the years, I have heard some misunderstandings about what SF practice is and it being dismissed as a shallow and simplistic approach. Through this book, I hope the reader catches a clearer glimpse of the subtle, yet profound process, not encumbered by complex theories, and is instead drawn to the simplicity and elegance of the tools we use, in the form of eloquent questions. The authors of the 35 chapters represent both novice and seasoned SF coaches. What they share in common is their commitment to and belief in this way of coaching. We hope readers will be inspired, pleasantly surprised, curious, intrigued, and left wanting more.

References

Anderson, H. & Goolishian, H. (1992). The client is the expert: A not-knowing approach to therapy. In S. McNamee & K. J. Gergen (Eds), *Therapy as a social construction* (pp. 25–39). Sage.

Berg, I. K., & de Shazer, S. (1993). *A tap on the shoulder: 6 useful questions in building solutions.* BFTC Press.

Berg, I. K. & Szabo, P. (2005). *Brief coaching for lasting solutions.* W.W. Norton & Co.

Brock, V. G. (2012). *Sourcebook of coaching history.* CreateSpace Independent Publishing Platform.

De Jong, P. & Berg, I. K. (2013). *Interviewing for solutions.* Brooks/Cole. Cengage Learning.

Dolan, Y. (2024). *Solution-focused therapy: The basics.* Routledge.

Haley, J. (1991). *Problem-solving therapy* (2nd ed.). Jossey-Bass.

Jackson P. Z. & McKergow M. (2007). *The solutions focus: Making coaching and change simple* (2nd ed.). Nicholas Brealey.

McKergow, M. (2023, November 2). Information-gathering and world-stretching questions: A key distinction in solution focused practice. Substack. https://markmckergow.substack.com/p/34-information-gathering-questions

Solution Focused Brief Therapy Association (2013). *Solution focused therapy treatment manual for working with individuals: 2nd version.* Solution Focused Brief Therapy Association.

2 History and Philosophy of the Solution Focused Approach

Kirsten Dierolf

As I am writing this, I am keenly aware that I am a white woman from Europe writing in a book on Solution Focused practice in Asia, which parts of me deem inappropriate. However, the topic is close to my heart, and I will do my best to represent the history and philosophy of the Solution Focused approach and the relations I see to Asian philosophies as best as I know. Please forgive any misunderstandings.

This book is a collection of chapters on the application of Solution Focused coaching in Asia. As "Asia" is not one context but a multitude of cultures, languages, and contexts, Solution Focused practice, too, is what Ludwig Wittgenstein might have compared to a family resemblance. All sorts of practices can claim that they are "Solution Focused." This is why we would like to provide an introduction to the aspects that the authors of this book would like to stress when they speak about the Solution Focused approach.

Very Short History of the Solution Focused Approach

Harry Korman, Peter De Jong, and Sara Smock Jordan created a very useful overview of the theory development of the Solution Focused approach in their 2020 article titled "Steve de Shazer's theory development" (Korman et al., 2020). They were able to identify four phases in the theory development of the approach which are summarised below.

Phase 1: The Young de Shazer, 1969–1978

This phase was focused on interpreting Milton Erickson's principles and experimenting with his own strategies. Theories used were Heider's balance theory to understand Erickson's therapeutic "rules" and "Expectation States Theory" to explore Erickson's crystal ball technique. In this phase, we also see the beginning of de Shazer's shift from observing clients' systems to emphasising the interaction between clients and therapists. This shift, articulated in his 1999 reflection "Beginnings," laid the groundwork for two fundamental axioms: therapy as an observable interactional process and the therapist-client interaction as the minimum unit of analysis.

DOI: 10.4324/9781003431480-3

Phase 2: Early Brief Family Therapy Center, 1978–1982

In the period from 1978 to 1982, Steve de Shazer, along with colleagues at the Brief Family Therapy Center (BFTC), critiqued traditional family therapy concepts like homeostasis, resistance, paradox, and power, deeming them inadequate for understanding therapy as a "change-promoting" system. The team observed families and therapists collaboratively producing client change, prompting de Shazer to shift from studying the family-as-a-system to family-therapy-as-a-system. They replaced homeostasis with "morphogenesis" and resistance with "clients as cooperating."

This conceptual shift led to a change in therapeutic practices. The team saw the therapist's role as initiating change through interventions and tasks. A pivotal axiom emerged: "Change is the purpose of the therapist and client meeting." Another axiom emphasised observable interactions and cooperation as the mechanisms for client change. This phase laid the foundation for Solution Focused therapy, differentiating it from other therapeutic approaches.

Phase 3: de Shazer at BFTC, 1982–1989: The Emergence of Solution Focused Brief Therapy

In 1982, a pivotal shift occurred in Solution Focused Brief Therapy (SFBT) development, as recounted by Hopwood and de Shazer (1994). During a therapy session with a family facing 27 problems, the therapist, following Ericksonian principles, introduced a vague task known as the "formula first session task" (FFST). This task instructed the family to observe and report what they wanted to continue experiencing in their lives before the next session.

Surprisingly, two weeks later, the family returned with descriptions of 27 different positive occurrences, with 25 directly related to their initial concerns. This led to a groundbreaking realisation: problems could be solved without explicitly identifying them. The FFST was then systematically applied to various cases, resulting in a significant shift from the traditional focus on isomorphic problem descriptions to a more outcome-oriented approach emphasising solutions.

This transformative process prompted the abandonment of a theory of change, which required matching problem descriptions. Instead, interventions only needed to "fit" the client's context. This shift was formalised in de Shazer's 1985 publication, *Keys to Solution in Brief Therapy*, marking a transition from problem resolution to solution development. The therapy process evolved to focus on exploring exceptions and pre-session changes as key elements in promoting solution development. In the late 1980s, the team at BFTC focused on refining the therapeutic process and understanding how change occurs. They emphasised organising therapy around client goals and believed goals should be specific, concrete, behavioural, and realistic.

Two significant therapeutic techniques emerged during this period: the crystal ball technique and the miracle question. The crystal ball technique, a precursor to the miracle question, involved having clients imagine their successful future. It aimed to prompt different behaviour, leading to solutions. de Shazer integrated theories like Berger's expectation states theory and Axelrod's theory of cooperation to explain how the crystal ball technique influenced client expectations for change.

The miracle question, introduced by Insoo Kim Berg, asked clients to envision a future without their problems, fostering a future-oriented perspective. de Shazer explored the impact of language on problem construction, highlighting the importance of exceptions to open the door to change. This period solidified the shift from problem-focused therapy to SFBT, characterised by solution development in collaboration with clients.

Phase 4: The Late de Shazer and Wittgenstein, 1989–2005: Co-constructing Client Change Through Language

In the late 1980s, the SFBT community, led by Steve de Shazer and Insoo Kim Berg, entered what some term the "post-structural phase." This marked a departure from traditional structuralist views of therapy, emphasising the interactional, dialogic process of negotiating meanings between therapists and clients. The post-structural perspective, influenced by philosophers like Ludwig Wittgenstein, emphasises that meaning-making is an interactive, social process rather than an internal, individual one. In this view, words don't have fixed, essential meanings; instead, they are negotiated through dialogue. SFBT began to be described as "interactional constructivism." The therapist's role is to engage in a language game with the client, co-constructing solutions based on the client's language and descriptions of their preferred future. Tasks, while still offered, became less prominent, serving as summaries of interactionally constructed solutions.

Further Development of the Approach

In the years after de Shazer's and Insoo Kim Berg's death, the Solution Focused approach was developed further, both in theory and in the application of the approach in various fields such as education, social work, counselling, coaching (as is visible in this book), and organisational development. The connection to other post-modern, post-structural, and social-constructionist philosophies was strengthened: discursive psychology (Dierolf, 2011), Wittgenstein and complexity theory (Miller & McKergow, 2012), enactive and embodied cognition (McKergow, 2020), and others.

In 2017, there was an initiative of Solution Focused, narrative and collaborative practitioners to state the shared values which culminated in the Galveston Declaration (Gosnell et al., 2017) stating joint preferences for pluralism – differences of view, flux – differences of state, opening space – expanding choice and responsibility – generativity over singularity – of view, static – fixed states, closing space – removing choice and deficit focus – constraint. There are renewed and ongoing contacts between practitioners of social-constructionist and interactional approaches and we are hopeful that this will result in more publications and the development of the approaches through the exchange.

Associations like EBTA, SOLWorld, SFBTA, UKASFP, SFIO, and IASTI were founded, certifications devised, a treatment manual was designed in 2011 (Trepper et al., 2011), and "Clues" to recognising that a piece of work is using the Solution Focused approach published by SFCT (2009).

Possible Areas Where the Solution Focused Approach May Fit Well with Asian Philosophies

As stated earlier, "the Solution Focused approach" is not one unified approach, and there is surely also not one "Asian philosophy." This article will focus on Buddhism, Taoist philosophy, and Hinduism, in full awareness that Islam is the most practiced religion in Asia and knowing that there is a huge gap in the exploration of Islamic uses of Solution Focused ideas (which the author knows nothing about and can therefore not contribute to). It is almost preposterous to attempt an overview of where the Solution Focused approach and "Asian philosophy" overlap. However, the Solution Focused approach does clash with many of the traditional tenets of Western psychology and philosophy of psychology: presumptions of a body/mind differentiation, internal forces guiding human behaviour, causal internal mechanisms needed for the treatment of human difficulties, individualism, context-free diagnoses, and so on. The Solution Focused approach seems much more in harmony with some tenets more prevalent in Asian philosophy. This has been noted by researchers working with Asian American families (Lee & Mjelde-Mossey, 2004) and others (Shudofsky, M., Stefan, L., & Tozzi, G., personal communication, 7 January 2024).

So let us attempt the impossible and mention some areas of possible "fit" between the Solution Focused approach and Asian philosophy.

Present-Focused Orientation

The Solution Focused Approach places a strong emphasis on the present and future rather than dwelling extensively on the past, as it is not deemed necessary to analyse a problem in order to achieve a "fitting" solution. Explanations of why the problem exists are not necessary. The present is accepted "as is." The Solution Focused approach encourages clients to identify and work towards solutions in the current moment. Many Asian philosophies, such as Zen Buddhism and Taoist philosophies (as differentiated from Taoist religion), advocate for mindfulness and being fully present in the current moment. The concept of mindfulness in Buddhism, for example, involves cultivating awareness of the present without attachment to the past or concern for the future. In both the Solution Focused approach and Asian philosophies, reflecting on the past is seen as a useful way to generate learning for the future. The past is not analysed for the root cause of "the problem" but used as a resource for the present. This may be an instance where it is easier for followers of Asian philosophies to engage with a Solution Focused approach than for followers of Western psychology who are looking for a root cause of the presenting problems in order to solve the clients' issues.

Holistic Perspective

Solution Focused practitioners consider individuals within the context of their whole lives, relationships, and environments. Especially the later developments of the Solution Focused approach are linked to social-constructionist (Gergen, 2015) and Wittgensteinian thought which view human beings and their experience as shaped by the interactions they have with others. In a sense, as in many Asian philosophies, there is no idea of the self as a "bounded entity" but more like a nexus of experiences and stories. There is no differentiation between "inner" and "outer" world of the client. Therefore, Solution Focused practitioners invite the clients to consider observable signs of instances in which their lives are better rather than "diving deep" into their inner world of emotions and memory. The approach takes a holistic view of clients and their strengths. Many Asian philosophies also emphasise a holistic understanding of life and well-being. Concepts like Tao in Taoism and the interconnectedness of all things reflect a holistic perspective on existence. Upanishadic philosophy also talks about the interconnectedness of all existence and the unity of the individual soul (Atman) with the universal soul (Brahman). In some Buddhist thoughts, the differentiation between "inner" and "outer," which is not important in the Solution Focused approach, seems important. The outer world is seen as a deceiving reality, a construct of the mind. Therefore, the investigation of "the inner," for example in meditation, is important. What unites the Solution Focused approach and Buddhism here may be the focus on the human experience rather than explanations and theory.

Non-Linearity

The Solution Focused model is non-linear, acknowledging that change can happen in unexpected ways and that progress is not necessarily a step-by-step process. This is especially well presented in Miller and McKergow's referencing complexity theory in their 2012 article. Several Asian philosophies, including Taoism, often express non-linearity in their teachings. The Taoist concept of the Tao, for instance, is described as the way that is inherently without a fixed path. This is also linked to the next point of "change is happening all the time." Upanishadic teachings often delve into non-dualistic thinking, emphasising that reality transcends dichotomies.

This aligns with the Solution Focused coaching approach, which encourages thinking beyond binary problem-solving methods and exploring diverse perspectives to find solutions.

Change Is Happening All the Time

Solution Focused practitioners assume that change is happening all the time and that practitioners invite clients to notice these changes and amplify them. As stated earlier, inviting clients to change their language around the problems they are experiencing to be able to note the positive changes that are happening and figure out what they are contributing to them is one of the essential shifts from a problem solving to a solution developing model and a characteristic of the Solution Focused approach. In Asian philosophies, the recognition and acceptance of the constant nature of change lie at the core of their worldview. Influenced by beliefs such as Taoism and Buddhism, the understanding that "change happens all the time" is crucial for navigating the complexities of life. In Taoism, the concept of the Tao emphasises the natural flow of the universe, where change is an inherent and essential aspect. Acceptance of this perpetual change allows individuals to align themselves with the rhythm of the Tao, fostering harmony and balance in their lives. Buddhism, with its emphasis on impermanence (Anicca), teaches that all phenomena are in a state of constant flux. This awareness serves as a foundation for the Buddhist path, encouraging practitioners to cultivate mindfulness and detachment from the transient nature of material existence. The Upanishads highlight the impermanent nature of reality and the concept of change (Maya).

As Few Assumptions as Possible

Solution Focused practice does not engage in analysing the client, putting them into diagnostic or other frameworks or classifying their hardships in any way. Other than assuming competence and the willingness to work on the desired goals, Solution Focused practitioners try not to have any assumptions about clients. In Asian philosophies, particularly influenced by Taoism and Zen Buddhism, the notion that having assumptions is detrimental stems from the emphasis on direct experience. Assumptions are seen as mental constructs that cloud the clarity of perception, hindering one's ability to engage with the present moment. By cultivating a mind free of preconceptions, individuals in Asian philosophies seek to approach situations with open-mindedness and receptivity. This absence of assumptions aligns with the ideals of spontaneity and non-attachment, fostering a deeper connection to reality and a more authentic experience of the unfolding present. Practitioners who hold a worldview like Asian philosophies will have a much easier time adopting a Solution Focused approach. Western psychologists with their impressive diagnostic toolkit have much more to unlearn.

While these similarities exist, it's important to note that the Solution Focused approach is a specific approach developed in the West by an Asian woman (Insoo Kim Berg), an American man (Steve de Shazer), and many other people mainly from North America and Europe. Any parallels with Asian philosophies may be conceptual rather than direct influences. It is unknown to me how much Insoo Kim Berg's thinking was influenced by Asian philosophies. Additionally, the diversity of Asian philosophies means that not all elements align with the Solution Focused Approach. Also, the Solution Focused approach is not monolithic, and different practices and strands of theories can be identified.

References

de Shazer, S. (1985). *Keys to solution in brief therapy*. Norton.

de Shazer, S. (1999). *Beginnings [from the BFTC website]*. Retrieved from: https://www.sikt.nu/wp-content/uploads/2020/06/SdeSBeginnings-.pdf

Dierolf, K. (2011). SF practice as an application of discursive psychology – discursive psychology as a theoretical backdrop of SF practice. *InterAction*, 3(1), 21–34.

Gergen, K. J. (2015). *Relational being: Beyond self and community*. University Press.

Gosnell, F., McKergow, M., Moore, B. H., Mudry, T. E., & Tomm, K. (2017). A Galveston declaration. *Journal of Systemic Therapies*, 36(3), 20–26.

Hopwood, L., & de Shazer, S. (1994). From here to there and who knows where: The continuing evolution of solution focused brief therapy. In M. Elkaim (Ed.), *Therapies familiales: Les approches principaux* (pp. 555–576). Editions de Seuil.

Korman, H., De Jong, P., & Jordan, S. S. (2020). Steve de Shazer's Theory Development. *Journal of Solution Focused Practices*, 4(2), Article 5.

Lee, M. Y., & Mjelde-Mossey, L. (2004). Cultural dissonance among generations: A solution-focused approach with East Asian elders and their families. *Journal of Marital and Family Therapy*, 30(4), 497–513.

McKergow, M. (2020). Stretching the world: A friendly explanation of SF practice. In K. Dierolf, D. Hogan, S. van der Hoorn, & S. Wignaraja (Eds), *Solution focused practice around the world* (pp. 50–56). Routledge/Taylor & Francis Group.

Miller, G. &. McKergow. M. (2012). From Wittgenstein, complexity, and narrative emergence: Discourse and solution-focused brief therapy. In A. Lock & T. Strong (Eds), *Discursive perspectives in therapeutic practice* (pp. 163–183). Oxford University Press.

SFCT (2009). Clues 1.0. *InterAction*, 1(1), 101–103.

Trepper, T. S., McCollum, E. E., De Jong, P., Korman, H., Gingerich, W. J., & Franklin, C. (2011). Solution-focused brief therapy treatment manual. In C. Franklin, T. S. Trepper, W. J. Gingerich, & E. E. McCollum (Eds.), *Solution-focused brief therapy: A handbook of evidence-based practice* (pp. 20–38). Oxford University Press.

Section 2

Coaching in Organisations

3   Solutions for Change

Change Management and Solution Focused Coaching

Juan Pablo Lisdero

Solution Focused Coaching at an Organisational Level

In this chapter, I describe a pilot project that shows how applying the Solution Focused (SF) coaching approach has both simplified and amplified a change process for 500 people in Asia. Following the success of the pilot, the project was then escalated to more than 5,000 people across different Asian countries.

By using an SF toolkit, I have been able to co-create a communication loop where employees of a large multinational company (MNC) have sustained a coaching conversation across five production facilities. This process involved setting clear objectives, scaling progress, affirming what was going well, and calibrating action plans as new opportunities emerged.

Following the SF paradigm, our methodology focused on communication as the key path to useful change. This included team talk routines, powerful questions through regular iterations, and leadership training in coaching principles.

What started as a transition into a new set of systems and rules gradually became a culture shift. SF practices proved to be highly transferable to new contexts, instilling in the team a renewed openness and desire for change and improvement.

As the project expanded throughout different regions, the SF framework gave us the advantage of 'not knowing': we started each stage with a fresh perspective, making use of what is unique to each culture. At the same time, the framework became a bridge between countries, where the achievements of each team were enablers for new units.

'Our role is to identify useful change and amplify it' (Bateson et al., 1956). This chapter serves as an example of how the transformative power of the SF approach can by far exceed the traditional sphere of individual or team coaching when we amplify its impact to reach an organisational level.

The Scope of Work: Operation Units in Asia

The project objective was to create a new way of working in the production facilities of Asia. As part of a continuous improvement emphasis coming

DOI: 10.4324/9781003431480-5

from the company's culture, the initiative pursued operational excellence in the production environments by seeking actions on multiple fronts such as maintenance, performance management, logistics, human resources, quality, safety, and many others. One distinctive feature of the programme was to identify opportunities to simplify, optimise, and make the everyday processes of the departments involved in the factories more agile and efficient, by allowing small and consistent steps that could be measured and communicated actively.

The project was conducted in phases, leveraging the lessons learnt in each stage to progress gradually. We decided to start with a smaller unit, to later scale and iterate the learning process, amplifying solutions for larger populations. While the final reach of the initiative impacted more than 5,000 employees, the initial pilot project was run in a production unit of 500 employees located in Asia.

The people in this unit comprised diverse nationalities and cultural backgrounds. The workforce included people from India, the Philippines, Nepal, Pakistan, Sri Lanka, and South Korea, as well as several countries from South East Asia and the Middle East. At the same time, the staff covered levels from senior management to technical experts and advisors, together with operators and technicians. The educational background of the personnel ranged from elementary school studies to postgraduate degrees.

An Inclusive Approach: The Importance of Coaching

The complexity of such cultural diversity demanded a flexible and inclusive approach. Knowing that change occurs when someone does something differently or looks at something differently, we wanted to make sure we could capture and appreciate the useful and positive differences that surfaced from such a multicultural environment. For our approach to be successful, we had to make use of this gift of diversity and utilise the resources that people brought in their interactions, relations, experiences, abilities, emotions, and environment.

For this reason, we chose to make coaching an essential element of our method: focusing on people and their own resources. Rather than explaining, we focused on listening and understanding, as a way to co-create useful actions. The SF coaching approach seemed especially fit for purpose, through its emphasis on leveraging the resources that every participant contributes towards unlocking new potential solutions.

Focusing on the useful differences between people allowed us to unlock some simple and surprising potential, as we were able to find what worked and do more of it (Jackson & McKergow, 2007). SF coaching provided a way to empower people to participate actively in their own change process, contributing to the success of the project. This is described in more detail below.

The Method: Four Guiding Principles

We created a methodology that integrated change management models with SF coaching practices, for a large-scale organisation with a rich cultural diversity. The assumption was that solutions and progress during the project would surface in the interaction with employees, rather than through the top-down hierarchical advice of experts or consultants. Our priority was to research best practices that people were already applying in different parts of the organisation and amplify them by creating a positive network of interactions.

For this reason, we designed an approach prioritising four main guidelines:

1 Frequent partnering with the employees, as main leaders of the direction throughout the project
2 Active focus on coaching conversations within each team
3 Systemic feedback loop to amplify useful actions
4 Scaling and measuring progress in an iterative way.

The following segments will explain in more detail how each of these items was deployed.

While a coaching conversation can occur with an individual or group, our approach had to enable a simultaneous collaboration of hundreds of people to define and calibrate continuously in the direction of our initiatives. To address this, we defined a monthly routine. Like the notes in a song, each week would have a specific function, following our monthly rhythm and starting the cycle again after four weeks. Small actions each time would allow a fresh new start and an opportunity to create new solutions.

Starting the Monthly Cycle: The Employee Survey

We began each month with an employee survey: we wanted to hear from people directly about their priorities, focus, and resources. In order to structure the inputs, we applied ADKAR (Awareness, Desire, Knowledge, Ability, and Reinforcement) methodology, an approach that gathers insights from employees in a brief and simple way (Hiatt, 2006). This method was explicitly chosen due to its proximity to SF principles and the OSKAR model (Outcome, Scaling, Know-How, Affirm and Action, Review). It allowed us to know more about the outcome that people expected, the know-how and resources they have, and provided opportunities to affirm their progress (Jackson & McKergow, 2007).

Multiplying Interactions: The Bi-Weekly Team Talks

The second important action in our monthly cycle was focused on the talks that happened within each team. In preparation for this step, we split the entire organisation into working teams of 5–20 people, each with an assigned team leader. To promote the SF approach, we also ran training sessions on coaching conversations with all the team leaders. The sessions involved theory and practice and were delivered by a certified ICF coach and advanced SF practitioner, covering 100% of the people in the organisation who had at least one direct report. Once we launched the monthly cycle, we ran a kick-off session with all employees and provided a simple routine and set of questions for the team talks. It was suggested to leaders that they use the following deck of questions:

• What is working well? Celebrate small successes?
• How will you notice things continuing to improve?
• What support do you need to keep going in the right direction?
• What actions will we implement to keep improving?
• Open feedback/comments.
• Schedule the next meeting.

After the meeting, the team leader filled out a 5-minute form with the following information:

• Key actions that your team will implement to keep improving
• What else you need to continue moving forward
• Share best practices that are working well in your team.

The qualitative outcomes from the forms were consolidated and provided a detailed view of the way each team and area were working and created a reservoir of numerous best practices. It was a bi-weekly continuous source of solutions that kept accumulating and renewing, and that were then ready to be shared across teams.

Scaling and Acting: The Monthly Committee

The third essential element of our monthly cycle was structured as a conversation. Every month the main stakeholders of the organisation met as a change management committee. For this conversation, our project team prepared a control panel with the main numerical and qualitative outcomes coming from three main sources:

• Employee survey
• Team talks
• Project progress indicators.

By combining the three inputs, the committee had visibility on the monthly progress. We saw how the organisation was progressing in their awareness, motivation, knowledge, skills, and actions towards the project completion. The panel also allowed us to:

- Identify teams that were performing remarkably well in certain processes or variables
- Read a detailed description of their best practices that took them to that level.

The committee systematically selected and shared the solutions applied by the most successful teams and with the teams that were in earlier stages or who had actively requested support through the team forms.

The key to the process was to promote interactions that reinforced the exchange of existing solutions across teams and people. Solutions would originate from within the organisation and employees were encouraged to collaborate with valuable inputs from their peers. As teams were coupled together to share best practices, they simultaneously supported each other to improve different procedures.

We assumed that the main source of action is in the interaction, so the committee initiatives fostered continuous connection across teams and departments to share solutions, creating a sustainable network and culture driven towards systemic solutions.

The cycle then repeated, and a new survey provided the chance to partner again with employees, to ensure that they remained protagonists of the process and that our committee remained curious to listen to what else surfaced through the continuous conversation.

What Went Well: Outcomes of the Method

One year after the project launch, the pilot unit had undergone a relevant number of iterations in the cycle of change that our method enabled.

We knew from previous research that, in organisations or groups, the SF approach helps to enable resources and symbols of desired change, which lend a motivational boost to any change project (Jackson & McKergow, 2007). Similarly, we identified clear outcomes, which reflected the impact of coaching practices when sustained over a prolonged process of change with a large group of people.

One of the most evident outcomes was the impact on engagement across levels and functions, as measured by the responses of employees about their general satisfaction with work and willingness to contribute to the company's objectives. Employees within the scope impacted, responded on average with a 93% engagement score, with 3% of neutral responses and only 4% of negative answers. More than 90% of the total population answered the survey, representing a relevant sample of participants. The specific items that were monitored during the project showed the following rates of improvement year to year, before and after the project:

- Leaders encouraging, recognising, and respecting diversity in the workplace improved from 87% to 93%

- Fairness of performance appraisals improved from 87% to 91%
- Leaders seeking solutions rather than giving justifications or assigning blame improved from 85% to 90%.

Qualitative feedback from employees correlated with the above scores to an improvement in the levels of trust in communication. They indicated that leaders were actively taking time to listen to employees' inputs, asking relevant questions, and discussing important topics in a direct way. Comments also highlighted the increase in awareness of people about action plans that impacted them and their teams.

A key element of the process was to empower people as protagonists in leading change. The views of two people who experienced the project first-hand are shared.

Ang was an experienced technical referent in the International Operations team, actively involved in the design and development of the programme. He shared his observations about the process:

Our main objective was to achieve "Operational Excellence to Improve People's Lives." On this journey, transparent communication and active listening were essential to understand how people were experiencing change and to identify what was working well. This allowed us to adjust the strategy in an agile manner. By having this involvement in a collaborative way, we immediately empowered people, making it possible to create an environment of trust and engagement, where everyone felt part of the change process and was motivated to contribute to the success of the excellence program. This approach helped us increase the chances of successful implementation of our excellence program in different countries and cultures.

Simi was a senior leader in the project team, participating throughout the entire pilot and further stages. These are her comments about the method:

When the project was launched in the unit, in the beginning, it was approached with some skepticism. Why would a unit that had been a benchmark on all fronts, need an operational excellence program? Still, I think that's exactly what made it more relevant for the team. It gave us a chance to take another careful look at the way we did things and discover our way to do it even better. During this project, we identified a lot of opportunities for improvement, simplification and synergies. More importantly, it made us aware of the preparedness and willingness of the people to accept and embrace change.

In an Asian cultural context characterised by being respectful of hierarchy and authority, the SF coaching framework provided a new way of interacting for leaders and employees. While some of the leaders questioned at first the need for this change, eventually they became more familiar with the advantages of a collaborative Solution Focused approach: the number of active supporters grew fast as the results showed that change was positive. The practice of listening actively to inputs across hierarchical layers allowed the organisation to leverage the contributions and solutions of diverse people and provided broader collaboration networks, which eventually led to improved solutions and results.

Conclusions

Through the impact of this initial pilot, the project was scaled to an even larger population, stretching to five units involving more than 5,000 employees in Asia. In the same way, as SF coaching evolves through small actions, our pilot programme represented a first step on the way to more comprehensive and ambitious solutions.

The method we developed and applied was able to harmonise and integrate SF conversations into a large-scale change management framework. It impacted people in a richly diverse environment, across hierarchical and educational levels, while providing a scaling process to measure and simplify action planning.

Actions surfaced through a systematic process, where existing solutions were shared with those teams who requested support, setting an active collaboration loop that increased motivation and belief in positive change. Keeping interaction as the main source of action, each iteration helped to develop an increasingly sustainable network.

The outcomes were visible and concrete. Coaching practices implemented over a prolonged process of change provided an impact on engagement levels, improving people's perception of diversity in the workplace, fairness of performance appraisals and solution orientation of leaders, and helping to sustain an overall high engagement score above 93%. Participants' qualitative feedback acknowledged an improvement in the levels of trust in communication and active listening practices from leaders. They also highlighted their increased awareness and willingness about action plans that impacted them and their teams and their empowerment as protagonists in leading change, helping them to identify opportunities for improvement, simplification, and synergies.

A real privilege of having participated in this project is witnessing how the organisation created a culture focused on possibilities and solutions, which translated into clear results. The focus on continuous improvement is a key priority for companies to remain competitive in a world of constant change. In this way, we have seen that the SF framework provides a relevant model both for organisations needing a turnaround and for those that want to find new ways to maintain a competitive advantage.

References

Bateson, G., Jackson, D. D., Haley, J., & Weakland, J. (1956). Toward a theory of schizophrenia. *Behavioral Science*, *1*(4), 251–264. 10.1002/bs.3830010402

Hiatt, J. (2006). *ADKAR: A model for change in business, government and our community*. Learning Center Publications.

Jackson, P. Z. & McKergow, M. (2007). *The solutions focus: Making coaching and change simple* (2nd ed.). Nicholas Brealey.

4 Making Organisations a Better Place to Work

Through a Solution Focused Coaching Culture

Kapila Ahuja

Introduction

A dedicated Diversity, Equity, and Inclusion (DEI) committee was formed within a large organisation in Singapore to address the challenge of promoting more women into senior leadership positions. This passionate group of individuals shared a common goal: to create a more diverse and inclusive workplace. This chapter describes the pilot project of forming a coaching incubator. The initial success of the project is described from both the coaches' and clients' perspectives. This chapter then goes on to describe how the project was scaled up and the positive differences this made to the organisation as a whole.

Background

Work, as we know it, takes place in complex organisations with processes that prioritise client and shareholder interests. In recent decades, employers and employees have recognised the importance of investing in workers, communities, and surrounding ecosystems for sustainable success (Majumder & Dey, 2024). This shift reflects the growing desire among the workforce to find meaning in their work.

One notable investment in this pursuit is the framework of DEI, which aims to foster fair treatment and full participation for all individuals. DEI committees have long recognised that surface efforts to improve DEI within organisations are wasted if they don't structurally change workplaces to incorporate a balance of quantifiable efforts (e.g. decreasing the gender pay gap) as well as focusing on the qualitative impact of those measures.

The Pilot

As mentioned earlier, a dedicated DEI committee was formed within a large organisation in Singapore with the goal of creating a more inclusive and diverse workplace. With a collective desire to drive change, the committee members shared their ideas, skills, and expertise. Among them were experienced and accredited coaches who recognised the potential of coaching in facilitating this

DOI: 10.4324/9781003431480-6

transformation. The aim was to work towards making structural changes in the organisation that had both a quantitative and qualitative impact, starting small and scaling over time.

Coaching helps transform the narrative we embrace that further influences our personal growth and identity. It guides our choices, shapes our perspectives, and ultimately molds the individuals we become (Schultz, 2021).

Most societies in Southeast Asia are predominantly patriarchal (Niaz & Hassan, 2006). As a result, the gender discrimination affects women in many ways throughout their lifetime: physically, mentally, socially, and economically, and this extends to workplaces. While supporting and empowering women within the company was an important aim, the programme was acutely aware that there may be a longer time period needed for women to adapt to feeling empowered from within. Coaching was thought to be a great way of achieving this aim as it would be able to support the women with the goals that were important to them. Coaching is client-driven so does not add to any further discrimination by imposing external ideas about what they should do. Allowing for several sessions over a longer time period allowed for change at a pace the women felt comfortable with.

After discussing obstacles and opportunities, the committee proposed the establishment of a coaching incubator to be supported by a team of ten existing coaches within the organisation. The coaches and clients met at a frequency of the clients' choice lasting between six and nine months. Objectives were driven by the clients and were mostly aligned to organisational success, for example, significant promotions, desired job transitions, or difficult conversations that helped them achieve success in their existing roles.

As the pilot programme concluded, the results surpassed expectations. It became evident that coaching had made a significant impact on the personal and professional development of the women who participated in the coaching pilot. Nearly 90% of the coaching clients achieved their goals in less than a year.

Widening the Impact

Recognising the potential impact of this coaching approach, the institution sought to replicate and expand its success to benefit a larger segment of the global workforce. To achieve this, they collaborated with the Academy of Solution Focused Training, a renowned organisation specialising in Solution Focused (SF) coaching, to train 20 high-quality internal coaches in the SF coaching approach.

SF coaching recognises that clients are experts in their own lives and have the resources and strengths to achieve what is important to them. The coach guides clients through a process of self-discovery, helping them to utilise their own knowledge and capabilities. This empowerment fosters a sense of ownership and motivation, as clients feel in control of their journey and responsible for their own success.

These newly trained internal SF coaches continued to provide coaching support to a wider range of internal clients within the organisation. By leveraging the power of coaching, the institution aimed to create a sustainable culture of support, growth, and empowerment. They hoped the coaching programme would enable the achievement of specific individual goals as well foster a more inclusive and diverse workplace by enabling more women in senior rungs of the organisational structure.

Through the continued efforts of the DEI committee, the coaching incubator, and collaboration with external coaching experts, the organisation aimed to solidify its commitment in creating an environment where individuals can thrive and lead with their unique talents.

A programme was designed to replicate the model above at scale and is described below.

The Programme

To build on the initial pool of coaches, programme sponsors disseminated information regarding the opportunity as well as a sponsorship incentive. Interested applicants were asked to fill out a comprehensive questionnaire that addressed their experience with coaching, the attributes of an effective coach, and how they would embody those attributes to add value to the organisation.

The commitment of the organisation was evident as they partially sponsored the coaching fee for 40 of the selected applicants. The successful applicants then completed an Accredited International Coaching Federation Level 1 Coach Training Program that enabled them to earn professional credentials as a coach.

The DEI committee then invited prospective clients to experience the benefits of coaching. As trust is paramount in any coaching contract, we endeavoured to embed maximum possible degrees of separation when matching a coach to a client, such as differing businesses, geography, or functions within the organisation.

Being a part of the DEI committee as well as the first cohort of SF coaches lent me a unique vantage point. Having previously been through several initiatives (internal mentoring, lean-in circles) that bore short-lived gains, the sponsors were very curious about the potential success of the scaled version of the programme. Coaching skills are typically embedded within HR functions; given the programme was the first to develop the skillset in non-HR functions it was met with some initial hesitation. The more we collectively discussed it, the more it made sense to continue to expand the coaching programme to all functions.

With these initial steps in place, and support from the leaders and high level of interest from the staff to join this programme, we proceeded to expand the availability to an even wider scale to develop internal coaches. As more internal coaches were trained, the impact of this programme on coaches and clients became more evident.

Transformed Perspectives: How Did It Change Us?

The Coaches

As an individual, the journey to become a coach is rooted in theory and self-examination, followed by practice to apply that theory. The training started with examining our own life and career pathways and how we managed to turn situations around by looking for solutions rather than dwelling on the problems. This approach not only helped me personally by moving past the problem statement but also equipped me with tools to guide others in discovering their own solutions and creating positive change in their lives.

Coaches across the globe came together to study beyond working hours. Within the safe spaces created by the cohort, coaches moved past their own career hurdles and defined their career purpose in peer coaching formats. Watching SF coaching come alive in a real-life classroom was incredible, and as the cohort grew closer, we were able to spend more time in the discomfort of charting new solutions to existing problems. I learnt how to be vulnerable about my feelings and impact of my work day, discuss solutions to some work habits that had stopped adding value to my newer career ambitions, and face difficult decisions with the support offered by peer coaches-in-training.

Increasing my skills as an SF coach in individual coaching conversations was one benefit. I was also able to engage and better manage members of my team using the coaching principles in regular catch-ups as well as in goal setting opportunities. Formal coaching sessions with employees outside my team (mostly women) enabled them to engage in more courageous conversations about what they needed from work, and their teams. The cherry on the cake was the joy of giving back to the organisation by seeing concrete results for the clients.

At the start of the programme, a ratio of one coach to two clients enabled ample time and support to clients. Coaches were given the option to add or reduce clients given their existing workloads that enabled them to embed a flexible coaching habit. Talking to various coaches in the wider International Coaching Federation (ICF) community, I understood that one of the biggest hurdles coaches-in-training often face is approaching new clients with confidence. Implementing this coaching initiative within the organisation had seamlessly bypassed that issue by tapping into a ready pool of existing clients that were then allocated to the new coaches.

Similarly, outside of the cohort of new coaches-in-training, existing coaches found it easy to source clients to pursue subsequent levels of their coaching journey. They also reported that their practice was improving while they experienced a heightened realisation of their purpose, especially as it was in alignment to that of the organisation, in providing value to the employees of the organisation in a meaningful way.

The Clients

Clients seeking SF coaching had various requests, including the need for clarity in their professional endeavours and to become better at voicing out their desires. Clients were given information about the coaching process and asked to simply be open to experiencing the transformative power of a coaching conversation.

It was important that each client was matched with a coach who was able to work on their specific goals and was someone with whom they felt comfortable. After an initial chemistry call, clients had the freedom to switch coaches if the connection didn't resonate. Trust was solidified through signed coaching contracts, ensuring a strong foundation for a successful and promising coaching programme.

Early feedback from clients showed that the clients reported clarity of purpose in their career direction and life as well as a feeling of empowerment and progress towards their goals.

Additionally, SF coaching promoted a positive mindset by being curious about what is important to the client and what their desired future looks like. Clients were encouraged to shift their focus away from problems and towards what is possible. This shift enabled clients to see new possibilities and identify new resources. It fostered a sense of hope, optimism, and resilience, which enhanced clients' motivation and belief in their ability to create positive change. By setting clear goals and taking incremental steps, clients created momentum and made progress towards their desired future.

Clients also expressed that engaging in coaching had cultivated a lifelong habit of seeking guidance. In a world where self-reliance and shouldering burdens alone are often emphasised, clients discovered the liberating realisation that they don't have to navigate life's challenges alone.

An added bonus was that many coaching clients were inspired to become coaches themselves. The transformative impact they experienced fuelled their desire to share the benefits with others, creating a ripple effect of empowerment and growth in the organisation.

As the programme grew, there were also noticeable benefits at an organisational level.

Benefits to the Organisation

Despite geographical or business separations, coaches and clients shared an understanding of the organisation's culture and product. Not only did the programme support individuals to meet their own goals, but it also fostered a shift in culture, promoting learning, open communication, trust, and constructive feedback. Regular feedback showed that employees felt valued, supported, and empowered, thus contributing to a positive work environment and overall organisational success.

The programme showcased the organisation's commitment to employee development and growth. By providing coaching as a valuable resource, clients reported feeling supported and invested in, resulting in improved retention rates.

Furthermore, the programme served as an excellent platform for empowering future-facing female talent. By offering coaching to aspiring and current leaders, we enhanced leadership capabilities, improved their decision-making skills, and cultivated a strong pipeline of female leaders who would be role models for budding leaders. Asia is one of the most dynamic regions when it comes to moving the needle in raising the role of women. In ASEAN, the percentage of women in senior management increased from 28% to 35% in 2023. Progress on the overall proportion of women in senior leadership increased in Southeast Asia, ahead of other markets globally (Thornton, 2023).

The programme not only helped individuals but also had a transformative effect on the organisation's overall culture by fostering a listening culture within the organisation. Coaches actively listened to clients, understanding their needs, challenges, and aspirations. These skills could also be used in conversations outside formal coaching sessions. This emphasis on listening created a safe and supportive space for open dialogue, where all employees felt heard and respected. This further enhanced collaboration, deeper understanding, problem-solving, and innovation within the organisation, contributing to its overall success and growth. The increasing number of internal coaches also strengthened the calibre of the leaders in the company.

As the coaching programme flourished and gained momentum, coaches were incentivised to expand their client base, accommodating more individuals as their workload permitted. The increasing success and impact of the programme attracted the attention of more businesses within the organisation, which were eager to become part of the supportive community and benefit from the transformative power of coaching. As a result, the programme's influence continued to expand, leaving a lasting legacy of positive cultural transformation and ongoing commitment to DEI principles. Coaching had evolved from a specific programme to a readily available product for all, offering timely support and guidance to individuals across the organisation, reinforcing the culture of growth, collaboration, and inclusivity.

Guidelines to Enhance Coaching Programmes of the Future

For anyone looking to embed a successful coaching programme within a large organisation, the following are some guidelines for consideration:

1 *Increased Exposure to Coaching*: For the senior leadership to empower leaders to champion diverse opportunities for exposure to coaching, including engaging in training sessions and story-sharing events that illuminate the transformative power of coaching. Foster a culture that deeply values coaching as a catalyst for personal and professional growth, enhanced performance, and positive change.

2 *Strategic Alignment*: Ensure that the coaching programme aligns with the organisation's strategic goals and priorities to increase its relevance, impact, and long-term sustainability.
3 *Consistency and Structure*: Establishing a consistent framework is key to the programme's success. Define clear goals, create a structured approach, and ensure regular coaching sessions. Consistency builds trust and reliability, allowing participants to fully engage and experience the programme's benefits.
4 *Agility and Adaptability*: Recognise that each organisation has unique needs and challenges. Be open to feedback, learn from experiences, and be willing to make necessary adjustments. Embrace agility and adaptability to respond to evolving circumstances, optimise the programme's effectiveness, and ensure its long-term sustainability.
5 *DEI Benefits*: Tailor coaching programmes to address DEI challenges. Offer diverse coaching options, including coaches from under-represented groups, and ensure coaches receive training on cultural competence and sensitivity. Encourage open dialogue, active listening, and empathy within coaching sessions to build trust and psychological safety.

SF coaching is transformative for both individuals and organisations. With coaching as a catalyst, organisations can create a culture that fosters personal growth, empowers individuals, and positions them for long-term success.

References

Majumder, S., & Dey, N. (2024). Investing in people and organizational transformation. In *The vogue of managing people in workplace. Innovations in sustainable technologies and computing*. Springer, Singapore. 10.1007/978-981-99-6070-5_2
Niaz, U., & Hassan, S. (2006). Culture and mental health of women in South-East Asia. *World Psychiatry: Official Journal of the World Psychiatric Association*, 5(2), 118–120. https://www.ncbi.nlm.nih.gov/pmc/articles/PMC1525125/
Schultz, J. (2021 January 21). *What is coaching in the workplace and why is this important?* Positive Psychology. https://positivepsychology.com/workplace-coaching/
Thornton, G. (2023). *Women in Business 2023. International business report*. Grant Thornton. https://www.grantthornton.sg/insights/women-in-business-2023/

5 The Power of Coaching in Everyday Conversations

Karen Leong

Introduction

Modern-day leaders are under tremendous and ever-escalating pressure to deliver results within tight timelines, with resource constraints induced by a Dilbertian do-more-with-less view that is so mainstream that it is now embedded in many corporate cultures. Consequently, there is a marked tendency to prioritise immediate and short-term business goals. Because of this, leaders may often lose sight of the importance of developing and empowering their people. This sets off an unhealthy spiral of reducing empowerment and engagement, thereby further increasing the pressure on leadership time.

One of our biggest priorities at Influence Solutions, an organisational development company headquartered in Singapore, is to support organisations in forging high trust, high-performance cultures. During many such projects, one of the most common refrains we hear from busy executives is: 'I know developing people is important, but right now I have no time because I have so many fires to fight … which I wouldn't have to, if my people stepped up more.'

Reminding them that if they invested more time in developing their people, they would perhaps feel more equipped to step up more, take charge of dealing with daily fires, and drive the business results expected from the team seldom yields any long-term results. What is required is to help these overloaded and overstressed business leaders find a way to leverage something they do a lot of every day, to energise, engage, and empower their people.

Analysis of an average workday of any working professional shows we spend an inordinately large time in some form of communication: about 45% listening, 30% speaking, 16% reading, and 9% writing (Ahmed, 2015).

We decided to help business leaders evolve a pragmatic process to leverage this time already being utilised in communication. This would ensure that they keep business operations moving forward, by empowering team members and enhancing their confidence to function independently.

While most coaching methodologies and frameworks help leaders to enable and engage, we noticed that Solution Focused coaching is one of the most effective. Additionally, it fosters a Solution Focused culture in the organisation.

DOI: 10.4324/9781003431480-7

The aim of this chapter is to highlight how the Solution Focused coaching approach and frameworks can be leveraged to power up daily conversations with all categories of stakeholders. Such conversations build rapport and trust, provide the required clarity, and create moments of learning.

This chapter will first explore the three most common biases while working with leaders in Asia, which hinder them from using coaching to engage and empower. We will then look at three practical ways to infuse coaching into daily conversations.

Bias 1: The Belief That Coaching Requires Special Skills

Many managers are reluctant to coach because they believe it requires specialised training. It is true that professional coaching requires considerable training. However, most line managers, just by mindfully applying some key coaching skills, can transform daily conversations into powerful, inspiring ones.

Effective coaching is not about asking complex questions. It is about being curious about what is important to the team member and exploring possible ways forward that leverage their ideas. These questions seek to provide clarity so the team members can take the actions required to deal with the situation and keep business operations moving forward.

It is not important for the coach-leader to have domain knowledge or subject matter expertise. At times, this knowledge might be useful in helping the leader generate workable options for the team member they are coaching. However, it is equally possible that this subject matter knowledge coupled with time pressures might motivate the leader to provide the team member with a solution to the problem, rather than helping them to evolve their own solutions. While this 'mentoring-style' approach gets quick business results in the short term, it is unlikely to empower the team members or develop their capability and confidence instead making the team members more reliant on their leader to generate solutions in the future.

As Einstein (n.d.) said: 'You cannot solve a problem with the same mind that created it.' Hence, the Solution Focused approach works very well, since it is not encumbered by the need to deeply understand or analyse the problem. Instead, the leader is interested in the team members' ideas, expertise, and exploration of what is desired and what a good outcome looks like.

These skills, while taking time to learn and develop, are shown to be effective and lead to greater engagement and productivity, in the long run. Employers who invest in understanding what their employees value, providing career paths and development opportunities will gain a significant edge in retaining their best talent (De Smet et al., 2021). In Asia, the world's largest economy and one of the fastest growing regions, there is also a growing recognition that developing a thriving coaching culture is key to increasing productivity and talent retention (Boccongelle, 2022).

Bias 2: Lack of Time

Most leaders feel that coaching, though useful, requires a lot of time, something they simply do not have. With the fast pace of work in many Asian countries, where executives report feeling the pressure to be constantly busy (MacCartney, 2022), coaching tends to take a back seat to the immediate and urgent tasks. However, it is precisely those leaders who lack time that seem to benefit most from using coaching skills. Once they start giving the same priority to people development that they give to business results, they begin to see an increase in engagement. As the confidence of their team members functioning independently increases, the team begins taking charge of daily issues, thus reducing the time investment of the leader. So, in essence, time management is priority management.

Bias 3: The Belief That Coaching Is Not Efficient or Fast Enough

Many leaders also believe that coaching takes time to deliver results. They know that directing people will get quick results; hence, they fall into the 'Telling Trap' and prefer to offer solutions rather than help people evolve their own solutions. This directive communication dynamic is rooted in the traditional Asian hierarchical style of leadership where seniority commands authority. Leaders are expected to know the answers, and the team members tend to defer to experience.

However, this approach does not build the teams' capacity, and will ensure that team members keep falling back to the leader to provide solutions. When this becomes the norm, the leader gets swamped and becomes the bottleneck, thus slowing things down. When the team is not empowered to respond to changing circumstances, there is increased fire-fighting and micromanagement required. The lack of autonomy usually results in lower morale and disengagement, thus reducing productivity further.

Many leaders overlook the fact that the difference between them and their team members is often just the date of birth. Their team members have been hired for their competence, and like themselves when they first started, have tremendous strengths and potential that can be harnessed.

When we learn to work past these biases and start leveraging coaching to power up daily conversations, everyone wins. The team members feel more empowered, and this enhances their engagement and morale, since everyone loves to learn and grow. The leader also benefits because as the capability, confidence, and engagement of their team members grow, they will start taking charge of issues independently saving the leader time and energy.

The aforementioned section not only challenges some of the biases that prevent leaders from wanting to try coaching but also shows the huge benefits of doing so. The rest of this chapter will share how at Influence Solutions, we have utilised a Solution Focused coaching approach to create a culture of leveraging daily conversations to enhance trust, which led to transformational business results.

The Solution: Using Coaching to Enhance the Impact of Daily Conversations

During the global pandemic, a client reached out to help them transform the impact of their entire leadership team. Managers were grappling with multiple challenges – managing remote working, loss of morale, and greater uncertainty all around. The discovery survey and conversations revealed that many of these leaders had a distinct bias against coaching and mentoring. Most of the participant leaders shared that these skills were 'good to have' when they had a lull in business and time to 'try them out.' It also became obvious that while they saw people development as important, in theory, it was given nothing more than lip service as most leaders were too busy with driving business results.

The first step of this transformation journey was therefore to shift the thinking of leaders at all levels from problem-talk to solution-talk and help them realise that people development would help them enhance business results and that this could be done fairly quickly.

We used the Executive Conversations Series – a series of four half-day workshops delivered four weeks apart. Tools generated from the Solution Focused model of coaching were mapped into daily conversations to ensure that these would achieve three things: build rapport, provide clarity about possible solutions, and create moments of learning. The participants used questions evolved from the Solution Focused OSKAR coaching model (McKergow & Jackson, 2007) and practiced role plays to ensure they were able to manage key stakeholders effectively.

Experiential activities and peer coaching helped participant leaders to deepen their awareness of the impact of the Solution Focused mindset. They were encouraged to try out these learnings and realisations between each half-day session.

The results of the Executive Conversations Series were remarkable. Daily conversations became forward-looking and inspiring, and there was a measurable increase in the levels of trust, empowerment, accountability, mental health and wellness, and the organisation being seen as an inspiring place to work.

These factors were measured before, at the end, and three to four months after the programme, combining self-reflection, organisation-wide surveys, and diagnostic tools developed by Influence Solutions such as the Team Trust survey.

Business results increased as well as productivity and talent retention, as reported in interviews with the senior leadership team from across Asia.

The four major factors that helped to drive the success of the Executive Conversations are discussed below.

Help Leaders to Demonstrate the Right Intention

The Executive Conversations Series involved about 100 leaders, attending the workshops in groups of 16. At the start of the first workshop, I asked each participant to share something about themselves and what they loved about what they did.

Interestingly, while most of the leaders shared that they liked to **solve problems**, a minority shared that they liked to *help* **people solve problems**.

This resulted in an animated discussion about the difference between these two statements, and what impact each had. They realised that when 'you like to solve problems, you are more prone to offering solutions to your team members' (the task-focused approach), whereas when 'you like to *help* people solve problems' you are likely to encourage people to evolve their own solutions (the people-focused) approach.

The group discussion also revealed a time and place for both approaches. In time-critical situations using the task-focused approach would be more logical, whereas in other situations it would be more useful to use the people-focused approach.

Consequently, we suggested to the participant leaders that whenever any of their team members came to them with a problem, the first thing the leader should do was to ask themselves if this was going to be a 'Coaching' or a 'Telling' moment.

In the second workshop, leaders shared they were surprised at how powerful this simple question was. They were able to move between their two top priorities of delivering business results, and people development with ease. Most leaders expressed satisfaction at the impact they were seeing on people development, without having to compromise on business results.

Also, as team members saw the leaders demonstrate their intention to help them learn and grow, there was a commensurate increase in trust.

Providing Structure to Daily Conversations

Once the leader had identified that it was a 'Coaching' moment, the second step was making their conversations shorter and more effective. To make this happen we used several activities that helped the leaders realise that they should *not* jump into either coaching or telling without first establishing what the team member wanted from that conversation i.e. their goal.

This simple but powerful realisation was even easier for the participants to act on since it required no skill or training. Just by asking what the team member wanted clarity on made the conversation more focused, hence shorter and more efficient. Once the goal is clear, this can be followed with simple questions such as:

• What have you done before, in a similar situation?
• What can you use now that will help?
• What is the next smallest step you can take?

Leveraging Your Problem-Solving Process to Create Learning

The final step was to help participant leaders break their habit of being solution-providers/problem-solvers. To enable this, we encouraged participants to become aware of the processes they were using to solve the problem. If you examine this process and break it down into three or four steps, then 'coaching' and 'telling' both become easy.

If one wants to *tell*, one simply needs to share the steps in the process they follow, and then allow the team member to personalise and contextualise the process for their situation and apply the steps.

If one wants to *coach*, then converting each step into open-ended questions, beginning with 'What' and 'How,' focused on the preferred future or the resourceful past, would help the team member identify their own solution, for example, 'What does success look like?' and 'How can you tap into your strengths to achieve this goal?'

By the final workshop, most of the participant leaders reported leveraging daily coaching conversations to help their team members learn and grow and deliver much higher levels of performance. Most reported an increase in trust and accountability, with people speaking up more proactively, escalating challenges earlier, and volunteering to take charge of ideas more readily.

These three steps led to daily conversations becoming more efficient and more effective in empowering team members. However, it was also important that these steps were 'seen' to be effective, by the stakeholders they were designed to influence.

Making Learning Visible

We suggested that at the end of conversations, leaders asked team members to share what they had learned or realised, and what they had 'found most useful.' This helped to make the learning of the conversation more visible and enhanced both the leaders' and team members' perceived value of this approach.

When tabulated, at the end of the Executive Conversation Series, and then again 120 days later, that organisation reported a double-digit increase in Trust, Empowerment, Accountability, and the Mental Health and Wellness of the team members, as well as their perception of the organisation as an inspiring place to work in. The impact was visible with an increase in indicators such as the frequency of performance management conversations, more proactive progress updates, issue escalation in time, and greater collaboration across business functions.

Conclusion

By integrating Solution Focused coaching into everyday conversations, you can create a culture of growth. The quality of our conversations is the biggest indicator of trust and culture. When you invest in Solution Focused thinking, it will have an exponential positive impact on both the qualitative experience of your organisational life as well as improving business results.

References

Ahmed, R. (2015, June 18). Five essential listening skills for English learners. *British Council*. https://www.britishcouncil.org/voices-magazine/five-essential-listening-skills-english-learners

Boccongelle, D. (2022, April 27). *Why your company needs a coaching culture*. DDI World. https://www.ddiworld.com/blog/why-is-a-coaching-culture-important

De Smet, A., Dowling, B., Mugayar-Baldocchi, M., & Schaninger, B. (2021, September 8). *'Great Attrition' or 'Great Attraction'? The choice is yours*. McKinsey. https://www.mckinsey.com/capabilities/people-and-organizational-performance/our-insights/great-attrition-or-great-attraction-the-choice-is-yours

Einstein. (n.d.). Quotespedia. https://www.quotespedia.org/authors/a/albert-einstein/we-cannot-solve-our-problems-with-the-same-thinking-we-used-when-we-created-them-albert-einstein/

Jackson, P. Z. & McKergow, M. (2007). *The solutions focus: Making coaching and change simple* (2nd ed.). Nicholas Brealey.

MacCartney, T. (2022, February 18). *Future of coaching in Southeast Asia*. HR World. https://hrsea.economictimes.indiatimes.com/news/workplace/future-of-coaching-in-southeast-asia/89637747

6 Leaders are Human Too!

Scaling Coaching Systematically

Abhishek Mehta and Sandeep Joshi

Introduction

*"I don't see a way forward from here, I feel I am stuck in my current role,"
John said to their coach Lucy. "I feel stuck because I don't see any growth in
my current role, I am doing the same tasks repetitively and not learning
anything new or using the best of my abilities."*

*Lucy empathetically nods and asks with a gentle tone "Imagine you are
already in a new role, what would it look like John?" Lucy asked him.*

*John took a pause to think for a moment. He kept thinking for a while and
Lucy patiently waited.*

*After some more time, Lucy asked again "What does growth mean to you,
John?" and this time John replied instantly "For me growth means solving new
challenges, meeting new people, having the power to make decisions and so on."*

This is a common scenario in a coaching session, where a client comes feeling
stuck. The follow-up questions by the coach Lucy are examples of Solution
Focused coaching questions that enable a client to see their situation differently
and start discovering what their life would look like as they move towards a
more hopeful future.

In this chapter, we will start with a brief outline of what Solution Focused
coaching is. We will share the benefits we noticed of using this with individual
clients. Based on the positive impact at a micro level, we decided to use this
approach to create and scale a coaching culture at a macro level at Standard
Chartered Bank. This chapter outlines what we did and the changes noticed
throughout the organisation. The challenges of the cultural context will also be
discussed.

Solution Focused Coaching

Solution Focused coaching is a hopeful approach to change management. It
focuses on shifting the client's view and reframing from problems towards

DOI: 10.4324/9781003431480-8

describing a more hopeful future which can lead to opening up possibilities and an expanded view of their situation. It creates a positive framing and greater emphasis on moving forward. Solution Focused coaching leads to a shift from "why" is there a problem to "what" is possible and how to manage it more effectively.

Over the last few years, we have been using the Solution Focused coaching approach in our coaching conversations and we found it to be particularly effective for smaller groups and teams due to its focused and collaborative nature. Here are some real-life examples that highlight its effectiveness:

1 Team alignment and goal setting:

- Smaller groups and teams benefit from Solution Focused coaching when aligning team members towards common goals. At a start-up incubator, we were engaged with a start-up team where each member had different perceptions of the company's direction. Through coaching, the team collaboratively defined a shared vision and set actionable goals aligned with individual strengths.

2 Enhancing communication and collaboration:

- Solution Focused coaching is instrumental in improving communication dynamics within small groups and teams. For instance, we coached a project team facing communication challenges. Using Solution Focused coaching we helped the team identify and implement effective communication strategies, fostering better collaboration and ensuring everyone's input was valued.

3 Adapting to change:

- Small businesses often face rapid changes. Solution Focused coaching helps teams adapt by focusing on what's working well and leveraging existing strengths. For example, during one of the transformational shifts we used the Solution Focused coaching approach to identify how current skills and resources can be redirected to support the shift in focus.

It is clear from these examples that Solution Focused coaching is not only effective but also highly adaptable to the specific needs of smaller groups and teams, helping them work towards targeted and actionable solutions to challenges they may face.

We have also seen how it manifests into a growth mindset when applied in a 1:1 setting. Solution Focused coaching in 1:1 sessions creates a growth mindset by promoting a focus on solutions, encouraging goal setting, fostering self-reflection, providing strength-based feedback, supporting experimentation, and facilitating individuals' ownership of their development journey.

When we put the benefits together, Solution Focused coaching clearly shows improvements in productivity and employee retention. A report by

Sheehan (2022) confirms that coaching can improve productivity by 53% and employee retention by 33%. The study by the International Coaching Federation (2023) revealed that more and more organisations are coming forward to scale coaching from individuals to small teams to the enterprise level in the post pandemic era. The scaling usually manifests into one of the following aspects such as driving a cultural transformation, ensuring a consistent problem-solving approach, enhancing employee engagement, empowering leaders, fostering agility, promoting innovation, achieving measurable performance improvements, and aligning with core organisational values. This scaling contributes to a resilient, adaptive, and high-performing organisation and it starts with culture change.

The Challenge of Cultural Diversity in the APAC Region

In APAC (Asia Pacific) region, enterprises are just getting started with the concept of coaching, understanding the approaches to a growth mindset, and creating a collaborative conversation culture. The cultural context plays a significant role. The culture in the Asia Pacific region is both deep and diverse, with a mixture of religions and 3000+ languages spoken across more than 23 countries (Temelkova, 2022). This presents a unique challenge for coaches and the overall coaching process.

Many coaches we spoke to have highlighted the challenges around an ingrained hierarchical culture in Asian societies and enterprises where employees are not comfortable asking questions or expressing their views in public. This is evident in social gatherings, business meetings, and company events. People often wait for the event or meeting to end and later queue up to ask questions or express a view. People are hesitant and do not speak out, and possibly withhold something that could be very valuable in these meetings. In workplaces, employees don't feel safe to challenge the status quo. According to the Asia Pacific Hopes and Fears Survey (PWC, 2023), only around 30% of employees believe their managers tolerate small-scale failures or encourage dissent and debate. It presents a difficult starting point for coaching conversations. Overcoming ingrained hierarchies and encouraging open communication across different levels of the organisation are crucial for successful scaling.

Second, different teams within an organisation may have diverse needs and challenges. Adapting Solution Focused coaching to address the specific requirements of various teams while maintaining a consistent organisational approach is a complex task.

Lastly, the COVID-19 pandemic has changed many aspects of coaching conversations. As the world moved from face-to-face conversations to online conversations (and now hybrid conversations), we are witnessing a shift in people management, leadership, and collaboration approaches. Organisations with a global presence encounter challenges in scaling coaching uniformly across diverse geographical and cultural contexts. Ensuring cultural sensitivity and adapting the coaching approach to local nuances are crucial.

Creating a Coaching Culture at Standard Chartered Bank

Transforming a large enterprise culture from a traditional culture to a coaching culture is an arduous exercise. In this section, we share the example of how Standard Chartered Bank has created the foundation for creating a coaching culture. For context, Standard Chartered Bank is a corporate and retail bank based out of London, with more than 653 branches in more than 50 countries.

Recognising the need for transformation, the initiative began with a top-down commitment from leadership to foster a more collaborative and solution-oriented organisational culture. The coaching strategy was strongly endorsed by the HR Management Team, with the intent to make it accessible to all employees in the moments that matter. A three-pillar approach (Shirke, 2023) was developed to realise an ambitious aspiration of upskilling leaders in conversational coaching ability, developing an internal cadre of certified coaches, and providing access to external coaching partners.

As the coaching approach demonstrated positive outcomes, the bank systematically expanded its application across diverse teams, ensuring cultural alignment and sensitivity to the unique challenges faced by different business units. We decided to expand the Solution Focused approach in the Client Coverage Technology division of the bank with over 1000 people. It started with creating teams of leaders and ensuring we move forward from one team to another once the team demonstrates that they embedded Solution Focused principles into their day-to-day practices.

We had two different aspects to deal with as part of this transformation. First, we had to ensure each team has a consistent approach to embed Solution Focused principles into their practices. Second, a consistent approach to roll out this across the teams and ensure that leaders are able to manage and sustain this going forward.

Embedding Solution Focused Coaching Principles into Practices

Reframing the problem statements into envisioning a hopeful future state is the first step towards a Solution Focused approach. It helps people envision what the changed or improved state will look like.

In order for us to embed the Solution Focused coaching principle into everyday practices, we defined a set of three questions that every leader should ask themselves and their respective team members. These three questions are as follows:

1 What does good look like?
2 What is working well already?
3 What small steps will you take to go forward?

These questions were embedded as part of a weekly huddle and fortnightly retrospective. When leaders started asking these questions, the shift towards a Solution Focused workplace was visible. For example, when leaders came together for a weekly huddle, they started discussing what was working well and how they could take things forward. There was a sense of progress and a hopeful future.

Approach to Ensure Sustainable Rollout and Scale

The second part of the puzzle was to ensure we scaled these practices from a selected few to the broader organisation i.e. leaders to teams.

We observed that once leaders understood the shifts and benefits from the Solution Focused coaching approach, there was a greater acceptance to adopting it and influencing others to adopt it.

We applied a few scaling techniques to drive a Solution Focused coaching approach for the larger organisation. Here are the top three techniques:

1 **Leadership Lessons from "The Last Dance" Documentary**
We found a great reference example in the documentary called "The Last Dance" on Netflix. It is a story about the National Basketball Association's (NBA) iconic athletes such as Michael Jordan and Scottie Pippen and their team the Chicago Bulls, journey to winning their 6th NBA title in 1997–1998. While most of the documentary focuses on the talented players, there was also a silent hero among them. His name was Phil Jackson, one of the most successful NBA coaches in NBA history. What was the reason for his success? He spent time connecting at a deeper level with each team member. The way he coached the team clearly demonstrated his use of Solution Focused principles in practice by coaching the who rather than just what. Players loved to play for him, as he brought out the best in each of them.

As part of our coaching approach, we asked them to watch the documentary and share the lessons they have learnt. As they shared, we connected these lessons to the Solution Focused principles and highlighted how they were intuitively learning a coaching style which provided a hopeful approach to problems and challenges.

The lessons from this documentary helped leaders relate to the shift in the expectation from their role towards servant leadership.

2 **Leadership Agreement Volunteer Signup**
We leveraged the bank's Leadership Agreement (Standard Chartered, n.d.) to guide the leaders on leadership behaviours they can inspire, aspire to, and execute on. Every leader in the organisation has been invited to sign the pledge voluntarily, making the leadership agreement the foundational element for leadership in the bank.

This helped us in establishing a common understanding of leadership principles across the bank. It helped leaders envision what good leadership behaviors look like in the bank. The leaders who were getting coached on a Solution Focused coaching approach had imagined a future state in their mind and the leadership agreement contributed to creating that future image in their individual context.

3 Reframing our Measures to Solution Focused Ideas

We started a regular cadence of sessions to check in with leaders around what was working well and how well they were applying the Solution Focused coaching approach for work as well as their team performance discussions. Keeping the focus on solutions was critical to explore possibilities and after a few iterations leaders started seeing the value of these check-ins and adapting them to their context. This also helped the cultural shift to one where people were more comfortable sharing.

To enhance awareness around Solution Focused coaching and its value, we organised weekly "ask-the-coach" sessions. These free sessions were open to everyone in the organisation and structured as open dialog sessions. These sessions helped attendees to clarify their queries about Solution Focused coaching and its application in their context.

Summary and Key Takeaways

Leadership is a demanding profession. In our day-to-day life, we all play distinct roles, yet we all are leaders in different capacities and contexts. The leader in us needs constant reminders to focus on the bigger picture or outcome while dealing with the practical details of everyday affairs. It is easy to get bogged down with the transactional nature of day-to-day work.

To stay focused, we all need tools and approaches that can help us get the desired outcomes. One such approach is the Solution Focused coaching approach. It helps leaders to focus on the bigger picture, create a sense of progress, and tackle contextual challenges using reframing and focusing on possibilities.

Throughout this chapter, we explored the key principles and techniques of Solution Focused coaching, emphasising its effectiveness in driving cultural change, fostering adaptive mindsets, and promoting continuous improvement. From its application in small teams to its successful scaling across enterprises, the approach has demonstrated its ability to empower individuals, enhance leadership effectiveness, and contribute to measurable performance improvements.

Despite challenges such as resistance to change and traditional Asian hierarchical organisational culture, organisations that invest in strategic communication, training, and ongoing evaluation stand poised to reap the numerous benefits of this coaching paradigm. As organisations increasingly recognise the value of a Solution Focused mindset in navigating today's complex business landscape, the insights and strategies shared in this chapter serve as a valuable guide for those looking to harness the full potential of Solution Focused coaching in their journey towards sustained success.

References

International Coaching Federation (2023). *Amid post-pandemic burnout, organizations increasing their investments in coaching.* https://coachingfederation.org/blog/amid-post-pandemic-burnout-organizations-increasing-their-investments-in-coaching

PWC (2023 June). *Asia Pacific workforce hopes and fears survey 2023.* PWC. https://www.pwc.com/gx/en/asia-pacific/hope-and-fears/2023/asia-pacific-hopes-and-fears-survey-2023.pdf

Sheehan, S. (2022, November 7). *The impact of executive coaching on business performance and employee performance.* Brainz Magazine. https://www.brainzmagazine.com/post/the-impact-of-executive-coaching-on-business-performance-and-employee-performance

Shirke, P. (2023). Building a coaching culture. In P. Ramanathan (Ed.), *Reflections on coaching: An anthology.* Coacharya Publications.

Standard Chartered (n.d.). *Leadership agreement.* Standard Chartered. Retrieved on 5 December 2023 from: https://av.sc.com/corp-en/content/docs/Final_Leadership_Agreement_Visual.pdf

Temelkova, K. (2022, September 8). *Everything about the languages of APAC.* Milestone Localization. https://www.milestoneloc.com/languages-of-apac/

Section 3

Executive and Leadership Coaching

7 Leadership Development in Asia Using Solution Focused Coaching

Sam Chia

Introduction

I wrote a chapter in 2010 to share the coaching trends and developments in Asia at that time including the selection criteria of an executive coach for an Asian leader (Chia, 2010). One of the important considerations for the coach is to be familiar with the Asian culture and leadership practices due to the unique way people interact and communicate which impacts the coaching relationship.

Asia has been at the forefront of the global economy in recent years. The role of the region's leaders has never been more important. Leadership transcends more than organisational hierarchies; it affects how societies and economies function. The importance of understanding leadership in Asia in this chapter is to grasp the broader dynamics and cultures of the region and how we can better develop leaders to navigate through those challenges with leadership coaching.

The primary objectives of this chapter are two-fold: firstly, to highlight the distinctive features of Asian leadership; and, secondly, to focus on cultural and historical factors shaping expectations and behaviours for leaders.

Secondly, I am recommending the use of Solution Focused (SF) coaching as a powerful development practice for improving leadership effectiveness in Asia. In an environment marked by cultural nuances and unique challenges, SF coaching offers a forward-looking and culturally sensitive approach to leadership development.

Unique Characteristics of Asian Leadership

One of the characteristics of Asian culture is the collectivist way in which groups take precedence over individuals. In such a context, leaders are often seen as managing a collective effort, and they are expected to maintain harmony, foster cooperation, and foster a sense of belonging to their teams. In Asia, this emphasis on interdependence and group cohesion creates a leadership expectation that requires leaders to be sensitive to the needs, harmony, and dynamics of their teams.

DOI: 10.4324/9781003431480-10

Steven Lam, a regional sales director located in China in the financial services industry, faced challenges when transforming his organisation and managing an underperforming leader in Japan. He received negative feedback from his clients regarding one of the leader's behaviours. He confronted the leader and shared the customer feedback, but the leader blamed his new processes as the cause of customer dissatisfaction. Steven also involved the support of the human resource (HR) manager to interview the team members to have a third-party perspective of the issues.

However, HR could not gather supportive evidence to initiate any actions. The leader's subordinates were not forthcoming with negative feedback about their boss's behaviour, despite the fact that they were not happy with him for unclear direction and lack of support to service their customers that resulted in the customer complaints.

The team members put priority on maintaining harmony and relationships within the team and were not willing to step forward and confront the leader.

Confucius' teachings ("Confucius," n.d.) encourage the idea that leaders are moral role models, fully responsible for the well-being of their followers. He stresses the importance of cultivating virtuous leaders that include kindness, goodness, honesty, modesty, wisdom, and trustworthiness. Leaders shall remain humble when working with people. Humble leaders are seen as more trustworthy and approachable, which enhances team cohesion and collaborative efforts.

Michael Tan, the Asia HR director of a global hospitality company located in Singapore, received feedback from his American boss that he needed to express his viewpoints more often, especially when meeting with senior management from the global team. Coaching conversations with him noted that he was holding back from giving his views because of the belief that he may embarrass his boss if he spoke on areas that may be overlooked by his boss. He did not want his boss to lose "face" in the meeting.

In conclusion, leadership in Asia is deeply intertwined with cultural values, historical legacies, and the expectations of collectivism, hierarchy, and humility. Understanding these unique characteristics is vital for anyone engaging in leadership development in Asia or coaching Asian leaders.

Solution Focused Coaching

SF coaching is a dynamic and forward-thinking coaching approach that focuses on solutions instead of problems, leveraging strengths, and taking small steps towards future possibilities.

SF coaching redirects attention towards exploring possibilities as coaches and leaders work together to envision a desired future and explore the steps needed to reach that outcome.

Such a forward-looking approach is well-received when working with Asian leaders. Focusing on mistakes in the problem-focused approach will face greater resistance as it may result in people being embarrassed, disrupting team harmony as they accept collective responsibilities, and the people responsible may lose face.

Traditional coaching approaches may highlight deficits, weaknesses, or gaps in a leader's skills. SF coaching, conversely, accentuates strengths and positive attributes as the foundation for change and growth. Engaging the leader in exploring past or current successes creates a different pathway towards exploring creative possibilities. By recognising and capitalising on the leader's strengths, talents, and resources, it encourages leaders to leverage these assets to overcome challenges and achieve their goals. This in turn further cultivates leader confidence.

Practical Tools and Techniques in Solution Focused Leadership Coaching

When applying SF principles in leadership coaching, several practical tools and techniques can be utilised. Some key tools are described below and illustrated with examples.

Miracle Question

The miracle question is powerful as it invites the client to imagine and describe what it would look and feel like when the problem that brought them to the session was somehow resolved, and the differences they would notice.

Using the miracle question helps the client see an ideal future without constraints by limiting beliefs and cultural constraints to focus on the solutions they would like to achieve. This is especially helpful when a younger leader is leading a team that is much older and more experienced than them.

Annie Sim, a Chinese senior director of a medical technology company, was promoted to lead a new team after a merger. Her subordinates included her former peers and team members who were much older than her. She was sensitive to the culture of respect for seniority and had been overly careful when communicating and setting new expectations for the team. As a result, change was not happening as she hoped. She was not assertive in driving her new direction with the team and was not comfortable providing feedback to older colleagues. She began to lose confidence in leading the new team.

During the coaching, she shared her frustrations. The miracle question helped her to shift her perspective and visualise a team of people with a depth of knowledge and wisdom helping one another in an open and supportive environment. She described herself influencing and gaining the trust and respect of the team with her respectful approach but firm and clear in her expectations and direction. She focused on leveraging the team's strengths rather than worrying about their age and experience. She shifted her mindset, viewing her team as a pool of consultants or expert resources instead of her subordinates.

The questions helped her to explore ways to use her strengths, seek her team's feedback and input like a consultant, and create an environment of a mastermind group to jointly explore solutions when working with issues.

Scaling

Scaling (Jackson & McKergow, 2007, pp. 94–95) provides a process and helps visually demonstrate the extent of the distance between the current state and the desired state in relation to any identified goal.

Scaling is a widely used coaching tool and can help to overcome the Asian value of humility, as Asians do not like to promote themselves and speak about how good they are. They normally rate themselves lower, even though they may be proficient. The tools help to surface their strengths and resources in an indirect way.

Scaling invites the client to think more deeply about the areas being scaled, irrespective of the number on the scale. It facilitates an increase in self-awareness and provides some valuable insight into the client's situation and thinking.

Johnson Wang was a Taiwanese director of an IT solutions provider. He hoped to develop greater visibility based on the feedback he received from stakeholders. The lack of visibility had hindered his opportunity for promotion, as his good work was not noted by others. Johnson personally felt that the development gap was too big and difficult to close. He shared that he did not like to promote himself and he believed his performance should speak for him.

Johnson was a classic example of an Asian leader whose values of humility had limited his visibility, which is an important practice in a large matrix global organisation. During the coaching sessions, he was asked to rate himself on visibility, and with no surprise, he gave himself a low score of 3.

I asked him to reflect on what made him a 3 and not a 1 or 2. Surprisingly even to himself, he shared a series of things he was doing well that helped him to build his visibility. He spoke about his strengths and how he contributed to some projects beyond his functions; he showed good initiative and was seen to be a reliable member of the organisation; he was hungry to learn and open to feedback. As he spoke, he thought he should be a 6 or 7 in visibility, and the gap towards his goals was not as big or scary as he thought.

The tools helped to build up Johnson's confidence and empowered him to further explore some small steps that would move him forward towards greater visibility. He realised that visibility was not only about himself but also about raising his team by sharing their achievements and successes through newsletters and internal forums. In addition, he put effort into developing his strategic network and building relationships with the right people.

He was promoted about a year later. Scaling helped to create greater awareness that he had the resources and strengths towards his goal. This gave him greater confidence to find some additional small steps to move forward.

Small Actions and Affirmation

SF coaching pivots around small actions that empower the client to step forward. Such small wins supported with affirmation will propel a series of new small actions that may result in a big difference in the client's journey towards his goals.

The case of Johnson in the earlier example reinforced this principle.

Case Study – Putting the Solution Focused Tools Together in Coaching Leaders

Case Context – Platform

Ashish, an Indian national, was a new country general manager based in Indonesia leading a team of about 50 people for a global IT solutions company. Ashish was previously the national sales director in India and had been a high achiever resulting in his recent promotion.

Ashish faced some major challenges during his first six months in Indonesia, as the attrition rate increased. In addition, he found that he had fumbled in presentations to some regional leaders when they visited.

Ashish sought the help of a coach to support his new leadership journey. They had a series of prior coaching sessions on a number of leadership challenges and this session focused on the effective presentation to regional leaders.

Switching the Conversation from Problems to Solutions

Coach: Hi Ashish, it's been two weeks since we met. What has been better for you?

Ashish: Hi Coach! We discussed how to build relationships and gain trust with my team. I started to have small talks with my team and during the 1 on 1 talks, I showed more care and concern instead of questioning their work progress. I can see that they are more open to me now. I think I am in the right direction to build a relationship and gain trust with my team.

Coach: Great. What would you like from today's session?

Ashish: Remember the incident I told you about, the presentation I made to the regional guys who visited my location last month? I hope to review my mistakes so that I will not repeat them.

Coach: Yes. I remember. Reflecting back on the presentation, what was different when you presented very well in India?

Ashish: Oops! Good questions. I just think about the mistakes I made. Let me recollect some of the good presentations previously. I was confident, I knew my content and numbers and I understood my Indian client's needs. I have been working with many of those clients before and I have good relationships with them. When I think about the difference, I don't know the regional people that well who were mainly from the United States, and I am meeting some of them for the first time.

Affirmation

Coach: Wow. You have just shared some important considerations for a good presentation, i.e. confidence, knowing the content and audience needs. I have also noted you have a different type of audience this time.

Ashish: Yes. Unlike presenting to the client in India, this time we have some senior people from the United States whom I don't know well. Whatever I say, I may be judged on my abilities, and I may lose their respect. I don't really like to have strangers in my presentation. Somehow, I just feel uneasy.

Using the Miracle Questions

Coach: Ashish. I am going to ask you a strange question. Hope it is OK?

Ashish: Sure!

Coach: Suppose there is another presentation tomorrow to another group of regional people whom you do not know well. You go home after our conversation and spend the day preparing the presentation. Tonight, you do your usual stuff, go to bed, and sleep early. Somehow while you sleep, some miracle happens! You have acquired some superpower during your sleep that makes you an amazing, fearless, and eloquent speaker tomorrow when you carry out the presentation to the regional team, many of whom you haven't met before.

What would you notice?

How would the regional team react to your presentation?

What difference does this make?

Ashish: Ha ha! I love to have this superpower. I would say hello to some of them whom I hadn't met before the presentation. I will be very confident and convincing in my presentation. I can handle any questions they throw at me. I will impress them that I know the market and product well and that they feel confident and trust me feeling assured they are putting the right GM in Indonesia. I feel very comfortable as if I know them well and have an established relationship with them. I am sure I will receive compliments from them after the presentations.

Scaling and Resources

Coach: I can see the smile on your face when you share this experience. Suppose this experience represents a perfect 10 experience. Assuming 10 is the ideal presentation and 0 is a poor presentation, how do you rate yourself currently?

Ashish: I think I am only 4. I am still afraid and not comfortable. Maybe I am not a native speaker. I just don't know why.

Coach: I'm curious about those areas that you felt you did well to give yourself a 4 and not lower.

Ashish: I believe I know my product and market well and I am pretty good at putting the information in the PowerPoint so that the flow of information is clear.

Coach: That is great. You have some strengths that you can leverage for a good presentation. You have good content and structure in the presentation format.

Small Actions

Coach: Suppose you start to move up to a 5. What would you notice?

Ashish: I would have more confidence. I would have a casual chat with the regional team before the presentation to gauge what is important to them. I would build some relationships with small talk and learn to calm myself before the presentation. You have to think of them, not as a stranger.

Coach: How have you managed that so far?

Ashish: I started practising meditation and yoga a year ago. I probably can use some of the techniques like breathing in and out a few times before I start the presentation to calm myself.

Coach: What else helps you to have the confidence you want?

Ashish: I think I should also change my presentation a bit. The American people are more direct and straight to the point. I should be more direct in sharing my ideas.

Coach: Sounds like you have some great ideas on what to do to cater to the audience.

Ashish: I can focus my eye contact with those that I know well as this relieves me from the thought of presenting to a stranger.

Coach: Sounds like you have gained some new ideas to impress your American colleagues. Can you summarise some of the points and some action steps you can do to make the killer presentation?

Outcome

The client overcame one of his presentation challenges to senior people whom he doesn't know well. The SF coaching approach helped navigate some concerns in the cultural differences in communication style, building relationships, and maintaining respect and seniority. The client was promoted subsequently and took up a larger regional role a year later.

Conclusion

Leadership coaching in Asia is a growing need with Asian leaders playing a more important role in global organisations. Understanding the unique traits and business practices in Asia and the use of SF coaching can help speed up the leadership development process.

The SF coaching approach harmonises seamlessly with Asian values like respect (recognising strengths and affirmation), emphasising harmony (what's working and doing more of it) and humility (small steps). It offers a culturally sensitive and agile approach that empowers leaders to address leadership challenges, enhance their communication and presentation skills, improve self-awareness, and develop greater self-confidence.

References

Chia, S. (2010). Coaching in Asia: Trends and development. In D. Wright, A. Leong, K. E. Weith, & S. Chia (Eds), *Coaching in Asia: The first decade* (pp. 153–162). Candid Creation Publishing LLP.

Confucius (n.d.). Retrieved on November 28, 2023, from https://en.wikipedia.org/wiki/Confucius

Jackson, P. Z. & McKergow, M. (2007). *The solutions focus: Making coaching and change SIMPLE*. Nicholas Brealey Publishing.

8 The Power of Imagination – The Future Perfect

Solution Focused Coaching in Hong Kong

Yee Lin Ng

Introduction

In 2020, the world came to a standstill, yet it was also evolving into something unfamiliar to most. I began to question myself and the work that I had confidently identified with for the past 30 years.

I was drawn to the quote "Problem talk creates problems, solution talk creates solutions" by Steve de Shazer. This paradigm aligned with my conduct in leadership and work in the creative industry that I was in. Solution Focused (SF) widened my perspective to re-discover who I am, what's important, and what my preferred Future Perfect would look like.

The transformational impact was so positive and powerful that it led to coaching adults going through transitions in life, as well as with youth. The SF framework guided me as a consultant at Community Business Hong Kong (a non-profit) to design and facilitate programmes with C-suites and organisations on their Diversity and Inclusion journey.

This chapter explores the power of imagination on one's "future perfect". I will share a case example of how transformative SF conversations led to a client's enhanced sense of confidence, discovered what's next, and shifted her perception that unleashes clarity and hope.

Case Example

CJ, a Hong Konger, and co-founder and director of a startup based in Thailand, greeted me with "I look tired ... I'm very tired". The company was expanding beyond her expectations. She wanted "to adjust my emotions". She felt lucky yet annoyed because of the work. She questioned her capability to handle all the opportunities coming in. She felt unable to follow the daily plan as she has "拖延症" *(Cantonese: procrastination)*. CJ was delaying tasks that were easy to do but were not a priority due to other tasks. Her time was compromised because she had to complete these routine tasks. It made her very "憫憎" *(Cantonese: agitated)*.

DOI: 10.4324/9781003431480-11

Excerpts of the Solution Focused Conversation

Coach: What would you prefer instead?
CJ: Well … I should do it right away.
Coach: What else?
CJ: I prefer someone else to do the routine work. *(smiles widely)*
Coach: What difference would that make?
CJ: Well … I will have some "alone" time to think about story concepts, story development related to drama, and performing arts. I prefer to use the night-time for these.
Coach: How come this is important for you?
CJ: Spending the amount of time on admin work … like till 1 am, 2 am, … the biggest difference is I end up with the creatives happily. It's like time well spent! While doing the admin tasks, I'm always annoyed why I'm doing it.

CJ shared two questions she had about her daily plan: "How do I stick to the plan?" and "How do I delegate to new people because the existing people are at full capacity?"

Coach: Suppose you stick to your plan and know how to delegate to the new people. Let's put on your imagination cap now *(pause)*, how does the 最佳场景 (Cantonese: *perfect scenario*) look in your future perfect daily plan?
CJ: I would be proactive. If I have a list of 20 tasks, I finish them before attending to something else. I know other work will keep coming in too.
Coach: What else?
CJ: Some tasks that are creative … working with the scriptwriter and show director to talk about stories, how to set up the workshop. This is what I like to do. Everything related to theatre or storytelling. Right now, we have this task, I've been quieter than I should be because I don't have time.
Coach: How would you be feeling?
CJ: I am reminded I'm not really involved in the theatre work. In fact, I'm not proactive in anything. Just supporting.
Coach: Suppose you are fully involved in the theatre work, how does it look in your 最佳场景 *(perfect scenario)*?
CJ: I would have a clear mind to suggest things.
Coach: What would you be suggesting?
CJ: Talking about the grand opening for the restaurant or other projects that we are doing. I get focused on doing one thing, just do, do, do. Then I can't do the rest of my other tasks.
Coach: What else would you be doing in your future perfect daily plan?

CJ: Talking to people. When I talk to people, it's a struggle. I get more information, then it goes into a loop, and I have more things to do.

Coach: Instead of feeling a struggle, how would you like to feel instead?

CJ: *(Laughs)* Then I would choose the people I talk to! I like the feeling that when I talk to certain people, I inspire them to do things differently … . and they feel relieved after talking to me. I feel useful.

Coach: Wow *(softly)*. How would you know who are the people to choose?

CJ: They are not related to work.

Coach: How else would you be feeling?

CJ: Contented. *(smiles)*

Coach: And what would you be thinking?

CJ: Oh … so deep … it is the way of living that I like. I want. *(nods her head)*

Coach: What else would you like to add to develop this storyline?

CJ: Spend time with kids.

Coach: How does that look in your 最佳场景 *(perfect scenario)*?

CJ: I feel contented. I feel I can help the parents when I interact with the young kids. I know I have the talent to talk or play with the kids.

Coach: Where do you meet these kids?

CJ: Kids I meet on the streets.

Coach: Suppose you are playing with kids, how would you feel?

CJ: I feel useful and contented. This is what I want to do.

When scaling CJ's current state in relation to her preferred future perfect daily plan, she wanted to give a scale of 3 or 4. CJ realised that being an Asian, one tends to underestimate oneself.

CJ: I feel I'm underestimating myself. If 6, I don't feel it yet. Maybe 6 is being too optimistic. If I want to improve I would need to delegate work. Do I have potential people? Actually, yes! I have but didn't do yet … so I make it a 5. We have projects, tools, people, a target audience. If I want to play with kids and inspire them, I have a way. The restaurant, the kids' education centre, friends' kids. All the things are here … 5 means all the things are here.

Coach: Wow! What else helped you to arrive at 5?

CJ: Myself!

Coach: What about yourself that helped you?

CJ: Two things. Original me and evolving me.

When asked what qualities of "original me" and "evolving me" helped her reach the current stage, upon "self-reflection", her perception changed and some of her ways of doing things.

Most importantly, she accepted certain things needed to get done, whether she liked it or not.

It helped her to adjust her emotions from being annoyed to being calm. Her best friend noticed she's brave as she had always "followed the flow" when the right opportunities related to theatre or entertainment knocked on her door.

Coach: What else?

CJ: When I talked to people in my Perfect 10 scenario, they pushed me to excel or sometimes transit to business opportunities.

Coach: Talking to people who inspire you ... sounds like this is another storyline to enrich your 最佳场景 *(perfect scenario)?*

CJ: *(Smiles and nods).* Can I add one more thing to my 最佳场景 *(perfect scenario)?* I will be speaking Thai. The young kids, graduates, students, working with us now or acting in the theatre production ... only 2–3 of them can speak basic English. When I speak in English, most of the time, they don't understand. We have facilitators who can communicate with them. However, during rehearsals when we work on storylines and brainstorm different ideas ... I cannot get involved because I do not understand Thai.

Coach: Suppose you can converse in Thai, what difference would that make?

CJ: I will be more involved, instead of in a supporting role.

Coach: Since we are back in your 最佳场景 *(perfect scenario),* I'm curious about what happens to the admin routine work.

CJ: I find experts to do it instead.

Coach: How can the experts help you?

CJ: Structure reorganisation and admin tasks. I will have more free time ... I will have more time to do what's in my 最佳场景 *(perfect scenario).*

Coach: Experts to assist you so you have more free time to live your way of living,

CJ: Yes, *(laughs)* Yes!

CJ ended the session with "When I work on my task list, I will imagine my Perfect 10 最佳场景 *(perfect scenario)*!" Later, CJ sent me a picture of her having coffee at a restaurant, while she was handling an unexpected task.

Quote from CJ – After my first session, something amazing happened. I was able to clearly identify the goals that mattered most to me. It felt like magic. Yee Lin skilfully guided me through a process of organising my thoughts and uncovering my true aspirations. She helped me understand what I really wanted to achieve.

Excerpts of the Follow-Up Session

Coach: Hello CJ. You are looking more refreshed than we last met.

CJ: The task list ... I thought about the future perfect 10. Let me summarise. To meet people ... to meet selected people ... to do some creative work that I like. Play with kids and ... learn Thai.

CJ shared what had happened: "When I see it, I make the effort, I enjoy the moment".

Coach: How come this changed in you?
CJ: I'm conscious of my 最佳場景 *(perfect scenario)* that I want to achieve.
Coach: What else have you noticed about yourself?
CJ: Things not related to the scenes; I need to make sure they are done faster so I can do those things in my 最佳場景 *(perfect scenario)*!
        It feels like I've changed my focus 重心 *(Cantonese: centre of gravity)*. The to-do list of tasks that do not make me happier ... sometimes even annoys me. It's because I want to achieve my perfect scenarios, I've got to attend to these tasks first or squeeze some time to do them. For example, I was at the visa office close to a friend's house. I needed to have lunch and grab a coffee so why not take the chance to ask her out?
Coach: Wow ... take the chance?
CJ: This is an accidental agenda. I planned 1–2 hours for admin work at some centre, but I have no control over the waiting time. While waiting, I went for coffee and played with my phone. I saw this massage place. Why not get an hour massage? The remaining time, I can still grab a coffee. It seemed to make more sense, more purposeful and practical. At least I will be relaxed ... quality time spent.
Coach: How do you feel after making a conscious effort to achieve better choices?
CJ: Happy. Recharged. Sometimes, I think we are too tense. Meetings all the time. Plenty of things to do. All back-to-back.
Coach: What did you learn about yourself?
CJ: It's very important to be independent.
Coach: How does independence look to you?
CJ: It's my relationship with my partner RJ. Despite being together, both of us need to be independent. We spent so much quality time together during COVID-19; my dependency on him became a habit. I'm trying to correct this.
Coach: What did you do that tells you are trying to be independent?
CJ: Each of us has different tasks to do, many of which I can do myself. I also rely too much on my PA but knowing she's leaving soon, I need to change. My PA speaks Thai and things get done quickly. I need to figure out a way I can work quickly, or does it matter I don't speak Thai?
Coach: You are thinking of ways to work differently. What else?

CJ: I look at my perfect scenarios. I tell myself I need to speed up while I'm doing all these tasks so I can do something else. All are interrelated. Because when I need to speed up … I need to be even more independent to figure out ways to do it. "Should I find time to discuss with him?" This wasted time since we're all so busy. I spent the last few days practicing how to speed up because I'm conscious of my 最佳场景 *(perfect scenario)*.

It's not about finishing the task, just because I get to do things in my 最佳场景 *(perfect scenario)*, my mood is better! *(Smiles)*

When asked how to sustain her progress, CJ shared that there's an app that teaches a few Thai words daily. She would learn Thai as part of a "daily routine morning habit". She would try conversing in Thai with her staff in the morning before everyone gets busy. In turn, she would know they appreciate her effort in learning Thai.

Quote from CJ – When I met with Yee Lin in the second session, I could sense the positive changes within myself. It's important to note that the transformation wasn't an overnight miracle; it involved taking gradual steps towards progress. The whole process allowed me to gain a deeper understanding of myself. What amazed me the most was that the methods for improvement were often surprisingly simple. Yee Lin never imposed her own ideas or solutions. Instead, I was able to think independently and find my own answers. It was truly an empowering experience. I could feel myself growing and evolving with each session.

Cultural Reflections

During the scaling exercise, CJ commented that she had initially underestimated her number – noting that Asians often do this. Modesty is an important Chinese cultural value (Chan & Chung, 2016). The beauty of SF is that the actual number does not matter. It is a means to explore what is working already and all the strengths and resources that got the person to that number, and ask what they will notice as they move up the scale. Therefore, the coach can respectfully accept the number offered.

A diverse and inclusive leadership team and organisation is visionary, empowering, and authentic. Teams will embrace multiple perspectives, experience wider engagement, and thus be constantly in the state of future readiness. When I design Diversity and Inclusion workshops, I incorporate future perfect and scaling exercises that stretch the boundaries of the leaders or team, to recognise and value the diverse voices and situations that went well and enable them to commit to small steps. In this way, the work is truly inclusive as it focuses on the preferred future that fits the client's or organisation's cultural context.

Paying attention to language is important in SF, which relates to the client's language and the words they use. While the majority of the session was conducted in English, CJ used specific Cantonese words when these fitted better for her. I used the term 最佳场景 *(perfect scenario)* as I felt CJ could relate to it. It is like speaking her language about developing storylines in the theatre for perfect scenarios.

CJ's preferred future perfect is where she can be her authentic self, fully express her strengths, and have her contributions valued through engaging with people who matter to her. With clarity, these transformational behaviours and positive emotions create an inclusive environment where all can thrive and for CJ to arrive at her future perfect scenes, the way of living she wants.

It is a hopeful virtuous cycle. It makes her happy.

Reference

Chan, S. T. M., & Chung, A. Y. L. (2016). Chinese cultural values and solution focused therapy. In *Solution focused practice in Asia* (pp. 48–53). Routledge.

9 Leadership Coaching with Entrepreneurs in Malaysia

Alex Tan and Jane Tuomola

Introduction

I (J.T.) had the privilege of interviewing Alex Tan about his work as a leadership coach in Malaysia. This chapter is a transcript of our interview sharing a wonderful case example of how he combined individual leadership coaching and team coaching with two founders of a company, to strengthen their partnership and business. Alex shares how he built a safe and trusting relationship, using Solution Focused (SF) coaching questions to help them realise their best hopes. What could have been a challenging situation full of conflicts was an inspiring piece of work that enabled the founders to grow and mature in their work and life. He shares tips he wishes he had when starting as a coach, and how to find your coaching voice and resonate with your clients. He offers reflections on the Asian cultural context and how the entrepreneurial culture differs from corporate settings. My hope is that you are as inspired reading this chapter as I was doing the interview.

Q: Alex, what are your best hopes in sharing this piece of coaching?
My intention was to share how SF coaching was impactful for my clients and for me as a coach. I want to share practical examples of coaching so that other people can find inspiration and find their own coaching voice. When I first started coaching, I didn't have any reference points from a case study. When I first learned coaching, it was about the techniques, versus when you actually coach, process that, and how you adapted coaching to different cultural contexts.

Q: Before we dive into the story, what is your context as a coach?
I am based in Malaysia, and work across Southeast Asia, including Singapore, and the Philippines. The coaching style of choice is SF which I've been practicing since 2010.

Q: What piece of work would you like to share?
This involves two founding partners: individual coaching with each founder and team coaching with them together. They were young and dynamic

DOI: 10.4324/9781003431480-12

entrepreneurs. They were in a new business and the business was flourishing. They wanted coaching as a safeguard to ensure their partnership would flourish and thrive.

Q: How did you approach this piece of work?
I always start with an alignment session to make sure that they know what they're getting into, and to understand what leadership coaching is. I wanted to make sure they understood what coaching is. I'm not here to fix their business. They were very smart and confident. What they needed was a coach to help them get to the next level.

Q: How did you manage meeting with the two founders - potentially there could have been a conflict of interest with each of them meeting you individually?
I had a preliminary conversation with one of the founders to size me up. Then the three of us met. I laid out the plan to include individual and team coaching. I explained confidentiality and they understood the professional nature of the engagement. They were both very open minded and humble.

Q: Can you share some of the background?
When I first met them, they had just gotten a prestigious business award. They wanted to make sure they were grounded. They both wanted to develop as founders and directors. They were young, successful people who were aggressive, eager, energetic, and sometimes impatient. They were growing their business very aggressively. You're talking about massive growth, sustainability, and managing the expectation and pressure.

Q: What were their hopes from coaching?
They each wanted to develop their leadership capacity and capability as they grew the company. They wanted to maintain the unity, strength, and synergy that they had as partners and keep growing. Team coaching was important that the coach remain neutral to enable open communication.

Q: What did the sessions look like? What did you do?
The two founders had very distinct backgrounds, characters, and different profiles, with an age gap of three years. I wanted to ensure consistency in the kind of things we covered, but in broad strokes. For example, we could be talking about the personal side, then work and then about the partnership, and lastly the business.

I maintained an SF mindset. I asked: What are key progress areas in your business that have happened since the last session? Then we'll explore what they were looking for from each conversation. What's important for us to talk about today? How would that make a difference for you? One of the important things in an engagement like this is building rapport and trust. It's always a relationship. If they don't feel that you're listening or interested in them, or if you go into the business first, then it's going to be dry and superficial.

It's about being able to build a cumulative relationship rather than just cumulative listening. It's about the relationship built over time, and references to where things were when we first met, to where they were at every point.

Q: What kinds of SF questions did you use?
I used the scaling question almost every session. They were corporate people, very cognitive and analytical. The scaling question always worked well. They liked to reflect on progress. I usually make references from the past: 'In the previous session you said you were at a five, right now you're at seven. What's different? What did others notice? What does this mean for you?"

Small change can lead to big change. Change in insight, change in their lens, how they look at things can be significant for their growth. Asking questions to identify and build on these small changes is useful.

Q: How did you bring their best hopes together during team coaching?
The team coaching worked well because they both had a very clear contractual goal – to ensure the partnership, the bond, the trust, and the loyalty were intact. In the event they had differences, which they did occasionally, I would remind them – 'Why are we here? Are we here to point fingers or are we here to resolve things?' They also had a promise to themselves that they would not leave things hanging, they would always address 'the smelly fish' on the table.

It's almost like couple counselling. You never go to bed angry. I think that was one of the contractual goals; we made reference to how this topic is useful and relevant in terms of our partnership. Is it a joint task? Are we talking about this because it strengthened the relationship? Everybody was just in tune.

There was one point where the partners had to appoint a CEO because in the beginning of the partnership both of them treated each other as equals. But as they grew, they needed to get investors to come in. In the corporate context, it's useful to have a hierarchy and to state clearly who is steering the ship. I personally thought that if they did not have a coach, it could become competitive and very aggressive. Coaching helped them see the bigger picture, as it could have escalated.

Coaching was one of the factors that kept them together. They created a cadence between themselves. Recently, I was in touch with them and they said that the cadence they created, meeting on weekends, regardless if they have any reasons to meet, worked well. They kept the brotherhood. They were friends first and partners second.

Q: What impact did the coaching have on them?
My perception is that they grew mentally. Looking at things from a broader perspective. The SF approach uses a lot of relationship questions: How would

this make a difference to your partner? How will this impact your team and those around you? How would they notice this?

One of them was very proud of his culture, and his values. It was never about him. I remember him saying that leaders eat last. I reflected back to them: How is that relevant to your values? In the event where there was friction, what did they want to do? I think maturity would be the biggest word. Both of them became more mature and more selfless. There was also a major impact in their partnership: they grew together. Their bond became very strong. There were many instances when it could have gone either way but until today they are good friends and partners, and their business is flourishing despite the pandemic.

Q: When you mention maturity or the bond was stronger, how did that show up?
Partner A, who is older, would say partner B is now a very different person. He used to be frivolous, and somewhat impulsive. He used to do things his way. Partner A has become more mature, empathetic and understanding. His tone is like a proud brother to Partner B, saying he's very grounded now. Partner A is more mature with who he wants to be, and the kind of leader he wants to be. There used to be a conflict between what he's expected to do and what he wanted to do. Now he is in alignment and there's a calmness. How they show up now is very different, more mature.

Q: What have you learned from your coaching?
I noticed that while we are coaches, we have to stay impartial, I realised that to do a good job, and to be a good coach, you have to grow together with your clients as well. And you don't take it as a job or contract; you have to genuinely care. And the coachee also genuinely cares about you. They said you're the one who keeps us grounded, every time we deviated, you kept us focused. I didn't realise these are the things that people appreciate about me – so now I have more awareness about myself too.

I've also grown from the perspective of my coaching skills because this was one of my longest coaching relationships – it lasted for about three years. In these three years, their business went through highs and lows. I could see how coaching worked when people are flourishing. But did it also work in times of crisis? I can conclude it works in bad times because it gives people hope. It gives people a sense of affirmation. It's one of the reasons why I love SF scaling; we scale the past to build on resources that are already available. What got you here? That question is very powerful because most people don't think of it like that. They usually say, I have so much more to go. I thought that was very profound, being able to test the SF approach with the same person through thick and thin.

Q: What cultural factors impacted your coaching?
What I'm going to say might sound stereotypical. For example, entrepreneurs are more sensitive about money. Every single cent counts. I think more so in

the Asian context – being concerned about the money rather than the value. How do you clearly quantify the value that you get from coaching? From a cultural perspective, it was a gamble for my coachees. Maybe that is the same everywhere, but I think more so in Asia. If your friend recommends it, the chances of you getting a coach is much higher. In Asia even if you have the best credential in the world, you may or may not get the job.

The cultural context was also about the entrepreneurial versus the corporate culture. I'm more accustomed to coaching leaders in the corporate setting which is very different because they have to answer to board members. I introduced concepts like 'optics' to them. Whether you like it or not, you have to show up in a certain way because now you own the business. You are the face of the business. There are many stakeholders that you have to be looking at.

The third adjustment is about how I match them in terms of their energy when it comes to their age. I'm more than ten years their senior. What they didn't need was a mentor. What they needed was a coach who could resonate with them from a thinking perspective. If the language is about marketing, I focus on marketing. Over and above our competency as a coach we need to be able to resonate at the same level that requires conscious adjustment.

Q: There are so many layers of culture: generational, corporate, entrepreneurial. What particular factors related to Asian cultural values emerged?
It's like asking a fish how it feels being in water. I'm an Asian. The easiest way I can explain this is to contrast when I coach clients from Europe. My European clients focus more on their personal development, how they show up, and how their leadership impacts others and the business. From an Asian context, we are a little bit more communal. It's about how I show up and how it impacts my team, how it impacts my partner. I've got to be good because my team depends on me rather than I want to be good, which I feel is more of a Western perspective: 'I want to be the best version of myself'. There's nothing wrong with that, but in the Asian context: 'I want to be the best that I can be so that I can protect my team, I can protect my family, I can protect my partner'. It is less self-centred. I don't say that in a bad way but here it is more community driven, more tribe driven.

Q: Is there anything I haven't asked that you want to share?
This piece of work was about building a relationship and growing together with my clients. The term partnership actually works really well and benefits both the coachees and the coach. You partner with them because they are in the driver's seat. I need to think about what is in their best interest and what kind of response would be helpful to them. I reflect, am I truly helping them? Is it my personal agenda? And when they are successful, I become more successful. So partnering in my context is really about growth from all parties.

Q: Any final tips for the readers?

My tip is find your coaching voice and find the most optimum way that your coaching voice can benefit your clients and you. Find what you like, and whether it works for your clients or not. So the tip is that there's a period of courtship from both parties. Enjoy this courtship and understand one another and be genuine about it. That's why I would say building trust and rapport is about making that conversation work. Because if your coaching voice resonates with them, they will respond more fluidly. So it's never about the technique. Although I love being SF, that should not be the reason why you coach using the SF approach. You should coach using SF because it works for your clients. They don't even know that it's SF, but they just know that they like it. So those would be my parting words: find your coaching voice and resonate with your clients.

10 Solution Focused Executive Coaching in Taiwan

Cheng-Tseng Lin and Ru-Ya Chang

Introduction

Solution Focused (SF) coaching uses positive language with clients to inspire them to make changes happen. Coaches aim to understand clients' perspectives, abilities, and resources. They look for signs of exceptions to the clients' problems and support a change to occur in small steps.

This chapter showcases the application of SF coaching in Taiwan. It starts with a description of the Taiwanese business context. In Taiwanese companies, coaches empower coachees through one-on-one sessions. The conversations can help managers develop an understanding of and appreciate the views of the staff they work with so that they can mentor their staff more effectively. A case study with transcripts is provided so that readers can see the powerful conversations that SF coaching enables, using the SOLUTION model (O'Connell, 2012).

The Taiwanese Business Context

Taiwan faces significant political risks and changes in international relations which bring about a high degree of uncertainty to economic and industrial development. Taiwanese managers face unique and complex challenges, such as policy changes, trade friction, political instability, international market competition, and industrial restructuring. With the advancement of globalisation and technological change, industries need to deftly adjust their corporate strategies to ensure long-term development. With the intensification of international corporate competition, attracting and retaining excellent talent has become increasingly difficult. Corporate managers need to develop more effective talent management strategies to attract and retain personnel. As companies expand globally, multicultural teams are an inevitable development that forces managers to adjust their strategies accordingly.

Case Example

Paul is a professional manager who has been with the current company for nearly 30 years. Prior to the outbreak of the pandemic, the net profit of his

DOI: 10.4324/9781003431480-13

company's products could reach 40%. However, over the past three years, catalysed by the pandemic, there have been significant changes in professional skills and market demands, resulting in the net profit dwindling to only 20%. The management team is under immense pressure.

In the 360-degree interviews conducted before the coaching conversation, the management team highlighted the following challenges, hoping that Paul could find some opportunities for resolution. In the past, the organisation prioritised performance without emphasising talent training and development. Now, a difficult economic environment has exposed the team's lack of manpower and talent gaps, putting Paul's leadership team in a state of disarray, and the atmosphere is extremely tense. Because there is no clear knowledge transfer process, a lack of willingness to share and collaborate among new and old employees, and a lack of effective communication and collaboration mechanisms, cultivating or finding new talent is a daunting challenge.

Modelling a Solution

Rather than discussing the reasons behind their clients' issues, SF coaches prioritise discussing what their clients have already. The coaches talk to their clients about their current situation and interests, without directly probing into the problems they are facing. This often allows coaches to uncover helpful information during the coaching session, such as how to collaborate with the client, what cases or metaphors are most likely to resonate with clients and touch them emotionally, and what resources can help their client build solutions related to their strengths, abilities, and values. Simultaneously, it empowers the conversation to become impactful and open by centring the discussion on the client's resources and strategy. It creates a positive starting point for the coach and the client.

O'Connell et al. (2012) summarised the SF coaching approach into the SOLUTION model, which serves as a foundation for coaches. The SOLUTION model consists of eight elements:

S	Share updates
O	Observe interests
L	Listen to hopes and goals
U	Understand exceptions
T	Tap potential
I	Imagine success
O	Own outcomes
N	Note contributions

Below is an example of the SOLUTION model being implemented in a coaching conversation with Paul in three different stages:

- Stage 1: illustrating the first three elements of the SOLUTION model (S, O, L)
- Stage 2: leveraging the fourth, fifth, and sixth elements of the model (U, T, I)
- Stage 3: wrapping up the conversation with the last two elements of the model (O and N).

The purpose of this conversation is to explore various common issues and situations many senior executives face in Taiwan.

Stage 1: S, O, and L in the SOLUTION Model

Paul sits with his hands clasped in front of a window in a high-rise building. The bright sunshine behind him makes his expression appear even more gloomy.

Paul:	Coach, are you here to convince me to quit my job?
Coach:	It sounds like you are worried about why we might be meeting. What are your hopes from our conversation?
Paul:	I seem to have misjudged the situation. With political factors and the rise in COVID-19 cases, we can't bring in enough inventory. The profit from our orders is not enough to cover the additional shipping costs.
Coach:	How do you see the situation now?
Paul:	It won't be resolved anytime soon!
Coach:	I see. If it's possible, how do you want things to look after this is resolved?
Paul:	That's a good question. In the long run, it can't always be me carrying the load. I hope I can have a successor sooner rather than later!
Coach:	What would be different for you if there was a successor?
Paul:	The younger generation on our team hasn't fully matured yet, so it's up to us old-timers! We'll work hard and then pass the baton!
Coach:	What does "pass the baton" mean?
Paul:	It means I can step back and no longer be in charge.

Although Paul started dour, for a coach, the more negative the client's emotions are, the larger his motivation to successfully turn things around. This is a very powerful message. An SF coach pays attention to the client's focus, accepts it, and then asks questions about the desired situation.

Stage 2: U, T, and I in the SOLUTION Model

The SF coach believes that clients are experts in solving their own problems, and they must have some past successful experiences and strategies to cope with current issues. Below, the coach uses exception questions to help the client identify successful experiences from difficult times in the past, see opportunities and resources, and guide them towards imagining a better future.

Coach: So, what is the situation now?

Paul: Currently, the three most important departments are manufacturing processes, finance, and sales. Finance has several managers with 10+ years of experience and is quite stable, but the manufacturing process department has a lot of issues. However, the sales department is the most concerning. Our old customers need new products and services to support their expansion, but the sales team's average age is too high, and they lack imagination and drive. They don't even know how to use the customer's products, so I don't know how to move forwards with the customer.

Coach: What have you done so far to help this situation?

Paul: Last year, the sales department recruited some experienced middle-aged and young salespeople. With the pandemic this year, we couldn't visit customers, but we became more familiar with them through online communication. The younger generation is proficient with video conferencing. They can converse more easily in front of a screen than face-to-face. We hold online lunch meetings and Christmas parties with clients, and the results seem to be good. It saves money and time!

Coach: What else?

Paul: The manufacturing process is variable and difficult to control. With the lockdowns, we can only follow the government's orders. I'm sitting in Taiwan, trying to reduce losses in shipments. Even if we lose money, we still must ship the goods! After all, the pandemic is temporary, but the company must last!

Coach: It sounds like you have some strategies in place for work. What do you hope will happen next?

Paul: Management training! Each department can provide professional training, but it is difficult to train a successor who has a comprehensive understanding of their department as well as a big-picture perspective. In the past, we had to do everything ourselves. But now, with more specialisation and a reluctance to take risks, it's not easy to produce successors within the organisation. However, bringing in outside managers is only a temporary solution, as differences in corporate culture can be an issue.

Coach: It's true that producing successors is not an overnight task, but if you hand things over to middle-aged and young salespeople and they step up, what difference do you hope that will make to the future situation of your company?

Paul: If the manufacturing process, finance, and sales departments all have stable and capable leaders, they will be better equipped to explore new markets and develop new products. The younger generation has many ideas, but they need to learn quickly. If they improve, our company's products will have a higher market share and we'll have more opportunities.

Stage 3: O and N in the SOLUTION Model

The coach continued with Paul and discussed his goals in more detail and then moved on to exploring what steps forwards he could take.

Coach: What ideas do you have for your next steps?

Paul: Perhaps we can first have each department propose candidates, and then plan the curriculum. It can be structured like graduate school programmes, with core subjects and specialised subjects for training. As for implementation, I should think about it some more. By the way, Coach, don't you also conduct training? Why don't you contribute as well?

Coach: Of course, that's great! But we need to establish training objectives and a timeline before I get involved. After all, you are the ones who have invested hard-earned time and money, so you understand the company's needs better than I do!

Paul: That's true. I wouldn't want to waste money or time.

Coach: In terms of training and human resources, what progress have you made so far?

Paul: I have brought in several middle-aged employees and assigned them to departments such as production, finance, research and development, and sales. Initially, I would attend every meeting with them, but later I let them handle it themselves. I also allowed them to handle overseas trips, like to Korea and Japan, with clients that I personally used to manage. They are now fully capable of handling such cases on their own.

Coach: How did these developments happen?

Paul: It required the endorsement of the senior executives and general manager. I put a lot of effort into mentoring these employees because there were many tasks needed to be done, but I couldn't do everything alone. It was crucial to cultivate a team, authorise and respect them, and let the younger generation do things in their own way. The most important thing was to instil confidence in them so that they could take the initiative to solve problems. Even though we had no time to spare, we managed to catch up with the teambuilding we had previously neglected.

The SF coach then used scaling questions to ask Paul on a scale of 1–10, where 1 represents the worst-case scenario and 10 represents the ideal future that he envisions, how he would rate his current position. This is represented by the "N score" in Figure 10.1, which helps Paul concretely identify his current position. When setting goals, the coach asks Paul where would be good enough on the scale i.e. his goal. This is the target score represented by the "G score" in Figure 10.1, which allows Paul to formulate a realistic and achievable goal that helps him progress smoothly towards his desired state.

Clients often mention their most difficult moments, so the coach asks Paul about the lowest score he has reached, represented by the "Min score" in Figure 10.1. Here, the discussion focuses on the gap between the Min score and the N score, which represents positive progress. It signifies that things are not entirely bad and improvement is possible. Even if the client says they have consistently remained at the lowest score, the coach can guide them to explore their current coping strategies. The SF coach believes that the client must have been doing something to prevent the score from further declining, indicating some effort even when staying at the Min score.

Furthermore, the coach asks Paul about the best score he has achieved in the past (Max score) to identify successful experiences. Asking about these times, or exceptions helps identify other strengths and resources that the client can draw on to move up the scale. The coach can ask the client how he would notice moving up the next small step on the scale (N+1) and then ask what first small step he could take towards reaching N+1, as shown in Figure 10.1. This helps

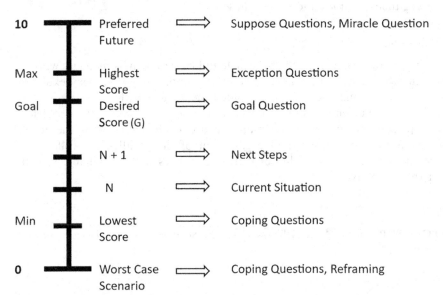

Figure 10.1 Illustration of scaling and associated SF questions to use (Cheng-Tseng Lin and Ru-Ya Chang).

Paul find practical, feasible, and goal-oriented next actions. These questions on the scale not only help Paul clarify his current situation and goals but also review past successful experiences and envision the future.

In this dialogue, the coach focused on what had already been done, what achievements had been made, and how to make further adjustments, and emphasised bringing responsibility back to the executives and igniting motivation.

Through the above exchange with Paul, several tips for successfully applying the SOLUTION coaching approach (O'Connell et al., 2012) are identifiable:

1 Break down big goals into actionable small goals to reduce anxiety and take gradual steps forwards.
2 Utilise scaling questions to help the client understand their progress so far and the next steps towards their goals.
3 Harness the client's abilities and resources to drive themselves towards their goal.

After this year, Paul became more confident and resolute in handling emergency situations. He made especially significant progress in leadership training. Although he still felt it had been too little too late, the younger generation in the company has at least begun to see opportunities, become more engaged, and now actively strive towards team transformation by voicing their opinions and putting in work.

Conclusions

Facing serious challenges, the SF coach and the company's manager worked together to identify the manager's current important goals. They explored the manager's ongoing efforts, expanded the range of effective solutions to address the challenges, and established action steps to solve the problems. The personal changes in the manager drove changes within the team, enhancing the motivation and engagement of the middle-aged colleagues. Training successors brought forth new initiatives and sustainable growth for the company.

Reference

O'Connell, B., Palmer, S., & Williams, H. (2012). *Solution focused coaching in practice*. Routledge.

11 Solution Focused Coaching in Japanese Business Management

An Exploration Through the Lens of Culture

David Macdonald

Introduction

Many scholarly works and business books have explored the uniqueness of Japan's business culture. Japanese business derives from a uniquely Asian set of values with a Japanese twist. It can sometimes be complex for global companies to navigate. This business style may have induced a slow recovery over the past 30 years since the economic bubble burst in the early 1990s. This chapter highlights the business differences in Japan, leveraging in part work by INSEAD Professor Erin Meyer on Culture Maps (Meyer, 2016). It then describes how a Solution Focused coaching framework, called the OSKAR model (Jackson & McKergow, 2007), can be used to support Japanese business leaders for better performance. While notable differences exist, the OSKAR method can extract what is already great from Japanese business leadership.

Background

Japan is well known for its unique business culture, based on Asian Confucianism (Watanabe, 2017), but with some special Japanese values. Chinese Confucianism has evolved over the centuries, but when adapted by the feudal ruling class of Japan, the concepts of obedience and loyalty outweighed other concepts such as benevolence and humanity. Many have an image of the Japanese "salaryman" working from graduation to retirement for the same company, committing his life to a hierarchical world where peace and harmony and "groupthink" take precedence over individualism and leadership. With new generations, this image is shifting, but that shift is taking time, especially in an ageing society.

This loyalty to the company and management style did well in the postwar reconstruction and boom years until the bubble of the late 1980s. However, when the bubble burst in the early 1990s, the economy fell into 30 years of stagnation, and the management principles of Japan came into question. Not only did economists and investors question those management principles but foreign direct investment in the country and market entry were also made

DOI: 10.4324/9781003431480-14

challenging by very different principles – a Western approach to business and that of Japan (Suleski, 1999).

In 2022 and 2023, we have seen an incredible rise in stocks traded in Japan, and Japan's value is rebounding (Kim, 2023). With geopolitical shifts and challenges, Japan is a safe and sound bet for business. Words like governance and transformation are now top of mind, and outside advisors and internal leaders are trying to steer their companies in a better direction. To that end, a Solution Focused coaching approach can help leaders bring out the best plans and the proper steps to move any business forward.

As a student coach and newly trained Solution Focused professional, I have started to apply this methodology to working with Japanese companies as part of my practice. I serve as an independent board member to public and non-profit organisations and coach leaders in emerging venture companies in Japan. While these roles require different modularities, being a coach to management is both personally rewarding and often provides the best results. To understand how to use the Solution Focused approach and OSKAR methodology in the Japanese context, let us first understand a framework to apply to the cultural situation in Japan.

Culture and Understanding Japanese Business Norms

Multiple theories and tools exist to understand and cope with differing business cultures. In the 1960s, while at IBM, Dutch social psychologist Geert Hofstede was one of the first to research and plot cultures on several dimensions (Hofstede, 2011). More recently, Professor Michele Gelfand of the Stanford Graduate School of Business has simplified the concept of cultural mapping by defining "tight" and "loose" cultures (Gelfand, 2018). Several other academic and business consulting organisations go further to map culture against a series of characteristics. In this chapter, I will focus on the work of INSEAD Professor Erin Meyer and her "Culture Maps" (Meyer, 2016).

As a student of the INSEAD executive education on leading across cultures, I took away Culture Maps as a valuable tool for understanding and navigating the complexities of cultural differences in international business environments. This concept involves visualising cultural behaviours and norms along eight key dimensions, enabling individuals and organisations to grasp the nuances and adapt their approaches accordingly. In a Japanese business environment, noticeable cultural differences emerge in several dimensions. One can bridge cultural gaps and foster successful collaborations by effectively applying Culture Maps in a Japanese business context, and as we will see later in this chapter, overlay the techniques of Solution Focused coaching and the OSKAR method.

Communication styles in Japan tend to be indirect and highly contextual. Respect for hierarchy and group harmony is paramount, leading to a preference for implicit communication and reading between the lines. Compared to the direct communication often seen in Western cultures, this can pose challenges in ensuring clear understanding and avoiding misunderstandings. While those inside the group will often understand the context and less needs to be said, those at different levels of hierarchy, different groups within the organisation, or across organisations often need more context to understand the meaning. However, if the context is not understood, problems arise.

Negative feedback is indirect, but it should not be misunderstood that there is no negative feedback. Many Japanese employees complain that managers give too much negative feedback, but like the communication style, this feedback is less direct, more subtle, and sometimes not constructive.

Trust-building in Japan takes the form of personal relationships versus task-based ones. While in many Western business settings, one would trust a colleague, team member, or leader based on results and output, in Japan, trust is built up over shared experiences and often over a long period. Sometimes it can take years to develop a client relationship in Japan; that relationship is based upon personal trust. However, once that relationship is established, for better or worse, it holds steady, and business will continue (Davies & Ikeno, 2002).

Meyer (2016) describes a continuum for persuasion from "principles-first" versus "applications-first." She expands on the concept to hypothesise that Asian cultures operate in a different state of mind, that of "holistic thinking." Asian business decision-making and persuasion tend to follow a pattern of seeing the "whole picture" versus its parts and adding up the sum.

Decision-making in Japan is typically a consensual process. The collectivist nature of Japanese culture emphasises group consensus and loyalty, making it essential to involve all stakeholders in decision-making. This approach can contrast with the more individualistic, top-down decision-making style prevalent in some Western business cultures.

The notion of hierarchy plays a central role in Japanese society. Seniority and age are critical factors in determining roles and responsibilities. Respect for authority and deference to superiors are deeply ingrained cultural norms impacting organisational interactions. This seems contradictory to the previous point on decision-making. However, while the senior member may appear responsible for the final decision, it has already been agreed upon through collaboration and discussion. This is often manifested in the voluminous Japanese presentations and a "ringisho" – an attachment for comments and affixing one's seal to include opinions and show approval (Davies & Ikeno, 2002).

When applying Culture Maps to a Japanese business environment, it is essential to recognise these differences and adapt accordingly. Emphasising active listening, respecting hierarchy, and fostering consensus-building are crucial strategies to promote effective communication and decision-making.

Solution Focused Coaching and the OSKAR Method Applied to Japanese Business

Many companies or business people in Japan have a hierarchical "problem-solving" mindset. Introducing more Solution Focused coaching skills can help counteract much of the silence in the meeting or board room. This approach is relevant to Japanese business, where focusing on harmony and consensus can hinder problem-solving. Solution Focused practice can encourage a more proactive and collaborative process by shifting the focus to strengths and resources. Others have already noted that Solution Focused practice is "so Japanese" (McKergow & Hogan, 2017, p. 234).

Solution Focused practice is a goal-oriented approach that concentrates on finding practical and innovative solutions to existing challenges. Unlike conventional problem-solving methods, which focus on identifying and dissecting problems, Solution Focused practice emphasises leveraging existing strengths and resources to achieve positive outcomes. By fostering a forward-thinking mindset, this approach encourages adaptability and creativity in adversity.

The OSKAR approach is an effective Solution Focused coaching model (Jackson & McKergow, 2007). OSKAR, an acronym for Outcome, Scaling, Know-how, Affirmation and Action, and Review, provides a structured framework for achieving desired outcomes. It empowers individuals and teams to define goals, measure progress, identify necessary expertise, acknowledge achievements, implement strategic actions, and continually evaluate results.

Outcome and Scaling

Japanese culture values long-term planning and commitment but often is challenged to envision and communicate it. From the 1950s to the 1980s, there was a rapid advancement of Japanese design and products. However, from the 1990s, many in management or senior executive roles became more cautious about defining a future (Suleski, 1999). Coaches can harness the OSKAR method's scaling element to help the leader define and measure progress by establishing clear and achievable goals in collaboration with employees. Regularly reviewing these goals ensures alignment and encourages adaptability when circumstances change. In my own experience coaching C-level Japanese executives at both small and large companies, the initial step is prompting them to think further ahead to an outcome through a "miracle question" – where do they really see their business, and themselves, in 5 years or more? By following this up using scaling it becomes easier to identify how far they still need to go in a clearly measurable way.

Leveraging Know-How and Trust

The OSKAR method's know-how component is particularly relevant in the Japanese context, where knowledge transfer often occurs through informal networks. As suggested by Professor Meyer's Culture Maps framework (2016), Japan is a culture where trust is based highly on relationships, and so developing trust through multiple and engaging conversations will help build credibility as a coach. In situations coaching leaders in Japan an active listening approach, leveraging the know-how the client or partner brings to the conversation, helps to demonstrate you're listening and want to understand what they do well. Once the leader has a better inventory of their own know-how, they can more easily pass both the knowledge and the process of collating the know-how of the group through to their teams.

Affirmation

Highlighting positive attributes and accomplishments in Japanese business settings fosters a conducive work environment, addressed by the previous section, while indirect feedback is often negative. By employing the Solution Focused approach, coaches can identify and amplify individual and team strengths, increasing motivation and confidence. Recognising achievements, even small ones, through the OSKAR method's affirmation component nurtures a culture of appreciation and boosts employee morale. Positive feedback calling out an individual in a group setting may often lead to embarrassment, but in a one-to-one coaching situation affirmation is welcome.

Action-Oriented Solutions and Gradual Change

Japanese business culture values action and diligence but is also allergic to radical change. By integrating the action component of the OSKAR method, coaches can support managers in facilitating pragmatic and incremental changes rather than imposing radical shifts. Such an approach aligns with the Japanese concept of continuous improvement, or "kaizen." Following a session, the follow-up at the next session continues in a similar cycle, so success should be measurable. Japanese business takes time to change, and so the process of the coach helping the leader identify small but measurable steps will help them try to also bring change to the organisation as a whole. As an example, in a recent coaching session, the leader was able to co-create a measurable solution to a resource challenge, which they could then more easily implement with their team.

Promoting Solution Focused Thinking and OSKAR in the Board Room

In Japanese boardrooms, the focus is often on consensus-building and avoiding conflict. Discussions happen outside the boardroom, or not at all, and group sessions tend to become venues for reporting. This can lead to a lack of decision-making progress. By taking on board Solution Focused coaching skills and the OSKAR method, board members can shift the focus to strengths and resources and encourage a more proactive and collaborative approach.

Summary

To summarise, the Outcome step of the OSKAR method can be used to clarify the desired outcome of the meeting and ensure that all participants are aligned. The Scaling step can be used to identify the current state of progress towards the desired outcome and to determine what needs to be done to achieve it. The Know-how step can be used to identify the resources and skills required to achieve the desired outcome. The Affirmation step can be used to build consensus and encourage participant buy-in. By highlighting the strengths and resources of each participant, a culture of collaboration and trust can be fostered. The Action step can be used to determine what actions need to be taken to achieve the desired outcome, and the Review step can be used to evaluate progress and adjust the approach as needed.

Conclusions

Every culture, and by extension business culture, is different, but arguably none so different as Japan. As Meyer's Culture Map (2016) demonstrates on multiple dimensions, Japan is very different from Western cultures, and while it shares similarities with other Asian cultures, it is still unique. By understanding the cultural norms and expectations related to communication, evaluation, persuasion, leadership, decision-making, and trust in the Japanese context, we can tailor Solution Focused coaching using the OSKAR method to ensure maximum effectiveness and cultural sensitivity.

Solution Focused coaches should be mindful of framing questions and feedback and using active listening techniques to encourage dialogue and build rapport. Japanese culture values consensus and group harmony in decision-making, with a tendency to avoid conflict. Solution Focused coaches should either directly involve all stakeholders in the decision-making process through team coaching, ensuring everyone has a voice and is heard, or indirectly support the manager they are coaching to do this.

Once Solution Focused ideas are understood and applied and the OSKAR method is used to work with clients and partners, it can be invaluable to the Japanese business situation.

References

Davies, R. J., & Ikeno, O. (2002). *The Japanese mind: Understanding contemporary Japanese culture.* Tuttle Publishing.

Gelfand, M. J. (2018). *Rule makers, rule breakers: How culture wires our minds, shapes our nations, and drives our differences.* Robinson.

Hofstede, G. (2011). Dimensionalizing cultures: The Hofstede model in context. *Online Readings in Psychology and Culture, 2*(1). 10.9707/2307-0919.1014

Jackson, P. Z., & McKergow, M. (2007). *The solutions focus: Making coaching and change simple.* Nicholas Brealey International.

Kim, L. (2023, November 20). *Japan's Nikkei average TOPS 33-year high thanks to strong earnings.* Nikkei Asia. https://asia.nikkei.com/Business/Markets/Japan-s-Nikkei-average-tops-33-year-high-thanks-to-strong-earnings

McKergow, M. & Hogan. (2017). Introduction to solution focused practice in organisations in Asia. In D. Hogan, D. Hogan, J. Tuomola, & A. K. L. Yeo (Eds). *Solution focused practice in Asia* (pp. 233–235). Routledge Taylor & Francis Group.

Meyer, E. (2016). *The culture map: Decoding how people think, lead, and get things done across cultures.* Public Affairs.

Suleski, R. (1999). Japan after the bubble burst: Traditional values inhibit quick comeback. *The Journal of the International Institute, 6*(3). http://hdl.handle.net/2027/spo.4750978.0006.303

Watanabe, T. (2017). The influence of Confucianism on the management philosophies of Japanese industries. *Scientific Society of Advanced Research and Social Change International Journal of Management, 3*(1), 1–5.

12 Begin with the End in Mind

Growing as a Solution Focused Coach

Jaime Ong-Yeoh

Introduction

In my work as a cultural consultant, I help clients understand and work with cultures across different countries, as well as how to determine and develop a corporate culture that will enable their organisation to succeed according to their business strategy. The most common and most palatable change management approach for large organisations is impersonal interventions at the system and process levels. To affect real change, I wanted to focus on behavioural change in individuals.

In hierarchical, collectivist societies such as in Asia, leaders play a major part in influencing culture in their organisation. However, leaders often think that it is something that the people below them are responsible for, while conversely many employees feel like they are powerless, and that culture and change can only be driven by the powers that be. I hope to highlight that in Asian corporate cultures, where top leaders are seen as the sanctioned conduit of corporate change, a coaching relationship can offer another platform where change can be implemented, one conversation, one client at a time.

Change Begins with Me

I decided that taking a coaching programme would enhance my capabilities as a change management and cultural consultant. The Solution Focused coaching approach was recommended by my CEO, and I enrolled in an International Coaching Federation (ICF) accredited programme. Before I could achieve my corporate coaching ambitions, I needed to build up the hundreds of hours required for certification. As a new coach, I was willing to coach anyone who was keen on receiving my services – friends, colleagues, referrals, and their network. Some sessions went surprisingly well, and some sessions were disappointing. Sometimes I did everything by the book, but sometimes I gripped the book so tightly that it slipped out of my inexperienced fingers. Upon reflection, I realised that as a new coach, sometimes one can get too caught up in the process or the 'how.' This distracts us from the end goal or the 'what,' so it is important to take a pause and reflect on what the client's goal truly is.

DOI: 10.4324/9781003431480-15

In this chapter, I will share my observations and learnings from a beginner's perspective as I developed my skills as a coach using the Solution Focused model, to help others taking the same journey.

Initial Frustrations

One of my first clients was a friend who had agreed to being coached. It was going to be easy, I thought; I was fresh out of training, feeling confident as I knew all the steps, and had all my questions ready to fire.

Aini had just started a new job. She had come from a small, local company where she was a director to becoming a regional head reporting directly to the regional CEO in a large, complex multinational that had just won a substantial contract. She joined this new company during the COVID-19 pandemic when everyone was working from home. She was new to the industry, knew nothing and no one, and yet to perform her job she had to depend on other people in the company to provide her with information. Adding to that was her lack of familiarity with remote working and the technology used by the company. It was a perfect storm.

Our first session started ok – Aini said she wanted to make connections, so that she could get information from people in a timely manner, and she wanted more autonomy to make decisions. All this would enable her work to proceed smoothly.

I took that at face value and tried to explore this further by asking her the miracle question. Aini's answers were short and not very descriptive.

Aini: I will have a smooth path without any hurdles so that I can proceed with my work faster and smoother.
Coach: What will be different from now?
Aini: I will be able to get on with my work without any hurdles.
Coach: What will other people notice is different about you?
Aini: Nothing. I don't think anyone will notice any difference.

It was the first place where we got stuck. She was unable to imagine a scenario beyond the absence of the immediate problem, and equally I was not sure how to develop this further.

Things continued to be a challenge as I tried to explore and leverage what she already knew and any past successes.

Coach: When have things worked for you? What did you do then?
Aini: I've been more successful with people I am familiar with, having worked with them on something before.
Coach: Ok, so how can you build relationships with other people and develop this familiarity?
Aini: I can't. Everyone is very task-focused, and they don't have time for small talk.

Aini then explained a few things she had tried doing, so I attempted to expand her thinking into new possibilities and action steps.

Coach: Is there anyone you can think of who might be able to help you?

Aini: Well, the CEO did say I could use his name to escalate things, but I don't want to. I don't want to be that person, the one who pulls rank to get their way.

Coach: What else can you do?

Aini: Nothing. I've already tried everything.

Coach: What can you do differently?

Aini: Nothing. I've already tried everything.

Aini was adamant that everything that could be done had been done and without success. Both of us became stuck in a loop where I repeated the same questions and she responded with the same answers, going nowhere fast. Becoming desperate for her to formulate some kind, any kind, of action plan, I regretfully broke out of coaching mode and started to offer specific suggestions. All were met with justifications of why it wouldn't work. After two painful sessions like this, she ended the session by saying, 'Thank you for trying, but I don't think this is helping.'

All my practice sessions during training had gone wonderfully, and I was aghast that this one had turned out so differently. I was frustrated – why couldn't I help her? And more importantly, why couldn't she help herself? To help me reflect on this, I looked up the definition of self-determination online: 'People are motivated to grow and change by three innate and universal psychological needs. This theory suggests that people are able to become self-determined when their needs for 1) competence, 2) connection, and 3) autonomy are fulfilled' (Cherry, 2022).

Aini had half of the first: competence – she was highly experienced in her profession, but she was new to the industry the company was involved in, and it was this missing half that made her suffer from impostor syndrome. Being new to the company and not knowing anyone also meant that she had none of the second: connection. In collectivist Asian cultures, work is not merely a task-oriented and transactional affair; it requires the building of relationships and trust between colleagues (Hofstede et al., 2010). However, the virtual working environment and tremendous work pressure at the time extinguished any opportunity for normal relationship building. The company culture also resulted in her not having the third need fulfilled: autonomy. Aini worked for the Asian office of a Scandinavian company, and in Scandinavian culture, it is important to get everyone's input and decisions are agreed by consensus (Hofstede et al., 2010), which can subsume one's authority and autonomy in the process. Aini found herself not only in the deep end of a completely new industry and company but also in a challenging emulsion of both Asian and Scandinavian cultures.

Reflections from Supervision

A coach supervisor helped me reflect on what I could have done differently. The most important realisation was that I had been using Solution Focused questions as a way of problem-solving to get Aini to change the situation, when in fact the situation was mostly beyond her control. No wonder nothing Aini tried had worked and she could not think of anything else to do! This changed my perspective tremendously as I had previously viewed Aini as a difficult client who refused to do anything to help herself. I could have used a solution-building approach to coach Aini into changing things that *were* under her control, such as the way she felt about herself, despite the situation. This would mean taking more time to explore what was truly important to her, acknowledging her frustrations, and using coping questions to bring out her strengths and resources.

Becoming More Comfortable

As I got more comfortable with coaching, I felt more relaxed. I allowed the client to direct the conversation and the actions, gently bringing them back using the Solution Focused coaching framework of OSKAR (Jackson & McKergow, 2007). I asked more evocative questions to help them uncover what was truly important to them beneath the initial outcomes they expressed, learned how to listen more, and developed a better sense of empathy. In the process, I began to care more about the person and less about ticking off boxes of steps to follow and things to do.

Avinash came to coaching feeling demotivated yet bearing a positive mindset. He was unhappy in his current job, but he didn't want to feel stuck. He wanted to make the best out of the situation by continuing to learn and grow whether in his current job or at a new job. Finding a new job would be ideal, but it was not an immediate priority as he didn't want to leapfrog to *any* job just as a way out, plus he had financial commitments that necessitated a stable paycheque.

A large part of Avinash's frustrations stemmed from the executive-level leaders he supported in the C-suite, in particular the new CEO. She was an expatriate from an Anglo-Saxon country; an egalitarian, individualistic culture where the leader is not necessarily better or smarter than the employees and not expected to know everything, plus where the communication style is very direct. Conversely, in more hierarchical, collectivist cultures in Asia, leaders are expected to lead, after all they are in that position for a reason, and the communication style is more diplomatic rather than direct. To Avinash, it felt like the CEO didn't know what she was doing and that she was very harsh with her comments. This was a difficult situation for him to manage. The capabilities of the CEO aside, Avinash had many opinions and ideas but speaking up and challenging someone directly, especially a superior, is not something that Asian cultures see as appropriate behaviour. Avinash's colleagues seemed to be more focused on not upsetting the CEO rather than doing what was best for the company and its employees.

Over the course of five coaching sessions, Avinash's mood lifted a little each time. We reflected on the progress he had made, what he was doing to cope with the situation, to the small successes he was achieving in managing upwards as well as job hunting. In the final session, he said, 'I can see you've changed too. You're more comfortable as a coach – you listen more, and you ask fewer questions.' I smiled as I realised that while I had been observing and helping Avinash, he had been observing and helping me too. The next time we met was informally, over a cup of coffee where he was clearly excited. 'I've got a new job,' Avinash said, 'It will be challenging but I'm really excited!' This time, for both of us, having a goal but not allowing it to consume us entirely ultimately led to us achieving those very goals.

Chong was a very experienced manager who unfortunately had recently been made redundant. He now needed to decide what to do next; he wanted to be financially comfortable but working in the corporate world had taken its toll, making him feel constantly agitated and distracted even at home. When I asked him the miracle question, Chong described that he had plans of eventually leaving the corporate world to become an independent consultant in a different field as that would allow him the flexibility to be more attentive to his family. What he said he wanted out of our coaching relationship was to develop the self-assurance that he had considered all that needed to be considered before making the big career change.

During our coaching session, we discussed what preparations he needed to make before deciding to embark on this new career. Chong had already thought through and done a lot on his own, and my role was to ask, 'What else?'; 'How would you do that?'; and 'What difference would that make?' to help him refine his actions. At the end of our first session, I felt that Chong was getting more comfortable with the idea of this career transition and doing what was necessary to move himself even further up the readiness scale.

In our second session, things were completely different, but not as I had expected. Chong told me he had attended a job interview with a new company. Despite his earlier desire to leave the corporate world, he realised that the salary he earned from this new job could be put aside to give him the financial cushion he would need when transitioning to becoming an independent consultant. Chong accepted the job, giving himself two years before pursuing his new career. Unlike before when it felt like there was no end in sight to the drudgery and frustration of corporate life, Chong was now happy that he had set an 'expiry date' and had something exciting to look forward to when it was over.

We often think of progress as change. Something needs to be visibly different for us to say we have progressed. However, Chong helped me realise that sometimes, especially in coaching, no outward change is also progress for it is the person's mindset that has changed.

Final Reflections

In my first few sessions as a new coach, I thought the objective was to drive as fast as I could to get my client to the A in the OSKAR framework: Action. I had been more task-oriented instead of outcome-oriented. I have since learnt to give due respect to each step of the coaching process, allowing my client the time and space to properly explore the possibilities. I realise now that the ultimate goal is less about doing and more about thinking, that is, achieving change in the client's mindset – either about themselves or the situation or both.

In my most recent session with a new client, we spent the better part of an hour exploring O-S-K: the Outcome, Scaling, and Know-How. We didn't get to the Action as we ran out of time and had to conclude the day's session, but this time I was fine with that. The client was ok too as he left saying, 'Thank you, that was very useful. Now I know what I *really* want.'

References

Cherry, K. (2022, November 8). How does self-determination theory explain motivation? Verywell Mind. https://www.verywellmind.com/what-is-self-determination-theory-2795387

Hofstede, G., Hofstede, G. J., & Minkov, M. (2010). *Cultures and organizations: Software of the mind: Intercultural cooperation and its importance for survival* (3rd ed.). McGraw-Hill.

Jackson P. Z., & McKergow M. (2007). *The solutions focus: Making coaching and change simple* (2nd ed.). Nicholas Brealey.

Section 4

Team Coaching

13 The Transformative Power of "And What Else?"

Team Coaching in Asia

Dave Hogan

Introduction

In this chapter, I delve into the impact of the "And what else?" question through two case studies in Asia, particularly highlighting its transformative role in coaching a team out of crisis in China. My initial experience with the outcomes of "And what else?" sparked a profound realisation, leading me to both practice it more and reflect deeply on its efficacy. The second pan-Asian team coaching case study offers a basis for reflecting on the commonalities in how the question operates within Solution Focused engagement. My hope is to guide readers in viewing "And what else?" not as a standalone magical question but as intricately embedded in the contexts of Solution Focused practice, serving as a valuable tool for practitioners in Asia.

Team Coaching in China: A Surprising Discovery

After the 2009 earthquake in Sichuan province, China, I coached a team of four families in a major city for an NGO. The NGO aimed to collaborate with local leaders for social service programmes. In their three-year journey, the team faced challenges such as leadership loss, administrative hurdles, language learning, and health issues. Amidst the devastating disaster, they were drawn into relief efforts, facing shock and despair. Asked to spend a week providing an "infusion of hope," my role was pivotal.

Solution Focused team coaching provided a roadmap for addressing the team's challenges, clarifying common goals, and facilitating desired changes. The most memorable change occurred almost accidentally during our initial session, following my red-eye flight from Singapore. For an introduction, I asked about positive aspects during their three years of adjustment and struggle amid trauma. That day, I uncovered the incredible hope-infusing power of the simple question: "And what else?"

One by one, they answered my initial question during our getting-to-know-each-other time, sharing what went well, followed by "And what else?" I recorded each response on my legal pad, occasionally inquiring about the process with a "How did you do that?" before continuing with "And what

DOI: 10.4324/9781003431480-17

else?" With each reply, their voices strengthened, postures improved, and smiles emerged. Gratitude for each other was expressed, leading to the list on my legal pad extending to the second page.

Some of the "And what else?" responses from the team include the following: becoming conversant in Mandarin, forming friendships with neighbours, connecting with local communities and leaders, creating opportunities for our programmes, navigating legal challenges, establishing and strengthening relationships, discovering more about each other, and deepening appreciation for diverse gifts. After more than twenty-five "And what else?" questions during introductions, tears, smiles, and hugs of gratitude marked the end, showcasing the transformative power of the question. Yet, it may not be definitive proof.

I invite my reader to also ask "And what else?" is at work when the question is effective. To start, we should understand where the question developed and fits.

The Origin of the "And What Else?" Question in the Solution Focused Approach

The transformative power of the "And what else?" question is not standalone magic but rather its integration into a Solution Focused conversation. "Solution Focused team coaching aligns with Solution Focused Brief Therapy, a progress and resource-oriented, social-constructionist practice, differing from deficit-oriented approaches" (Dierolf, Muhl, Perfetto, & Szaniawski, 2024, p. 5). The concise query "What else?" is part of an interactive, co-constructive process that encourages clients to contemplate change. Solution Focused coaches, focused on client desires, existing strengths, and resources, leverage this question to raise awareness of progress and resources throughout the process.

Consider, for instance, if I had posed "And what else?" following questions like "What's wrong?" or "Where are you having problems?". Such a series of repetitive questions would have yielded a vastly different list, potentially overwhelming hope with accumulating obstacles. This emphasises the critical role of orientation in shaping the question's outcome. It suggests that for effectiveness, the "And what else?" question must be directed by other Solution Focused questions like "What's gone well?" (positive exceptions), "What's better?" (progress), and "How did you do that?" (resources). These questions collectively guide the "And what else?" to identify team resources and tangible examples of ongoing progress, revealing its dependence on and service to other Solution Focused questions.

In the appendix to their *Brief Coaching: A Solution Focused Approach*, Iveson, George, and Ratner (2012, p. 194) include "What Else?" as the final entry to their six-page long list of Solution Focused questions. Under the entry "What else?" they just repeat it ten times! One might get the wrong impression that coaches are encouraged to pummel clients with this interrogation. However, the two final paragraphs of the appendix clarify how they think about questions in Solution Focused coaching:

> Questions lie at the heart of solution focused brief therapy. In the solution focused approach the coach does not 'tell' clients, she asks questions that allows the client to 'tell' herself and in so doing to reconstruct her world in a way that can make a difference. In asking questions the coach is not seeking to gain information about the content of the client's answer and thus to become more and more expert on the client and the client's world. Rather the questions are a provocation to the client to think differently. (Iveson et al., 2012, p. 194)

This seems to suggest two things. First, the extreme openness of the "And what else?" question is the means by which our question shifts the leadership of world-building from the coach or therapist to the client. It requires the client to make sense of open space by giving significance to particular things they name and describe as better, as evidence of progress towards their hopes. As we shall see later in this chapter, this applies to "things" clients name and describe in the past, present, and future. Second, the repetition of the "And what else?" question helps extend and accumulate the client's work beyond just single one-offs. In terms of the client building belief in their resources, for example, the amassing of multiple, and mutually reinforcing pieces of evidence can prove important.

And in the case of the client's task of building a better future, the more detail they are able to describe, the greater the scale and momentum of change. A list of one lonely "What else?" detail would hardly be sufficient to construct a whole world. It is the proliferation and integration of relevant detail that makes a fictional world in a movie credible. The "And what else?" question serves a similar function to help clients reinforce and realise the new world they are becoming aware of and building. More recently, McKergow (2023) elaborates on this idea of the key difference between SF questions being that they help "stretch the client's world", compared to many approaches which ask questions to gather information that is already known. Thus, the repetition of the "what else?" question helps stretch the client to think differently both about their resourceful past and their preferred future.

The EARS Process

In my first training as a Solution Focused counsellor, I learned that the "And what else?" question was first introduced by the Brief Family Therapy Center (BFTC) in the early 1990s as a way of building solutions in second and subsequent brief therapy sessions. The practitioners at BFTC (De Jong & Berg, 2012, p. 149) developed the acronym EARS to summarise the interviewer's work in helping clients explore details of even the vaguest exceptions to their initial problem that they had experienced since the first session.

E stands for *Elicit*: find the exceptions that have occurred since the first session regardless of any persistent problems.

A refers to *Amplify*: ask what was different and how it happened. What did the client do to make it happen?

R is for *Reinforcing*: the successes and strengths the exception represents for the client.

S is a reminder to the practitioner to *Start* again: ask "What else is better?"

Does this mean that the "And what else?" question should only fit in the S stage of the EARS process? In her recently published *Solution-Focused Therapy: The Basics,* Yvonne Dolan identifies the "solution focused what else question" as a version of the "solution focused detail question" which she defines as "An inquiry designed to further clarify various specific aspects of a goal, exception, position on a scale, coping or solution description" (Dolan, 2024, p. 160, 162). This well describes my own discovery by using the "And what else?" question. It is not just a follow-up question for second and subsequent sessions but a brief question that could, when appropriate, enrich every aspect of a Solution Focused conversation, filling it with detail that anchors and enriches what each client needs to hear for and from themselves. As in the case with the team in China, the "And what else?" question served as the "What's better?" question in the team's very first Solution Focused conversation. This suggests when we say that the "And what else?" question is transformative because it fits into the context of Solution Focused conversations, it clearly means more than merely fitting into a specific step in a Solution Focused process. A more recent team coaching experience illustrates this.

Pan-Asian Team Coaching: Intentional Experience Informed Practice

I had the privilege of coaching a commercial team in a major technology company that was in the process of moving from product-based to cloud-based services with members from over ten Asian countries. Their responsibility involved aligning a variety of internal and external customers in order to structure and finalise deals. The team leader was convinced that his team could benefit from Solution Focused team coaching.

During my initial interview with the team leader, I aimed to get a clear picture of his work, his team and their strengths and challenges, and the difference he hoped the team coaching would make, using questions such as "What will you notice if your best hopes from this team coaching are realised?"; "Who else will notice? And what will they notice?"; "What do you already appreciate about your team?"; and "What difference will it make for them?" Each question is enriched with granular detail by as many "And what else?" questions as needed.

The team leader's hopes were to strengthen his team ownership of their company's objectives, to co-construct team shared objectives and values, and to adopt a common and simplified framework to facilitate their shared objectives. Once we had a clear agreement, we designed a three-phase process. Each phase of the overall process was enriched by liberally asking "And what else?" at the appropriate moments.

Phase 1: Pre-Session One-on-One Interviews with Each Team Member

I interviewed each team member, asking about their best hopes, concerns, and expectations for the upcoming event. Some of the questions included were as follows:

1 What do you understand about the purpose of today's meeting?
2 What are some ways that the last retreat has helped you in your efforts to enhance customer experience?
3 What would enhance this further?
4 What capabilities/strengths do you bring to your team?
5 What is one area you would like to develop further?

Through "And what else?" questions more details emerged, helping create a strong sense of co-creation and co-ownership of outcomes in all the participants, as well as assisting me in my preparation for the two-day off-site retreat and team coaching process.

Phase 2: Two-Day Team-Coaching Retreat

The second and central phase of the process was the two-day retreat. It was a reunion of a diverse, gifted, and committed team who worked collaboratively together on the Internet daily but had not seen each other in person since their previous team retreat. There were two elements of the retreat: the first day was an experiential workshop on Mark McKergow and Helen Bailey's *Host Leadership*. The final day was an interactive four-round team coaching process. Team members self-organised into "project teams" based on their own areas of expertise and responsibility for the team coaching rounds. The projects that emerged focused on things like increasing compliance turn-around, and enhancing customer satisfaction. Each project team created a name for their group and went through a four-round team coaching process.

The "And what else?" question enriched the process at this stage with one significant difference: the team members were asking each other the question and enriching their own collaboration during their project work together.

Phase 3: Post-Retreat One-on-One Interviews

The following are some of Solution Focused questions we decided to use:

• What's better?

- How have you incorporated some of the new ideas and hard skills you learned at the team meeting?
- What difference did it make?
- What needs to be adjusted/refined/altered?
- What do you need to do to keep going in the right direction?

In the personal interviews, the powerful effect of asking "And what else?" was palpable; especially, the post-retreat interviews. I vividly remember one member of the team describing what she had noticed was better since the retreat. I forget how many times I asked "And what else?" but her final answer stays with me. "I've moved from miserable to miracle", she said with a big smile.

Conclusions and Cultural Reflections

Perhaps the greatest discovery I've made in my Solution Focused practice in Asia is the sense of awe I feel in observing the creativity and progress of coachees and teams individually and collectively. The radical respect of being humbly curious about what clients want as shaped by their own cultural context invites them to draw upon their own skills, experience, and resources, which is empowering and inspiring. I can attest that the open-ended "And what else?" question does not impose its own cultural qualities (or mine!) but allows what is significant in the Asian cultural context to emerge and receive its proper weight in the lists generated by those answering the question. "And what else?" presupposes that there is more – and when we dare to repeatedly ask it of our clients, more likely than not, we discover more about their resourcefulness, resilience, creativity, and possibility, which they find their own ways to describe in great and granular detail.

If you turn "And what else?" into an acronym, you get AWE which exactly captures what I continue to feel every time I use the question … Awe!

References

De Jong, P., & Berg, I. (2012). *Interviewing for solutions* (4th Ed). Brooks/Cole, Cengage Learning.
Dierolf, K., Muhl, C., Perfetto, C., & Szaniaswski, R. (2024). *Solution focused team coaching (2nd Ed)*. Routledge.
Dolan, Y. (2024). *Solution-focused therapy: The basics*. Routledge.
Iveson, C., George, E., & Ratner, H. (2012). *Brief coaching: A solution focused approach*. Routledge.
McKergow, M. (2023, November 2). Information-gathering and world-stretching questions: A key distinction in solution focused practice. Substack. https://markmckergow.substack.com/p/34-information-gathering-questions
McKergow, M. & Bailey, H. (2014). *Host, six new rules roles of engagement for teams, organizations, communities, movements*. Solutions Books.

14 Strengthening Organisations through Team Coaching

Debbie Hogan and Jane Tuomola

Introduction

In Southeast Asia, coaching is predicted to continue its rapid growth over the coming years, and team coaching has emerged as one of the fastest growing areas (Passmore, 2021).

The rise of team coaching in Asia can be attributed to many factors: organisational, cultural, and global trends that highlight a growing awareness of the importance of effective teamwork and collaboration in the workplace, to enhance organisational effectiveness. As a result of its rapid growth, coaching associations, such as the International Coaching Federation, the European Mentoring and Coaching Council, and the Association for Coaching, developed team coaching competencies (International Coaching Federation, n.d.; European Mentoring and Coaching Council, 2020; Association for Coaching, n.d.). There is a recognition that team coaching differs from individual coaching and each requires specialised skills.

Southeast Asia has more than 100 ethnic groups and 655 million people speaking over 1000 languages and dialects, making it one of the most diverse regions in the world (MacCartney, 2022). Team coaches in this environment need cross-cultural sensitivity and awareness, plus skills in team dynamics and group facilitation.

Both authors reside in Asia and have worked with local and culturally diverse teams. This chapter highlights the Solution Focused team coaching process and the positive impact this has on teams. Factors to be aware of when team coaching in the Asian context are offered.

Post COVID-19 Pandemic Impact on the Workforce in Asia

The post-pandemic period has had a profound impact on the state of mental health within the workforce in Asia. Many found the transition from remote working in silos to blended work environments very difficult. They felt disconnected from their colleagues, with a growing desire for better work-life balance and for finding meaning and purpose in their lives. The 'Great Resignation' led to the 'Great Renegotiation' as more in the workforce began

DOI: 10.4324/9781003431480-18

to grapple with what was important and how they wanted to restructure their lives. Recent surveys show that uncaring and uninspiring leaders are a big part of why people leave their jobs, along with a lack of career development. How leaders support and connect with their direct reports are a big factor in retaining talent (McKinsey, 2022).

Decision makers in organisations are evaluating how to adjust to the changing landscape within the workforce. There are encouraging signs that decision makers are increasing their support programmes to address the mental and psychosocial aspects of employee wellness to retain their talent.

In Singapore and other parts of Asia, there has been a surge in Employee Assistance Programmes (EAP), corporate wellness programmes, and a growing appetite for better work and life environments. Sponsoring team coaching is a popular intervention to enhance performance, engagement, and productivity.

Solution Focused team coaching is embedded in the core principles and assumptions of Solution Focused practice (De Jong & Berg, 2013) and adapted to team coaching (Dierolf et al., 2024; McKergow & Jackson, 2007; Meier, 2005). The basic steps and processes implemented by the team coaches are outlined below.

Solution Focused Team Coaching in a Nutshell

Phase 1: Initial Consultation with Stakeholders and Sponsors and Team Coaching Agreement

Most team coaching engagements begin with a request from Human Resources (HR) or a leader from the organisation. The discussion begins with a consultation session with the stakeholders, in which the right intervention or process is explored, which fits the needs of the team and the organisation. In the rest of the chapter, we use a typical example to illustrate the process.

An HR Director was interested in helping the management team to a higher degree of functioning, leading to more cohesion and better customer care. The management team was struggling in several areas. We explored how the stakeholders would recognise 'higher functioning', 'more cohesion', and 'better customer care', to gain clarity on their expectations. After exploring options, the request was made for team coaching.

Further discussions with top management clarified specifics around expectations from third-party stakeholders and the team coaching process was outlined. The HR Director had discussions with the management team and they agreed to the team coaching process.

Phase 2: Meetings with Individual Team Members

The co-coaches contacted each member of the management team for a 15–20 minute call, to explore their ideas regarding a successful team coaching experience. These individual sessions are important to maximise the team coaching sessions and help facilitate buy-in from each team member.

Additionally, it created a safe space for the team member to express their concerns without judgement. We kept in mind that the focus of team coaching is the functioning of the team as a unit. Team members were informed that these conversations were confidential and only broad themes would be shared in the team coaching sessions.

In Asia, where the group is valued over the individual, maintaining harmony and cohesion within teams is important. It can be hard to speak up when things are not going well for fear of losing face. It can therefore take longer in this context for team members to open up to an external facilitator (Kaul, 2016). The Solution Focused coaching approach therefore fits well in this cultural context as we don't ask for details about the problem and are not looking to name, blame, and shame. The individual calls with team members helped kick-start the process of building trust. Questions exploring what the team as a whole wanted and what is going well already demonstrate the kinds of questions we ask when the team gathers, and enable the team to feel safe to share ideas, focused on what is useful going forwards rather than what is not working. We emphasise that there are a variety of exercises in pairs and small groups to build trust before sharing in the large group, which maximises the chance that every voice is heard. When feeding back to the large group, no one individual contribution is identified.

Another cultural factor in the Asian context is the perception that the team coaches may be seen as experts and coming to tell them what to do. This is important to clarify in the individual calls that while we have expertise in designing the process and useful conversations, we see them as the experts within their team and organisation.

During individual consultations, questions were asked to check their understanding of the purpose of team coaching, any concerns, and their best hopes from team coaching.

• *What is your understanding of team coaching and its purpose for your team?*
• *What is your best hope for the team?*
• *What difference would a successful team coaching experience make for the team?*
• *What concerns do you have that might impact the team?*

The co-coaches exchanged information and noted themes related to the desire to connect, develop trust and openness, concerns about team members who seemed disconnected, and lack of clarity on procedures from top management. A schedule and process for Sessions 1–3 was then planned.

Phase 3: Team Coaching Process

Each session was half a day, a month apart. The format included team discussions, small group discussions, and individual reflections. Mediums used were flipchart paper, sticky notes, pens, markers, space to walk, and posters on a wall.

Session 1: Half Day

• Welcome and introductions
• Setting the agenda: an overview of the team coaching process and role of the co-coaches.
• Ground rules – small group discussions and feedback to the large group.
    Ground rules are co-constructed with the team using questions such as:

> *What are important ground rules for us?*
> *How should we manage conflicts or tensions?*
> *How do we honour all the voices in the room?*
> *How will we share the process and information with absent team members?*
> *What will you be noticing when everyone is at their best in behaviour, attitude, and participation?*
> *How will we manage confidentiality – what will stay in the room and what needs to be shared and with whom?*

Taking time co-creating a safe space is key and important to get details about what these behaviours would look like to enable everyone to be at their best and feel safe to contribute.

• Best hopes: reflect and discuss in small groups:

> *What are your best hopes for the team?*
> *Suppose this was a valuable and successful experience for the team, how would you know?*

• Collect the best hopes for the team
    Group post notes on flip charts according to themes; prioritise
    Team coaches ask:

> *What are your observations? What are common themes?*

Some best hopes included: working better as a team; getting to know one another better; trusting each other more; feeling understood and appreciated by leaders; having clarity about the team's vision and purpose; and more balance in their lives. After prioritising, the team chose to focus on working better as a team.

Lessons from the Geese

We ask teams to watch a motivational video called the Wisdom of the Geese (Ideal Motivation, 2020) and explore what is relevant to their team. The way each goose flies in formation creates uplift and reduces friction for the birds behind. By flying together in a V-formation, the whole flock achieves a 70%

greater flying range than any single goose would alone. The team resonated with wanting to share a common goal and get where they are going quicker and with less effort.

- Choose a project name
  Several project names were put forth, and the team voted for a common project name: Engaged and Energised
- Miracle question – individual reflection; draw a picture of your miracle

  Imagine a miracle happens and your best hopes for this project were realised.

  What would you notice about yourself and your team that were indicators of this change? What would be different about you, the team, management?

  What would you observe about others?

  What would they observe about you?

  What difference would this make?

- Each person shares their picture. The team is asked:

  What are you noticing?

  What does this say about your team?

The team realised that they actually all wanted the same things for the team and this already helped them feel more connected. The energy in the room was palpable.

- Scaling walk: Where are we already?

  Imagine this wall is a line from 1 to 10. If '10' represents the team at their best in relation to your project, and '1' is the opposite, where is the team on the scale already?

  Place yourself there. Turn to your neighbours and discuss:

  What tells you the team is at that number?

  What is working well already?

The group is reminded that there is no correct number. The intent is to hear what each person sees is already working well, which can be built on, and a way of measuring progress over time.

Those at the higher end of the scale were eager to share what they had noticed going well already. Those lower down expressed caution and scepticism about change. The co-coaches reframed their concerns as valuable and used these to explore what helped in the past when changes have been successful. This led to useful discussions around challenging perceptions of some team members being disconnected. It was not because they did not care about the team, but that their concern was about whether this change would be sustainable. This understanding became key to the progress of the team.

- Scaling walk: What would one step higher look like?

  Suppose you move up one point, what would you notice? Your Team? Management?
  Discuss and then feedback to the larger group.

Using culturally appropriate metaphors and idioms can be helpful, such as 'A journey of a thousand miles starts with one step' (Laozi, quoted in Yeo, 2016). This raised the energy and optimism of the team as they began to see that moving forwards was possible when exploring one small step at a time.

- Action steps
  Each team member committed to take one small action step, as they worked together to move one step higher. These were listed and they agreed on who would do what and when.
- Positive gossip from co-coaches
  The co-coaches demonstrated positive gossip by sharing observations about the team they had noticed during the morning. They affirmed the behaviours and comments, which demonstrated individual and team resources, skills, and capabilities, related to their project.
- Positive gossip in small groups
  Participants were asked to take turns sitting with their back to their group and the others would positively gossip about them:

  A personal strength you have observed in your colleague
  Something you appreciate in the way we work together
  Something positive you heard from others about your colleague
  Something you have valued in how they contributed to these workshops.

An important Chinese cultural value is modesty (Chan & Chung, 2016). It is not the norm to speak up about yourself or give compliments to others. When introducing the positive gossip exercise, it was important to acknowledge that this may initially feel uncomfortable but that it is important to feel valued and appreciated by those we work with. The team loved this exercise. There were many smiles, and some tears as people were so moved by what colleagues had noticed but never shared. This is useful for facilitators to know not to shy away from doing something that seemingly goes against the cultural norm, but introduce these in a culturally sensitive way, as the results are powerful.

   Another lesson from the geese (Ideal Motivation, 2020) – the geese honk to provide encouragement to those around them to keep up their speed. Giving people the recognition they deserve is so important as lack of recognition is one of the main reasons people feel dissatisfied with work and resign. We find that teams often want to follow this exercise with plans about how to keep recognising and motivating each other as they find it so valuable.

• End of session reflections as a group

> *What have you learned about yourself? Your team?*
> *What has been a surprise?*
> *What has changed in how you feel or think about the team?*
> *What has been helpful?*

A pleasant surprise was that everyone, including the quieter team members, spoke out and expressed their views and contributed to the team discussions. They found it helpful to realise they all wanted the same thing for the team and that many things were already going well. They felt more hopeful and excited about the next steps.

Sessions 2 and 3: Team Coaching – Half Day

Sessions 2 and 3 were very similar in structure and spaced a month after each previous session. The aim was to review progress and plan the next steps forwards to keep the progress going.

• Welcome and setting the agenda
• Ground rules – anything to add or change to the ground rules?
• Explore progress since session 1: Pair and share then feedback with the large group

> *What's been going well since we last met?*
> *How did you manage that?*
> *Who did what, when, where?*
> *What did you notice others do? How did you respond?*
> *How did you contribute to the progress?*
> *What difference did it make?*

• Managing challenges – small groups then feedback to large group

> *Any challenges faced along the way?*
> *How did you manage these?*
> *What did you learn from that?*
> *What ideas emerged about what else you could do instead??*

• Scaling walk – Where are you now? Share in small groups and feedback to the large group

> *What has got you to that number?*
> *If higher, what has been better? If the same, how did you keep things at the same level?*
> *If lower, how did you stop things from going even further down?*

• Scaling walk – what would the next step forwards look like?

> *How will you notice moving up the scale?*

- Action points, positive gossip, and end of session reflections (as outlined above)

At the end of the final session, additional exercises included:

- Celebration – large group discussion

  How would you like to celebrate your progress as a team?

- Team Tool Kit – self-reflection, share in small groups, then large group

  What is in your tool kit to help you continue your journey?
  What are you contributing to the team tool kit (skills, strengths, resources)?
  What do you notice others contributing?
  What support do you need from each other to keep going?

- Maintaining progress

  How will you keep things going forwards?
  What would you need to do to get back on track?

- Sharing information

  Who needs to be informed of what we covered in the team coaching sessions?
  Who will share what with whom and how?

Impact on the Team

The team reported that the team coaching sessions had led to a more cohesive team, enhanced individual and team engagement, and clarity on their common purpose. They realised they were all on the same page and had seen many signs of positive change. They were interacting more positively and intentionally with each other – simple things like saying hello and asking about the weekend. They were creating more opportunities to get to know each other better which helped them trust and support each other better. They felt less burdened and had more energy to focus on their day-to-day work.

Reflections

As team coaches, it is so heartening to see that by creating time and space to come together as a team, amazing things can happen. Changes in conversations lead to change in the organisation at a wider level such that people reconnect with why they do their job, are more positive about coming to work, and team performance increases.

References

Association for Coaching (n.d.). *AC Team coaching competency model V0F*. Retrieved from: https://www.associationforcoaching.com/page/TeamCoachingAccreditation

Chan, S. T. M., & Chung, A. Y. L. (2016). Chinese cultural values and solution focused therapy. In D. Hogan, D. Hogan. J. Tuomola, & A. Yeo (Eds), *Solution focused practice in Asia* (pp. 48–53). Routledge.

De Jong, P. & Berg, I. K. (2013). *Interviewing for solutions*. Brooks/Cole. Cengage Learning.

Dierolf, K., Mühl, C., Perfetto, C., & Szaniawski, R. (2024). *Solution focused team coaching (2nd Ed.)*. Routledge.

European Mentoring and Coaching Council (2020). EMCC global team coaching assessment and accreditation framework. Retrieved from: https://www.emccglobal. org/accreditation/itca/

Ideal Motivation (2020, December 10). Wisdom of the geese – best motivational video [Video]. YouTube https://www.youtube.com/watch?v=y-ezwb-lyw8

International Coaching Federation (n.d.). Team coaching competencies. International Coach Federation. Retrieved on 5 December 2023 from: https://coachingfederation. org/credentials-and-standards/team-coaching/competencies

Kaul, A. (2016). Co-creating our shared future. In D. Hogan, D. Hogan, J. Tuomola, & A. Yeo (Eds), *Solution focused practice in Asia*. Routledge.

MacCartney, T. (2022, February 18). *Future of coaching in Southeast Asia*. HR World. https://hrsea.economictimes.indiatimes.com/news/workplace/future-of-coaching-in-southeast-asia/89637747

McKergow, M. & Jackson, P. Z. (2007). Team coaching. *The solutions focus: Making coaching and change SIMPLE* (pp. 178–200). Nicholas Brealey International.

McKinsey & Company (2022). *The great resignation*.

Meier, D. (2005). *Team coaching with the solution circle*. Solutions Books.

Passmore, J. (2021). *Executive report: Future trends in coaching*. Henley Business School. https://assets.henley.ac.uk/v3/fileUploads/Future-Trends-in-Coaching.pdf

Yeo, A. (2016). Pulling up the shoots to help them grow and other oriental pearls of solution focused wisdom. In D. Hogan, D. Hogan, J. Tuomola, & A. Yeo (Eds), *Solution focused practice in Asia*. Routledge.

15 Solution Focused Team Coaching in Taiwan

Cheng-Tseng Lin and Ru-Ya Chang

Introduction

The development of team coaching has increased rapidly as workspaces learn to manage in this VUCA (volatility, uncertainty, complexity, ambiguity) generation. The team coach sees team members as one coaching unit and sets up the coaching agreement based on the group's goals, rather than the individuals' goals. Solution Focused team coaching does not explore the team's current conflicts but focuses on the existing strengths of teams and helps them draw on their own experiences to support the team in developing new practice models and behaviours.

In this chapter, the authors describe the Taiwanese business context and the specific cultural challenges that can affect the role of a team coach. They share a Taiwanese enterprise case study using a Solution Focused team coaching process with eight stages. They reflect on how this can address the cultural challenges described and the positive impact this has on teams.

The Taiwanese Business Context

Taiwan's high-tech industry has many advantages in the global market, but it also faces international competition and changes. Team leaders need to make decisions in terms of human relations and operational management. Taiwanese culture values interpersonal harmony and places great emphasis on the past emotional connections of teams. Enterprises that value these cultural traits face challenges in quickly restructuring organisations and choosing the right talent. The economic rise of emerging countries has prompted many talented individuals to leave Taiwan in search of better opportunities, making it a challenge for most business leaders to retain and attract global talent to join their companies.

Senior executives in Taiwan understand that simply providing new knowledge to employees is not enough. They strive to create a culture of continuous improvement, enabling their teams to successfully tackle challenges and constantly progress towards their goals. Therefore, team coaching has flourished in Taiwan. Coaches view team members as learners and work together with the team to set objectives.

DOI: 10.4324/9781003431480-19

In Taiwan, coaches often encounter challenges when entering a corporate team. Firstly, they are easily perceived as experts within the organisation. Team members therefore tend to respond to coaches in a passive, observant, and silent manner during the coaching process. There is an expectation for the coach to provide solutions and guidance similar to that of an expert or a consultant. Secondly, many companies are facing a generational shift in their workforce. The older generation of Taiwanese employees are accustomed to obedience and being managed, while the newer generation of employees are independent, innovative, and more willing to take on challenges. The diverse traits and values across different generations of employees bring both challenges and positive inspirations to the team. Thirdly, numerous Taiwanese companies engage in cross-cultural collaborations, testing the leadership's ability in cross-cultural management and communication within diverse teams.

Team Coaching

We share a team coaching model based on the Solution Focused approach. Through years of practical experience in team coaching, we have witnessed the transformation and growth of teams, and have summarised the essence of the team coaching process into eight stages.

Step 1: Positioning, Contracting, and Collaboration

In Chinese culture, it is customary to view an external coach as an expert. Therefore, at the outset, it is important to clarify the coach's position and establish a collaborative contract, which sets a positive start for the team coaching process. The coach needs to inform the members of the team coaching session that they are all important executives within the company, intimately familiar with the company's situation, and are experts in company issues.

In the first coaching session, the coach needs to understand who the team manager is and what role they play. They also need to identify the team members and their respective roles, assess the team's performance, determine the challenges the team is facing, identify the desired achievements, and assess the current team culture. Understanding the team dynamics is crucial for effective collaboration.

A Solution Focused coach can use the following questions to facilitate effective collaboration and understand the team's situation. For example, "What do you think your role and responsibilities are as a team manager/member?" "What kind of state do you hope the team can achieve?" "What roles do each team member play in the team? What are their expertise and contributions?" "How is the cooperation and coordination among team members? Are there any challenges or conflicts?" "How is the team currently performing? What achievements do you think have been made?" "What are the main challenges the team faces in achieving its goals? What is the impact of these challenges on the team?" "Please describe the current team culture. What are your expectations for the team culture? What achievements and changes do you hope to accomplish through collaboration?"

These questions can help the coach understand the team's members, roles, challenges, and expectations, establishing a common foundation for cooperation and enhancing the enthusiasm and participation of the team.

Step 2: Listening and Solution Talk

Firstly, allow the participants to discuss the problems they are facing in order to clarify the difficulties they are encountering. You can ask team members to listen to each other's perspectives on the issue and suggest the future they desire instead of the problem.

The Solution Focused coach can employ scaling questions to evaluate the present circumstances. On a scale of 1–10 (with 10 representing the best): "How strongly do you endorse this vision?" "On a scale of 1 to 10, how significant are these visions to the team?" "What do you think is achievable with this vision?" "How would you rate the team's confidence in overcoming current challenges?" "What steps can be taken to boost confidence by one point?"

Culturally, the Taiwanese are more accustomed to accepting scaling questions than the miracle question. In the team coaching session, through scaling questions, participants are asked to rate the difficulty they are facing on a scale of 1–10, where 10 represents smooth progress and 1 indicates significant challenges or obstacles. This helps further understand the nature of the difficulties they are encountering and where they want to get to.

This lays the foundation for subsequent solution-setting. Additionally, these questions help members to become aware of their current position and, through responses from other members, gain insights and perspectives, thereby enhancing client engagement, proactive thinking, and exploration, and motivating them to collectively face and resolve problems.

Step 3: Suppose Questions Lead to Preferred Future Imagery

The coach uses suppose questions to guide the team towards envisioning a positive future. They may ask the team, "Suppose the problem has been resolved, how would you know things are getting better?" Alternatively, they can use a miracle question such as "Suppose tonight, while you were sleeping, a miracle happened but you didn't know how it happened, what differences would you notice tomorrow morning?" Suppose questions and miracle questions allow the team to imagine a better future.

Based on coaching experience in Taiwan, suppose questions are generally more accepted by clients compared to miracle questions. For many team members who struggle with imagination, suppose questions are easier to answer. In reality, whether it's a suppose question or a miracle question, the key is to set goals based on the preferred future imagery. For example, "Imagine that we travel through time and arrive six months later, and the situation you desired has been achieved. How is the company different from the present? From which aspects would you know that the desired outcome has occurred? If we were to ask your customers, what would they say is different about you?" Members may provide answers such as "There will be more transparent communication, and colleagues will have access to current information, effectively reducing anxiety" or "Team members will feel valued and receive professional training. Even if the company develops new products and takes a new direction, employees will feel secure and able to keep up with the company's growth." These answers represent future talk and allow participating members to express their desired future.

Step 4: Goal Clarification and Setting

Once the members have a vision of a better future, it is necessary to transition towards reality and keep the members in solution talk. The team needs to further refine their goals with precision. For example, "How will you know when you have achieved it?" "What will be happening at that time?" "What might you need to do to achieve what you just mentioned?" "How committed are you to taking action?"

As a Solution Focused coach assists members in setting good goals, they need to consider the SMART elements: specific, measurable, attainable, resourced, and time-bound. Furthermore, they need to consider specificity, such as "Who will do it? How will they do it? What will they do?" By using outcome questions, they can explore what the final outcome will be and return to the individual's own part and responsibility. Questions like "What can you commit to doing?"; "How confident are you in completing the steps you just mentioned?"; and "What resources do you need assistance with?" can be asked. In addition to these principles, the Solution Focused approach, compared to other models, places more emphasis on the system. Therefore, the coach needs to inquire about the interpersonal dynamics from within. For example, "When your team is developing a new product, what adjustments do your team members need to make?" "Regarding the goal of developing new products and technologies, if you want to provide corresponding professional training to team members, what might their responses be? How can you increase their cooperation?" "If the company's direction is as such, what kind of training and skills do team members feel they need to increase?" "Regarding the aspect of 'information transparency,' how would the core members within your team define what it means for something to be 'information transparent'?"

A Solution Focused coach guides members in exploring goals, clarifying them, and setting them in a concrete manner. This greatly influences the initiation and implementation of actions for change. The clarification and setting of goals are crucial in linking actions, solutions, and evaluation.

Step 5: Identifying Strengths and Doing the Right Thing

A Solution Focused coach believes that the team must possess certain strategies and competencies to cope with the challenges they encounter. The coach's job is to support the team in identifying the most effective approaches. The coach may ask the team some questions such as: "Given the talent shortage and the communication issues the team is currently facing, in what aspects the team has done well so far?" "What have you done well to generate more efficiency?" "What signature strengths does your company possess that have contributed to its successes?" What has made your company stand out from all your competitors?" "What products, technologies, or practices enable your company to maintain its solid competitive position in the market?"

Here, it is important not only to identify organisational strengths but also to recognise individual strengths. "In the past, your company has achieved impressive results. What individual qualities and abilities have contributed to these accomplishments?"

Step 6: Extracting and Utilising Effective Experiences

In the Solution Focused team coaching process, the coach asks the team about their effective experiences, such as: "What past experiences have come close to the situation you desire?" "When have you come even a little bit close to the description you just mentioned?" "What methods have you tried in the past?" These questions amplify the team's successful experiences and instil a sense of hope.

When team members bring up some past practices they have had, the coach needs to pause and explore these valuable experiences. They should ask for details, allowing the members to outline the actions and steps taken in those successful experiences. For example, when team members mention experiences like "Engineers in the department proactively developed a messaging platform to stay updated on information and work progress, saving time on back-and-forth emails ..." or "During the pandemic, certain tasks were outsourced, reducing the workload for internal colleagues and enabling organisational restructuring ..." the coach then asks, "How did these past approaches work?" "What value or insights do the methods you previously used have in addressing the current challenges?" "Based on the experiences you just mentioned, what have you learned?" "Building upon the project experiences you just shared, what similar or different approaches will you take this time?"

Step 7: Expanding the Next Small Step

"A journey of a thousand miles begins with a single step." Even with a vision of a better future and clear goals, it is essential to start with the first small step. Therefore, in the aforementioned team coaching process, focusing on listening to the problem, assessing the problem, setting goals, and identifying past successful experiences and strengths, the Solution Focused coach needs to guide the team members to concentrate on the first small step. By identifying the first step that team members need to take, they can initiate action and resolution. Asking the team members about their first step and where to begin is crucial for fostering unity and cooperation within the group, ensuring that efforts are directed to the right place.

In addition to identifying the first step that team members need to take, the Solution Focused coach often engages in the process of "expanding" by helping team members think outside the box and consider other possibilities. The phrase "What else?" is a commonly used expansive questioning technique. This simple question implies that there are other possibilities and signifies the coach's trust in the client. Through open-ended questioning, the coach aims to explore additional methods. In addition to exploration, Solution Focused coaching emphasises focusing on the client's first step. The coach asks the team where they will begin with the next small step. "How will you notice that you have taken a small step forward on the scale?" "If your score increased by one point, what would your colleagues say you did that you are not currently doing?"

Step 8: Review, Appreciative Feedback, and Closure

In Solution Focused team coaching, it is important to review the process, assess the progress made towards the action steps and goals, identify areas that require adjustments, and determine which methods have been effective. The coach asks questions such as "How far have we come?" "What needs to be corrected?" "What methods have been successful?" "What else needs to be done?" These reflections help shape the subsequent steps and actions.

The team coach provides positive and appreciative feedback throughout the process, acknowledging the team's performance and growth. This feedback empowers the team, fostering their development and enabling them to take ownership of their progress. In the context of Solution Focused coaching, a 360-degree feedback approach is employed, using questionnaires to identify the strengths and areas of excellence demonstrated by the team members. This feedback helps individuals and the team as a whole to achieve the desired outcomes.

In our practical experience with the eight-step process mentioned earlier, we have identified two crucial points. Firstly, these steps are not linear or rigid; they need to be developed in accordance with the organisation's culture and climate. When an organisation decides to adopt Solution Focused team coaching, their behaviours, language, and interactions begin to change. The coach needs to observe the organisation's dynamics and adapt accordingly. Secondly, the role of organisational managers is crucial. They need to understand the principles and practices of Solution Focused coaching. Their support and demonstration within the organisation have a significant impact. Therefore, it is important to educate and involve managers in the process to ensure their understanding and active participation.

Conclusion

By following the steps outlined, many of the challenges faced in the Taiwanese business context mentioned earlier can be addressed. Starting the coaching process well with a clear discussion of the coach's role helps the team engage with the collaborative process. Asking about what is already working well brings in perspectives from all team members and can help recognise each other's strengths even when from different cultures or generations. Creating the preferred future together brings in the best of everyone's ideas and allows them to design the outcome that makes sense in their particular organisation and cultural context.

Usually, after 4–6 rounds of team coaching, the majority of teams have shown excellent results, such as increased team consensus and identity, rediscovering organisational advantages, finding solutions, and formulating action steps to solve problems. According to the feedback from team members, it is due to the coach's communication and guidance there is an increase in motivation and participation, and the quality of team communication and collaboration has improved which has, in turn, increased productivity and job satisfaction.

Section 5

Life Coaching

16   Thriving through Transitions

Using Solution Focused Coaching

Jane Tuomola

Introduction

Many clients come for coaching when facing a change in their life circumstances such as changing jobs, moving country, or transitioning to a new stage of life such as marriage, becoming a parent, or retiring. Changes involve both opportunities and losses and navigating these can be a challenge. The aim of the work is the same as any other Solution Focused (SF) coaching – establishing what outcome the client wants, creating a detailed picture of their preferred future, and exploring where they already are in relation to this and their next steps forwards. However, many clients may not feel ready to move forwards until the losses have been acknowledged.

This chapter will illustrate with excerpts from transcripts, how to listen to the client's story with an SF mindset and balance acknowledging their struggles while looking for signs of progress. Exploring what was important to the client about what they just lost can help them move towards the future where what is valued can be incorporated. Talking about losses can also lead to opportunities to highlight a client's strengths and how these could support them with the current change.

Being aware of when there might be a need to refer for therapy is also important, such as when strong emotions may be interfering with making progress in coaching. This chapter will also include cultural considerations when working in the Asian context.

Background

When I moved to Asia as a psychologist, I worked with expat clients who were struggling with the transition to life in Singapore. I would assess their problems and offer psychoeducation based on ideas such as the five stages of culture shock (Pedersen, 1995) and Berry's (1992) model of acculturation. I would assign homework based on where I as the expert assessed them to be struggling. Working with people from all around the world meant they differed in where they had moved from, where and what home meant to them, the reasons for their move, and their expectations of life in Singapore. I felt I was missing the mark as many of my suggestions did not fit well.

DOI: 10.4324/9781003431480-21

They did not want to pay for several sessions of therapy to assess the history of their problem, but just move on and thrive. This is what led me to train in Solution Focused Brief Therapy (SFBT) and then SF coaching. The SF coaching approach is a good fit for this work. I no longer had to worry about offering the right advice but asking questions that enable the client to construct the future they want, based on their own cultural frame of reference and what is important to them.

Below are some sample dialogues about how to set up a coaching agreement and other useful SF questions when working with clients in transition.

Setting Up the Coaching Agreement

As with all coaching clients, it is important to explore what the client wants out of the coaching sessions. Sometimes this can be relatively straightforward, as outlined in the dialogue below. In the solution building process, each question builds on the previous answer and uses the client's exact words as far as possible.

Coach: What are your best hopes from our session?
Client: I'm not really sure. I recently moved to Singapore with my husband and children. We have moved countries twice before, but this is the first time I have lived in Asia and it's much harder than I expected. I'm not feeling depressed but I'm not happy either. The kids seem to have settled well at school and my husband is busy at work. I'm just feeling lost all day on my own at home.
Coach: What would you like to be noticing instead of feeling lost?
Client: I just want to feel myself again. I'd feel happier.
Coach: What would that look like when you are happier and feeling like yourself?
Client: I'd have more energy. I'd be exercising and seeing friends and feel I was accomplishing something each day.
Coach: How would you notice by the end of the session today that you were getting closer to that?
Client: I'd feel more optimistic about my life in Singapore and have some ideas about steps forwards.

Once there is a clear coaching agreement, the coach can use the miracle or other SF preferred future questions to explore in more detail what they want, scale where they are already in relation to this, and explore how they would notice moving forwards step by step.

However, sometimes, the dialogue may go in a different direction.

Coach: So what would you like to be noticing instead of feeling lost?
Client: I don't know. The heat and humidity are tiring – I can't do anything without sweating. I can't even get basic tasks done – I was out

looking for a greeting card and found so many malls but not a single shop selling what I wanted. I haven't found anyone I connected with yet. I miss all my family and friends back home (client tears up).

Balancing Acknowledgement and Progress

The client has answered the question with many complaints about life in Singapore and what they are missing. This is very common when clients are in transition as they are often grieving what they have lost. Acknowledging and validating these concerns is important so that the client feels heard and that you are taking them seriously. McKergow (2021, p. 119) talks about imagining two circles on the ground: the circle of progress and the circle of acknowledgement. The aim is to stand with one foot in each circle and never lose contact with either. This is done by balancing statements of acknowledgement with questions about coping, progress so far, or what is wanted instead. If the client is struggling and finding things tough, more emphasis needs to be placed on the acknowledgement foot. Slow down and accept the client is finding it tough for now. There is a difference between being problem focused (exploring the problem in detail) and taking the client seriously. When things are going well we can focus more on progress and expanding what is better. If we only look for progress we may risk going faster than the client. If we only acknowledge, then they may slow down or stop and get even more stuck in the problem situation.

The coach continues the conversation by making an empathic acknowledgement and asking a coping question.

Coach: It sounds as if it has been tough trying to get every day things done in a new country and you are missing those you care about. How have you been managing?

Client: Just taking things one day at a time. Luckily, I have moved countries before and I know it takes time to adjust.

Coach: What did you learn from the previous moves that is helping you now?

Client: Trying to be kind to myself helps. I burst into tears last week as the supermarket didn't have something I wanted. When that happened years ago I thought I was going crazy! Now I know that is just part of the process. I also need to keep in touch with friends back home while making friends here. There are some great Facebook groups I can ask for advice.

Coach: It sounds like you have figured out a lot of things that help already. How did you do that?

Client: I figured that out by trial and error from the previous move. I also got advice from others about what helps cope with culture shock. Talking to friends who know me well keeps me grounded and means I can share some of the stresses. But I also need to focus on life in the new country, not just look back to what I am missing.

Coach: If our conversation today is useful to you and builds on what you are already doing, what are you hoping for?

Client: This time, I didn't really want to move here so I am fighting against it. I want to be happy, but I feel I am counting down the time until my husband's posting ends and we can go home.

Coach: So if you figured out what would make the time here as good as it can be, even though it's not the ideal place, would that be something you want to explore?

Client: Yes.

Solution Focused Listening

One of the concepts that I find really helps when listening to clients talking about what they don't want or what they miss is the Chinese character tīng (to listen) (Figure 16.1). I first came across this idea in the SFBT training I did at the Academy of Solution Focused Training (2009, p. 8).

The character tīng is made up of several parts:

- Ear: using your ears to listen and gather information about what the client has said
- King: showing respect and listening as if the person in front of you is as important and valued as a king
- 10 or maximum: giving clients 100% of your attention
- Eye: noticing what your client may be communicating non-verbally
- Heart: listening wholeheartedly to feel what the person needs
- One: through embracing all these ways of listening we can become of one heart.

Figure 16.1 The Chinese character Tīng meaning to listen (Illustrated by Chee Seng Cha, Reproduced with permission).

By really listening with all our senses, we can look for what the client values and what is important to them.

Useful Questions for Coaching Clients in Transition

We can move on to asking questions about what they valued from the previous place they lived, a previous job or relationship and what this would look like when they have more of this going forwards. Asking both what they want to keep and what they want to be different is helpful (SolutionsAcademy, n.d.). All SF coaching conversations are co-created and each question can only be constructed when we hear the client's previous answer. The questions below are a useful starting point which can then be adapted by using what the client has already shared.

- What did you value from your relationship with X?
- What do you think they would like to see live on from your relationship?
- What did you appreciate about your old job/life in the previous country and want to keep?
- What would you be noticing that tells you have more X in your current day to day life?
- What would you like to be different in your new job?
- Suppose you were connecting with your friends and family back home while also making friends here what would you be noticing?
- How would you notice moving forwards, despite this big change in your life?
- How would you know you are coping as well as possible in this situation?
- Suppose on a scale of 0–10, where 10 is you're satisfied you are doing as well as possible, where are you already? What has got you to that number and not lower? How would you notice moving up to the next point on the scale?
- Who would notice that you are moving on? What would they be noticing?
- Suppose you were thriving in your new job/role/country what would that look like?
- How would you notice embracing this change a little more each day?
- As you move to this new phase of your life (e.g. becoming a parent, getting married, retiring) what would you like to be noticing?
- What kind of partner/parent do you want to be?
- What would your partner/child be noticing about you?

Coaching Emotions and When to Refer to Therapy

When working with clients in transition, there are often feelings of sadness and loss. Unlike traditional models of working with grief, we don't assume the client needs to express and work through their emotions.

We give space and acknowledge these feelings as outlined earlier at a pace that feels right for the client. However there may be times that the client's emotions are overwhelming and interfering with making progress in coaching.

The International Coaching Federation (n.d.) has a guide about when and how to refer a client for therapy. If you notice any of the following, it is important to discuss with your client whether therapy would be a better fit for them and refer them on if needed:

• Issue is outside your competency and experience level
• Issue interferes with daily functioning
• Issue is a barrier to making progress in coaching
• Issue is psychological in nature and deals with deep-seated emotions.

Cultural Considerations

The beauty of the SF coaching approach is that the coach does not bring preconceived ideas of how a person should be coping while going through a transition, or what thriving in their new life should involve. The questions we use focus on establishing what the client's preferred future looks like and takes into account whatever is important to them. This therefore is a good fit no matter what cultural background the client is from.

However, there are certain factors that mean it fits well in the Asian cultural context. Chan and Chung (2016) describe how SFBT fits well with Chinese cultural values such as interdependence, face, filial piety, modesty, and pragmatism. As the theoretical stance of SF is the same whether the conversation is therapy or coaching, these ideas are also relevant in the coaching context.

Chan and Chung (2016) state that Chinese people place more importance on family bonds and unity than individuality, independence, and self-reliance. The SF approach frequently uses relationship questions to explore how significant others would notice the client changing, so it is important to ask about what family members or work colleagues would be noticing and how they would respond. Questions may also include what the client would be noticing when the client is thriving in a way that also supports good family relationships or harmony in the team (using words and concepts that the client has mentioned are important to them).

This can be especially important to clients who are repatriating to Asia after living abroad. Through being exposed to other cultures, clients can find it harder than they expected to fit in when back home. They may place a different priority on family relationships or work harmony than they did before. Useful questions can include: how might you notice getting the right balance between what's important to you and what's important to your family as you settle back to life here?

Chinese people value a pragmatic approach that is goal oriented (Chan & Chung, 2016). The SF approach to coaching is therefore a good fit as it is forward looking, starts from where they want to get to rather than understanding the root cause of any problems and through the use of scaling helps clients move forwards step by step.

Asian clients are likely to demonstrate modesty when asked about their strengths. Acknowledging strengths however also bring honour to the family and strengths are often defined through the collective strength of the family (Chan & Chung, 2016). Therefore, when exploring how clients have been coping with any transition, it can also be important to ask what the family has noticed the client doing well, or how the client may draw on the family to support them through the transition. Asking for factual evidence about what they have done may be more culturally sensitive than asking what general strengths they have. However, as always, be guided by how your client responds to specific types of questions and adjust accordingly.

Conclusions

This chapter has highlighted the need for balancing acknowledgement and progress when coaching clients in transition, who are often struggling with many losses. Noticing how clients respond to your questions can guide when to move forwards and when to slow down as you work towards a coaching agreement.

The Chinese character tīng is a wonderful analogy of SF listening – using our eyes, ears, and heart and focusing all our attention on our clients to understand what is important to them and what they want more of going forwards.

SF coaching fits well across cultural contexts as it focuses on constructing a preferred future that takes into account whatever is important to a client from their frame of reference. However, it also fits particularly well with certain Chinese cultural values such as interdependence, modesty, and pragmatism and questions can be adapted to be even more culturally sensitive such as asking clients how they notice the balance being right between what's important to them as individuals and to their family or work context.

References

Academy of Solution Focused Training. (2009). *Training manual solution focused brief therapy training level 1*. Academy of Solution Focused Training.

Berry, J. W. (1992). Acculturation and adaptation in a new society. *International Migration, 30*, 69–85.

Chan, S. T. M., & Chung, A. Y. L. (2016). Chinese cultural values and solution focused therapy. In D. Hogan, D. Hogan. J. Tuomola, & A. Yeo (Eds), *Solution focused practice in Asia* (pp. 48–53). Routledge.

International Coaching Federation. (n.d.). *Referring a client to therapy*. Retrieved on 5 December 2023 from: https://coachingfederation.org/app/uploads/2021/01/ReferringaClienttoTherapy.pdf

McKergow, M. (2021). *The next generation of solution focused practice. Stretching the world for new opportunities and progress.* Routledge.

Pedersen, P. (1995). *The five stages of culture shock: Critical incidents around the world.* Greenwood Press.

SolutionsAcademy (n.d.). *Coaching grief and loss*. Retrieved on 5 December 2023 from: https://www.solutionsacademy.com/blog/coaching-loss-and-grief

17 The Challenges of Decision-Making

A Case Study Using Solution Focused Coaching

Sukanya Wignaraja

Introduction

Of all the scenarios coaches encounter in their work, decision-making is one of the most common. Clients are often grappling with a dilemma that requires them to make a decision and feel stuck. We all know that for every decision made, there is a consequence and this is what makes decision-making challenging. Common questions clients bring to coaching sessions are as follows: "How do I know if I am doing the right thing?" "How can I be sure if this is the best way forward?" "How do I make a decision that keeps everyone happy?" In this chapter, I will examine how Solution Focused (SF) coaching can be used to help clients work their way through difficult decision-making situations and dilemmas. To illustrate the process, I will use a real case example and provide transcripts from sessions.

Background

I was certified as an SF coach in 2016 and received my Professional Certified Coach credential the same year. Prior to this, I had been practicing as an SF therapist. I am in private practice in Sri Lanka and see clients for both coaching and therapy. The 2023 Global Coaching Study commissioned by the International Coach Federation found that the number of coach practitioners has increased in all global regions, and most notably in Asia with an increase of 86% in this region. To provide some country context, it is worth mentioning that coaching in Sri Lanka is still in its nascent stages. However, there is growing interest in coaching as a profession. A significant development has been the setting up two years ago of the first ICF Colombo Chapter. This has brought coaching into the spotlight. The Colombo Chapter is active in promoting the benefits of coaching and organises a range of events on coach education and training.

The collaborative nature of SF practice was what drew me to this modality originally. SF coaching pays attention to what is already working for the client and in particular to the client's strengths and capabilities. The SF coach makes an assumption that the client is capable and competent which results in

DOI: 10.4324/9781003431480-22

the client starting to see themselves in the same light. SF questions are very carefully worded and intentional; they convey the coach's assumptions to the client. The entire coaching process is on a level playing field; it is co-created between client and coach.

Case Background

Dilan self-referred for coaching. At the time, he was working as a team manager for a multinational company in Colombo, Sri Lanka. He had been in this job for several years and was doing well. Dilan had plans for the future; he wanted to go abroad for post-graduate studies and he planned, further down the line, to set up his own consultancy. When Dilan came for his first session, he had just handed in his resignation and was working out his notice period. Although it had been Dilan's plan all along to move on from his current job to pursue his longer term goals, his resignation was prompted by HR asking him to let go of some employees on grounds of performance rankings. Dilan however knew that the real reason was a cost-cutting exercise, so felt unable to do as directed and thus saw no other option than to resign. Following his resignation, the four-person team Dilan had created and developed was asked to leave. Dilan felt deeply guilty and responsible for these four individuals as he had personally recruited them. He was visibly stressed and exhausted, wondering whether his decision to resign was the right one and how he would get through his notice period.

Decisions and Dilemmas

Below is an excerpt from the first session. Dilan began, as clients often do, by talking about the difficulties he was facing which were very real and challenging. While acknowledging the client's difficulties, my questions are within the SF framework. The coping question is one of the most commonly used in SF coaching. In this instance, asking Dilan how he had been managing conveys an assumption on the coach's part that the client is somehow coping despite how difficult and severe the problem is. At the same time, I am trying to establish what it is that Dilan would like from the session. It is most often the case that clients will initially articulate what it is they do not want (for Dilan, this is not wanting to feel worried and angry). As it is important to establish what the client does actually want, the SF question about what would be present instead is crucial.

Coach: What needs to happen here today for our time together to be helpful for you?

Dilan: I'm really struggling ... I can't sleep ... I dread going into work. I have no idea how I'm going to get through the next 2 months. I keep thinking I've made a terrible mistake.

Coach:	That does sound extremely difficult. How have you been managing?
Dilan:	I don't know ... I'm not sure I have, to be honest. I don't have a choice ... I have to keep going.
Coach:	So supposing today's session was to be helpful in some way, how would you know?
Dilan:	(is silent for a bit as he thinks): Well ... if I didn't feel so angry and worried all the time, that would help ... I suppose...
Coach:	Ok ... so what would be there instead? Instead of the anger and the worry?
Dilan:	(looks a bit surprised for a moment) Oh ... I don't know ... maybe some acceptance?
Coach:	Hmmm ... acceptance? And how would that make a difference?
Dilan:	Well ... I might start to feel a bit better about what I've done ... you know ... the decisions I've taken ... .
Dilan:	Ah ... I see ... and if you start to feel better about the decisions you've taken, how would that make a difference to you, going forward?

Dilan's response to what would be there instead of the anger and worry is "acceptance". Dilan was struggling with the consequences of his decision-making for those around him. His dilemma had been whether to do as directed by HR, an action that would go against his own ethical stance, or to exit his organisation. The latter appeared to be the more acceptable course of action at the time, but then Dilan was faced with what he believed were the knock-on effects of his decision to resign (i.e. junior colleagues' job security threatened). Acceptance, as Dilan saw it, was not only about him feeling comfortable about his decision-making but also about managing his disappointment with how certain senior colleagues/mentors had responded to the situation at hand.

Part of Dilan's dilemma was the relationship he had established with his team. This is where the cultural angle is especially relevant as there is often a fine line between the professional and the personal. The team that Dilan had built up and developed comprised younger people whom he had personally recruited and mentored. In the Sri Lankan context, he had created more than just a team; it was more of a community. At one level, Dilan's sense of responsibility for them extended beyond his managerial duties and he was anxious about how they would cope in their new roles within the organisation and their overall job security. He was acutely aware that they had always looked up to him as a mentor cum protector and that, in deciding to resign, he had somehow let them down.

Working with the Client in an Solution Focused Way

SF coaching is a collaborative process wherein the coach works alongside the client to help them find a way forward. As mentioned before, the questions are carefully worded to convey the coach's belief in the client's abilities and this results in the client gradually seeing themselves as inherently capable of working towards a solution. In working with Dilan, this approach proved very effective. He not only began to recover his confidence but also was able to look at his situation in a different way and work out where he could exercise control and try a different approach, and where matters were truly out of his hands.

The following is an excerpt from a later session where Dilan considered ways in which he might feel more at ease with his decision.

Dilan: I wish I could feel happier about my decision to resign. I know this was part of my plan but I didn't think I would have to decide in this way ... I feel I've put other people at risk ... or at least their jobs. They're so much younger than me ... they look up to me. I don't know what to tell them ... I feel I've put my own interests first ... .

Coach: It wasn't an easy decision to make ... I can see that. What enabled you to make the decision?

Dilan: (pauses as he thinks for a while) I guess I had always planned to move on ... that was in line with what I wanted to do career-wise. I've put a lot of thought into my career progression ... I know what I want for myself ... I know what I'm capable of.

Coach: So what needs to happen for you to feel happier about your decision?

Dilan: Well ... at one level, I know I've done the right thing ... for myself, for my career, and my job satisfaction. It's also important for me to know that my team members are ok ... .

Coach: And how would that make a difference to you? Knowing your team members are ok?

Dilan: Well ... I recruited and trained these people myself. I built up this team. It would put my mind at rest if I knew their jobs were secure.

Coach: I see ... and if your mind were at rest, what would then be different for you going forward?

Dilan: (pauses and then smiles) For a start, I would stop feeling guilty ... I would be able to focus fully on all the things I have planned without constantly worrying about my team.

It is important to note that in keeping with SF practice, I continually asked Dilan questions about how he was able to do various things and what difference something would make in concrete terms. These SF questions helped Dilan to focus on all the things he had achieved and had planned for his future as well as highlighting his belief in his abilities to accomplish his plans. All of this culminated in him acknowledging that the decision he made, however challenging, was ultimately the right one for him.

Scaling Confidence

Scaling questions are also an important part of the SF toolkit. They can be used to help the client situate themselves as to how confident or hopeful they are about a particular issue or consider the likelihood of success. Scaling questions came in very useful in working with Dilan as they enabled him to think about his decision-making in different ways.

Coach: I'm going to ask you a slightly different question. On a scale of 1–10, where 10 represents you feeling completely confident about your decision, and 1 is where you are not at all sure, where would you place yourself today on that scale?

Dilan: Let's see ... maybe a 4 ... yes ... I think that's where I am ... at a 4 ... .

Coach: Ok ... so now tell me, what are all the things that have happened already and are happening now, that get you to that 4 on the scale?

Dilan: Well ... to begin with, my decision to resign was not sudden. I had given it a lot of thought. It was planned. Also, I know that in order to progress in my career goals, I would have to leave my current job. With regard to my team members, although I am anxious about their futures, I can see that for now they have kept their jobs ... that definitely gives me greater confidence.

Coach: And what would be the smallest sign that your confidence had increased to a 5 on the scale?

Dilan: (pauses to think) I would start to feel comfortable at work again ... instead of feeling anxious and stressed all the time.

Coach: What else?

Dilan: I would probably be able to focus on all the tasks I have left to do in these final few weeks.

Coach: And if you were able to do that ... focus on all the tasks, then what would be different for you?

Dilan: (thinks and starts to smile) Well, I think I would feel I've achieved something by the end of each day ... feel productive again ... .

Coach: So, if all these things started to happen and you felt more comfortable at work, then what else would you notice?

Dilan: (smiles again) I would be chatting with my colleagues again ... you know, like I used to before ... in a relaxed way ... .

In the above exchange, the focus is very much on Dilan's confidence levels rather than on the merits of his decision-making. This helped Dilan to feel more secure and comfortable about his decision which is something he had been struggling with at the outset. The coach asks Dilan for a lot of detail on what he might notice when he does move up the scale. This is the purpose of scaling questions in SF coaching; it is not about what the client needs to do to move up. This is an important distinction to remember.

When a Decision Is Still to Be Made

This case example is about a client who has already made a decision and is struggling with the aftermath. I shall briefly touch upon how to work with a client who is debating whether or not to make a decision. The process is similar in that the coach would explore what difference it would make to the client once the decision is made. Scaling questions could be used: 10 on the scale representing the client having clarity about the decision to be made and 1 being the polar opposite where the client has no clue what to do. This would be followed by questions about what the client would notice as he moves up the scale. Additionally, questions about how the client has dealt with tough decisions in the past will be useful in exploring past resources which might be utilised in the current situation.

Conclusion

Dilan came for four coaching sessions. He eventually arrived at a place where he did feel more secure vis à vis his decision. He found that separating out factors that were within his control (focusing on his career plans, maintaining good relations with his colleagues, and exiting the organisation on good terms) and those that were not (the future of his team members, the behaviour of certain colleagues) was helpful in reducing his stress levels at work. The future of his team members held particular significance for Dilan and while he understood that this was out of his control, he nonetheless found this knowledge hard to accept. From a cultural perspective, even with all professional boundaries in place, he straddled a role that was part manager/part community elder. In such a situation, SF coaching is particularly efficacious, as it enabled me to explore with Dilan how he might come to terms with the consequences of his decision-making and what factors made his (unintended) dual role easier to manage.

This case study highlights the unique aspects of SF coaching and the manner in which it steers away from passing judgement or offering advice. Its emphasis is always on the collaborative process, the assumption that the client does have inherent strengths and capabilities, and the intentional questions that open up possibilities for the client and make them think about their issues in a new and different light.

Reference

International Coach Federation (2023). *Global coaching study*. Retrieved from: https://coachingfederation.org/research/global-coaching-study

18 Addressing a Culture of Patriarchy

Using Solution Focused Coaching with Female Clients in China

Joseph Wang

Introduction

This chapter demonstrates the use of the Solution Focused OSKAR coaching model with female clients in China who are looking for effective ways of handling the impact of growing up in a patriarchal culture. These clients are looking to find effective resources and meaning in their lives. The Solution Focused coaching approach shifts the conversation from talking about past discrimination to future solutions. It gives these clients hope in difficult situations, focusing on the future they want, and enabling them to create a clear path ahead. Transcripts of coaching conversations will be included to illustrate the process.

The Impact of Chinese Culture

In the course of my work with female clients, a common question I hear is: "Why should I be ignored because I'm a girl?" When I first began working with this demographic, I would often hear such sentiments expressed by women who had been deeply affected by the patriarchal culture they grew up in. These women were prone to self-doubt, believing that they were not good enough and did not deserve to be treated well. They sought approval and validation first from their parents and then from their husbands. The belief that they had to continuously sacrifice their self-interest was deeply entrenched.

Culturally, there is a tacit acceptance that women are destined to set aside their self-interest. Women are conditioned from an early age to put their own needs last. For example, if there is a younger brother, it is assumed that the older sister will take care of him. In some families, women are not allowed to eat at the table even though they may have prepared the food. While it is true that education can help to change women's lives in terms of offering greater opportunities, it is not always enough. Many clients choose to study psychology, read self-help books, or seek help. However, due to financial constraints, especially as a result of the pandemic, as well as the fact that traditional models of helping people are more problem-focused, many clients

DOI: 10.4324/9781003431480-23

are left still feeling disempowered. I have been exploring whether there is a more effective model and found Solution Focused coaching is a good fit for working with this client group.

Solution Focused Coaching

The assumptions of Solution Focused coaching are different from the traditional models of helping people. The role of the Solution Focused coach is not to be an expert but to enable clients to decide where they wish to go. The coach helps clients identify the future they want, not by focusing on the past, but on their inherent strengths. The relationship between the coach and the coachee is based on gender equality, cooperation, and trust and it is in contrast to traditional Chinese culture. The coach also believes that the clients have their own expertise, and despite having encountered difficulties in the past, they already possess inherent resources and the ability to solve problems.

The following are the common assumptions of Solution Focused thinking:

- Focusing on the positive, solutions and the future facilitates change in the desired direction.
- No problem happens all the time. Exceptions to most problems can be identified.
- Small change leads to larger change.
- Clients are always cooperating.
- Clients are the expert of their own life.
- Clues to the solution are often right in front of us; we just need to recognise them.
- Change happens as people experience themselves as competent and successful.
- Complex problems do not necessarily need a complex solution.
- The solution is not necessarily connected to the problem.
- People have innate capabilities and resources that can be identified and utilised.
- It is important to stay Solution Focused and not solution forced.

Separating the person from their problems helps clients regain the self-esteem they once lost. Every girl deserves to be loved and respected without having to doubt herself or try to please others because of her experiences. Many of my clients told me later that instead of feeling ashamed of their past, they discovered something new from their upbringing while using their experiences to help others with similar experiences.

OSKAR

The OSKAR coaching approach (Jackson & McKergow, 2007) is a Solution Focused framework for coaching and includes five areas:

O: Outcome – preferred outcome
S: Scaling tool
K: Know-How – past, present knowledge, and know-how of the client
A: Affirm and Action – giving evidence-based compliments; small action
       steps
R: Review – wrap up the sessions

The OSKAR model in Solution Focused coaching conveys acceptance, compassion, and respect for clients; reconstructs their past experiences; explores their own strengths; and builds their desired future step by step. In addition, OSKAR is concise and effective, saving clients' time. I have found that clients are able to grasp these techniques in the process of our dialogue and then internalise them in their own life experiences.

Case Example

Xiao Yu is a mother of three and a junior leader in an insurance company. When she came to meet me, she was struggling with various difficulties both professionally and personally. Like most Chinese women, she worked hard, and raised her children while also trying to meet her husband's needs. In the first session, she talked about how her parents, who had wanted a son, decided to give her away soon after she was born. Xiao Yu knew from a young age that her biological parents had given her away and that they considered this to be natural. Moreover, they paid extra attention to her brother and tried their best to meet his needs. Xiao Yu felt deeply neglected by them.

Listening Respectfully and Identifying Resources

The OSKAR model does not force clients to identify positives immediately. Many women are used to focusing on their pain and problems because this is what they have always done. I usually ask questions about the future slowly after establishing a safe atmosphere of cooperation, and respecting the client's lived experience. When I first met with Xiao Yu, she was tearful and struggled to think about goals. She was conflicted and didn't know how to alleviate her distress. I needed to give her time and explore how she had been coping so far before exploring what she wanted going forwards.

Coach: I've heard about your hardships and I'm sorry for what happened to you in the past. What I'm curious about is: How did you get through those tough times?
Xiao Yu: Probably my faith and church life.
Coach: Wow, your faith? And church life? How were those helpful?

Gradually, her face began to change, and the conversation seemed to open another door as she spoke about the amazing things that had happened over the years with God's help, and the support of her church partners. And then there was her own discovery from life experience of the need to stop those ineffective patterns of interaction. I was amazed to see her transformation, gradually starting from sadness to gratitude and beginning to have a gradual joy.

Slowly Focusing on the Client's Desired Future Life Goals

After several sessions I asked Xiao Yu: "What has changed for the better?" She was excited about the many changes in her life, and over the course of subsequent conversations she gradually clarified the direction of her future goals. She wanted to live out her mission in the workplace and inculcate her faith in her work with her clients.

Coach: What makes this so important to you?

Xiao Yu: Because I don't want to suffer like I did in the past. I want to be financially independent and be able to make my own choices. I would like to improve my living environment, my children's education and live out my faith through my work.

Coach: It's great to hear you talk about all these things and about wanting to feel more capable. What would that look like?

Using Scaling to Explore Client's Strengths

In responding to the Miracle Question, as Xiao Yu focused more on what she wanted to do with her life in the future, realistic details began to unfold. She talked about her differences, her temperament, her tone of voice, and the different reactions of her family and children around her. Scaling questions helped to highlight exceptions and successes. She had many talents, and was skilled in dealing with people. The changes did not always happen smoothly and she encountered challenges along the way but I continued to ask her scaling questions.

Coach: Where are you on the scale now?

Xiao Yu: 4 out of 5

Coach: What makes you at a 4 and not 3?

Xiao Yu: Because at least I'm not as vulnerable as I used to be. Not falling into the ineffective patterns of the past.

Coach: Wow, how did you do that?

Xiao Yu: I realised that I'm not the same as I used to be. I used to give in easily, but now I'm starting to have my own boundaries.

Coach: What else?

Despite occasional setbacks, Xiao Yu continued to move forwards. These ups and downs are a normal part of change. Later, as she became more familiar with the OSKAR model, she found she could face difficulties and re-focus on her future. She was able to transform challenges from her past into resources for moving forwards.

Through regular coaching sessions, Xiao Yu found she was getting much better at her work compared to the previous year. She gained confidence in her abilities and also knew what she wanted going forwards. Her communication with customers had improved and she was exploring ideas that went beyond selling only insurance and included looking at the financial and mental health needs of her clients' families.

She recalled that last year she had several colleagues who had conflicts but started to slowly resolve them, and they still particularly liked working with her because of her openness, her character, and her humanistic focus.

New Ways of Looking at the Past

The OSKAR model enabled Xiao Yu to open the window to her future, allowing her to see herself in a new light, to discover more possibilities and hidden strengths in the past, and also helped her to appreciate and accept herself.

During the coaching conversations, she found her way and constructed a new meaning for herself. She no longer saw herself as a victim, or a survivor, but actively lived out the meaning and mission of her life. Her family, her church, and her co-workers were all influenced by her as she moved forwards with the many changes in her life.

Focusing on Small Changes

Solution Focused coaching focuses on small changes, so each conversation explores small, practical steps. Clarity about current goals, exceptions, resourcefulness, all lead to greater change in her life.

She found that God began to bring clients into her life at work, and she had an apprentice at work, and her income increased. Her self-confidence increased and continued to add value to her life.

She also spoke about how she reconciled with herself and how she was no longer overly anxious and worried, and that her surroundings were also changing along with her. Looking back, she found that she was more anxious and miserable when she focused on her negative suffering and complained to others. By taking care of herself, being emotionally peaceful and joyful, she not only changed her family but also made her work and her circumstances less difficult.

I found that these small steps were making a big difference for her. At the end of a coaching conversation, I usually ask the following questions:

- What might you do to take a small step forwards?
- What is the first thing you do when you finish the conversation?
- What will change your life?
- What did you learn today?
- What are some of the takeaways for you from this session?

These conversations prompted her to be motivated and I was amazed to see that during the coaching, she was able to make changes quickly. Focusing on her temperament, her mindset, and her relationship with her children all produced positive results. Later, she also made positive changes in her career and was able to influence her clients as a result of this. She was also able to pay off major debts.

Today, Xaio Yu continues to move forwards. She now leads her team and positively influences people around her, whether in her family, church, or work. She is no longer the wounded and helpless person she was at the beginning but has transcended her suffering and focused on exploring the future she wants. She too has become a coach who influences others.

Conclusion

There are many similar stories, and the experience of working with Solution Focused coaching is always surprising; it is a concise and powerful tool. Over the years, I have met many clients like Xiao Yu. While these women may have experienced difficulties in their pasts, Solution Focused coaching provides them with the means to reframe those past challenges into something constructive that can help them move forwards towards their goals. It enables them to place boundaries where helpful and increase their self confidence in dealing with others.

Reference

Jackson, P. Z., & McKergow, M. (2007). *The solutions focus: Making coaching and change SIMPLE* (2nd ed.). London, UK: Nicholas Brealey International.

19 Being at Your Best

Single Session Performance Coaching

Chris Iveson and Jane Tuomola

Introduction

There are times in our lives when we have a task or event where we hope to do well. Occasionally, these events have life-changing potential: a job interview, a qualifying sports event, an exam, a first date, or a pitch for a major piece of work. At these times our performance is crucial, we want to be at our very best so that, whatever the outcome, we know we did our best and the rest is out of our hands.

This chapter describes the process of Solution Focused coaching at these critical points in life using an exercise called 'Being at Your Best' and illustrates this using a transcript. This exercise can be useful when a client comes for a single session of coaching to prepare for a specific event, or in a single session within a longer piece of coaching.

An example of using this in an Asian setting is given to show the applicability of the exercise across cultural contexts.

Background

This exercise was originally born out of desperation, when Chris Iveson was working with client stuck in an impossible situation, trying to escape an abuser but with little chance of moving from the run-down council estate where she lived. She felt a move was the only solution so had arranged a meeting with a housing officer to put forward her case but was realistic in expecting nothing. All the therapist could think of was to build the conversation around a possible future in which the client did justice to herself at the meeting but without stepping outside the harsh realities of social housing policies. At the time it seemed a poor response to the client's distress.

A few days later the client phoned saying she didn't know the outcome of the meeting, but was very pleased with herself and that whatever the outcome we did not need to worry about her. At our next meeting (by which time her move had been approved) I asked her about this new belief that even if she had to stay where she was she and her child would be safe. She said something changed in her. Because she came away from the meeting very proud of the

DOI: 10.4324/9781003431480-24

way she had handled it, she began to realise that the outcome was beyond her control. She had done her best and if they refused to move her it wasn't her fault. This seemed to open up a whole new understanding of her life.

Being at Your Best

After noticing similar results with other clients, came an idea that has stayed a part of BRIEF's practice ever since. When a person has an event coming up, especially one that will have a substantial impact on his life and where his performance will have a significant impact on outcome, then 'being at his best' during the event is likely to make a difference to his future life. One of the most common such events is a job interview but there are many more: board meetings, court appearances, presentations and pitches, even first dates. At stake might be future employment or income, whether or not you obtain a much-needed resource, or future relationships. What became obvious was that Solution Focused coaching at these critical points in life can make a major difference to their outcome.

Less obvious but possibly more significant is the impact the coaching session has on the client's view of their future irrespective of whether or not the hoped-for outcome was achieved. The client's experience of 'being at their best' frees them from a sense of responsibility for the outcome, or more particularly a bad outcome which might otherwise have led them to blame the misfortune on themselves.

This format is especially useful for events involving strangers and containing unpredictable elements. In these cases it is not possible for the client to describe the actual event in great detail because there are too many unknowns. For key events with known participants, such as a team meeting, it is possible to build an 'at your best' picture of the event itself or even do both: begin the 'at your best' description from the start of the day, include the 'successful' meeting, and perhaps finish with arriving home at the end of the day. In this way a key but isolated event is embedded in a wider life and thus a wider array of potential resourcefulness.

An example of a student facing her first university interview is shown below.

Coach: What are your best hopes from this meeting?
Louise: I'll get an offer!
Coach: So if this meeting boosts your chances of an offer, will it have been worth it?
Louise: Yes, absolutely!!
Coach: Let's imagine then that it's the day of your interview and –
Louise: Tomorrow!
Coach: Tomorrow! So let's imagine tomorrow is one of those days when you are at your best and absolutely ready for whatever the day has

in store for you! What's the first thing you notice when you wake
up in the morning?

Louise: I wouldn't have that horrible sinking feeling.

Coach: What would you have instead?

Louise: A positive feeling, maybe.

Coach: What time is that likely to be?

Louise: About eight.

Coach: What difference will it make to waking up at around eight
tomorrow with a positive feeling?

Louise: I'd be in a more positive state of mind and have that feeling of
being able to do it, of handling the day well.

Coach: What difference will that make to the way you get up?

Louise: I'll get out of bed straight away which I don't at the moment.

Coach: Who'll notice?

Louise: No one, everyone else will have gone.

Coach: And then? Do you have breakfast, what's the usual routine?

Louise: I'd make some tea and look on the internet for the stories that I
might be asked about at the interview.

Coach: As you were waiting for the computer to open what would you be
noticing about yourself that told you that you were at your best?

Louise: Maybe I'd relax a bit first and read my book.

Coach: So if you were reading your book, drinking your tea, and feeling
relaxed, how would you know you were ready for the day ahead?

Louise: I'd just be relaxing, not panicking, prepared to let the day unfold –
and concentrating on the book.

Coach: And what time will you have to leave for the interview?

Louise: I'm getting a taxi to the station at about 11.

Coach: What else in that couple of hours would tell you that you were
ready?

Louise: Well, I'll have packed the night before so I'll have plenty of time to
get ready.

Coach: So you're thinking about getting ready for this probably most
challenging event in your life; what at that point would tell you that
you really were at your best?

Louise: I wouldn't be putting it off, seeing it as a chore. I'd be enthusiastic
and thinking 'you can do this!' Feeling positive about what I've got
to offer and being able to impress and getting a place.

Coach: And so the taxi arrives. What sort of young woman will the taxi
driver see?

Louise: A woman who is smartly dressed!

Coach: So what else will the taxi driver notice about you?

Louise: Smiling, confident, polite.

Coach: And on the train. What will you notice then?

Louise: I'll be getting nervous then! I think nervousness can sometimes be
healthy; it can give you an adrenalin rush which means you can face

	things better. And I suppose it's tinged with excitement as well. That would be good!
Coach:	And how will you know it's the right sort of nervousness?
Louise:	It will just be a feeling that I'm ready for this and can really make a good impression.
Coach:	So, as you were sitting on the train, what would you be remembering about yourself that gave you good reason for your confidence?
Louise:	I want to be a lawyer and have the skills to be one.
Coach:	What else?
Louise:	I'm capable, I've already worked hard and got one degree, well nearly, and know I can do another one.
Coach:	What else?
Louise:	I've already got one offer so I know I've got what it takes.
Coach:	What else?
Louise:	I'll look the part and feel the part!
Coach:	So what else might you be remembering that was helpful?
Louise:	I'm really enthusiastic about it. And prepared. I've had work experience, I'm good with people. I know I can do it!
Coach:	And eventually, you come out of the station and you're walking towards the college – what will tell you that you are still at your best at that point?
Louise:	I'll probably be thinking about how my hair looks and if I'm still looking smart! I'll be walking along thinking I can do this! I'm smart, I'm capable, I can do it!
Coach:	What do you think the students who pass you by would notice that suggests you are smart, capable and ready for this challenge?
Louise:	My posture – I'll have my head up and my shoulders relaxed, not hunched up.
Coach:	What time is the interview?
Louise:	2.30.
Coach:	And what's the format?
Louise:	There'll be a questionnaire that takes about 30 minutes asking why this college, why law, and what can you offer; then there'll be an ethical case scenario to look at and then the interview.
Coach:	So what will the other applicants notice about you as you arrive?
Louise:	I'll be relaxed – hopefully! I'd do the form, then I'd read the scenario and think about it for a while. I'd probably chat with them about ordinary things, have they come far, that sort of thing.
Coach:	Let's say someone started talking about the questionnaires and what they'd said made you feel a bit wobbly about what you'd put, how would you react then if you were at your best?
Louise:	I'd remind myself of my reasons for becoming a lawyer and that it didn't matter if other people had different ones. So I'd stick with my own ideas.

Coach:	Let's say you are reading your scenario and you think oh dear, I've never even thought of a situation like that. How will you know then that you are at your best?
Louise:	Just stay calm and look at all the angles: responsibility to the client, what is the central legal issue. And also the moral side. It's just being systematic and trying to cover everything. And sometimes there isn't a 'right' answer!
Coach:	And now the interview itself is looming! What will tell you at that point that you couldn't be more ready, that you're at your best?
Louise:	I know there's nothing more you can do about your preparation – just relax and put your best foot forward in the interview.
Coach:	And as they come out to get you what would you notice about the way you walked to the interview?
Louise:	Relaxed, probably trying to talk to the person, keeping my head up and shoulders back – but not too far back!
Coach:	So what sort of young woman would the panel see coming into the room?
Louise:	A young woman smiling, going forward, shaking hands. Being polite and open.
Coach:	What else will they notice about you even before you speak that makes them think you are a potential barrister?
Louise:	It sounds funny but it's something about the way you sit – not too upright and not slouched but concentrating on them and the questions.

During the interview Louise is asked to describe both her inner states and the outer actions which signify these states. She is asked to locate herself at specific places and specific times and attention is paid to the most humdrum details such as the period during which her computer turns on or sitting on a train. She is asked to think about what this will look like to others (and as Louise will not be seeing anyone who knows her these others will all be strangers). In the middle there is the opportunity to list some of the reasons why Louise might be justified in feeling confident and there is also a potential setback to include the vagaries of life.

Of the many ways a Solution Focused conversation can be constructed, this particular format is one of the most effective and economical. It is also a perfect example of how the client leaves with no more than she came with: she was asked to describe nothing that was not already within her experience of herself; no 'miracles', no imagining you can do something you've never done before, just simply a description of what she might ordinarily do when she is at her best. Only a closer look reveals the extraordinariness of the questions and therefore the never-before-spoken answers. Louise is unlikely to have been asked what a taxi driver might notice about her so her answer is likely to be one that she has never heard herself say before that moment. At least half of her answers will also be new to her and many of the rest, though not necessarily new, will have new meanings.

The beauty of this process is that it works equally well across different cultural contexts.

Qi Feng

Qi Feng was a Chinese man in his early 40s. He wanted coaching as he had multiple interviews to prepare for. Unlike a typical Singaporean who may stay with the same firm for several years, he had changed industries and roles every 3–4 years. He felt it was time for another change but was not sure how to describe what he had done in a positive way given this is not the cultural norm. He reported having lost much of his confidence. Not being able to change his past, he felt stuck moving forward.

We used the same 'Being at Your Best' interview to prepare for an upcoming technical interview at a large multinational corporation. He described the day, waking up rested and calm, and the positive impact this would have on his family. He shared that he would be relaxed, have a coffee, and prepare the right amount for the interview. He described facing the interview panel in a calm and confident manner, taking time to answer the questions, and thinking 'I've got this'. We ended the conversation with a question asking him to look back on the day and what he had been most pleased to notice that told him that whatever the outcome, he knew he had done his best. The next session he shared he had unexpectedly had to face an interview panel of five people. Normally this would have thrown him but instead, he described how he had taken it in his stride and confidently answered their questions. He later got offered the job. He said realising he could be his confident self, even in a challenging interview, had significantly impacted how he saw himself in all areas of his life.

When asked to share his reflections for this chapter, he said he found the process really intriguing as he had never located an interview within the whole day before. While he knew he could not control what was asked in the interview, he hadn't realised the impact other parts of the day could have on preparing to be at his best. He said he would now notice if he went off course during the morning and prompt himself back on track.

What was interesting was the impact this had on other areas of his life. He noticed being more optimistic and conscious of the positives in his life. He was more productive at work, engaging his team more, and building better client relationships which brought in more business. He was also more present for his family and enjoying time with them.

Cultural Reflections

The two clients above are different ages, genders, have different family situations, and live in different cultures – yet the impact of the process is strikingly similar. One of the great 'discoveries' of de Shazer was that 'solutions' had more in common with each other than they do with 'problems'. His *Keys to Solution in Brief Therapy* (1985) is a fascinating description of the cusp between problem focused and solution focused conversations and where the idea that many different problems might have the same solution was first explored.

If you are familiar with the cultural expectations of the event, you can bring these in during your questions. For example, in a Japanese interview, you need to knock on the door three times, and say excuse me ('Shitsurei shimasu' 失礼します/しつれいします) before being asked to enter the room: 'As you knock on the door three times, what are you noticing that tells you, you are at your best?' Alternatively, you can ask the client at different points what they know about the process and what will happen next, and include this in the questions you ask.

What is entirely missing is the coach's own experience or advice about being interviewed and interviewing others. There is no place for this knowledge in a Solution Focused interview and having it is unlikely to make a difference. Indeed, it could even be unhelpful to share ideas of what would work in your cultural context, which may not be appropriate elsewhere.

Here again the simplicity of Solution Focused coaching is clearly evident as is the challenge it presents: being simple isn't easy. To refrain from the desire to pass on the benefits of our own experience requires great discipline and continues to do so even for the most experienced Solution Focused coaches.

References

BRIEF. London. https://www.brief.org.uk/
de Shazer, S. (1985). *Keys to solution in brief therapy*. W. W. Norton & Company.

20 From Shame to Freedom

Addressing Sexual Shame with Solution Focused Sex Coaching

Dian Handayani

Introduction

In this chapter, I discuss working with emotions in Solution Focused (SF) sex coaching within a Southeast Asian context, specifically with Indonesian clients. Internal and external factors can hinder clients from reaching their sexual goals and being empowered. In Southeast Asia, including Indonesia, conservative values and cultural norms inhibit open discussion and education on sexuality and sexual health. Furthermore, misinformation and negative messaging are rife on social media and in the broader society. My clients are typically exposed to these influences, perpetuating stigmas and sexual shame (Litam & Speciale, 2021). Sexual shame can negatively impact desire, arousal, and orgasm and contribute to relationship issues such as infidelity and conflict. SF sex coaches must be prepared to work with their clients' emotions to break down this shame, which will eventually facilitate empowerment on the way to the client's desired outcomes.

A case vignette will be used to demonstrate the SF sex coaching approach. Coaches will gain new insight into the application of SF tools and skills in addressing sexual concerns and working with emotions that surface in their sessions.

Coaching Context

I began my counselling career in 2010 as an art psychotherapist specialising in mental health at an acute hospital in Singapore. I completed a master's degree in sexual health counselling in 2019 and began offering sex therapy services at the hospital. That same year, I enroled with Sex Coach U (SCU). SCU is an online, US-based sex coaching programme that provides a comprehensive, evidence-based, and holistic framework of sexuality through its signature system of the MEBES™ model, an acronym signifying Mind, Emotions, Body/ Behaviour, Energy, and Spirit. I opened my private practice in 2021 and offered sex coaching to clients with the blessing of SCU. In 2023, I became a certified sex coach and a sexologist. I work with adults from diverse cultural backgrounds and nationalities, all genders, abilities, and sexual orientations.

DOI: 10.4324/9781003431480-25

Solution Focused Sex Coaching

Sex coaching itself combines coaching with the scientific study of human sexuality, incorporating cognition, behaviours, and sociocultural norms and values (Britton, 2005). SF sex coaching combines sex coaching with an SF coaching framework. The SF coaching framework is ideal for sex coaching, given its resiliency-based and non-pathological approach, since these factors correspond well to the human sexual experience. SF sex coaches facilitate the building of the desired sexual and relationship outcomes via empowerment (Britton, 2005).

The Indonesian Cultural Context

Indonesia is a tropical archipelago and the world's fourth most populous country. According to a 2018 Indonesian government survey, 86.7% of the population is Muslim (Diamant, 2019). A combination of Islam, a patriarchal culture, and increasing conservatism since the late 1990s plays a significant role in the daily lives of most Indonesians (Halim, 2021).

These conservative, religious, and traditional values permeate many Indonesian Muslims' views on sexuality. Sex and discussion of sexuality are considered taboo and sinful outside of the context of marriage (Riyani, 2021), which is viewed as fulfilling social, cultural, and religious obligations. Sex is commonly considered to be the husband's prerogative, whereas the wife's role is to fulfil his needs. These beliefs are reinforced and justified through religious doctrines that equate obedience to one's husband with strict Islamic observance (ibadah). As suggested by Riyani (2021), various Qu'ranic verses and prophetic sayings advocate male superiority and consider women as 'libaas' (garments).

Furthermore, these doctrines stigmatise women who openly discuss, initiate, or express their sexual desires, labelling them as 'naughty' or 'bad women.' Many women, therefore, believe that refusing sex or being overtly sexual with their husbands is sinful and culturally taboo, and they fear negative backlash from their family and community, which would bring feelings of shame and failure (Riyani, 2021). We must consider this emotional component of clients' worldview in the coaching process.

Embracing Emotions: The Role of Emotional Exploration for Effective Sex Coaching

In general, those in the coaching field are cautious when dealing with clients' emotions and typically recommend therapy or counselling referrals when difficult emotions arise. The coach's role is to acknowledge the presence of emotions and shift the focus back to the client's desired outcomes. Similarly, SF coaching is rooted in Solution Focused Brief Therapy (SFBT), which emphasises behavioural change and goal setting and typically excludes the emotional aspects of clients' experiences.

The International Coaching Federation (ICF, 2019) include as part of their core competencies that a coach should acknowledge and support the client's expressions of feelings (4.5) and demonstrate confidence in working with strong client emotions (5.4).

A growing body of research suggests that neglecting emotional exploration can negatively impact the coach/coachee relationship (Duffell & Lawton-Smith, 2015). This avoidance may reduce effectiveness and client engagement in the coaching process. Furthermore, the exploration is especially pertinent to sensitive taboo topics such as sexuality.

Exploring emotions, including shame, can provide valuable information to enhance the coaching process (Cremona, 2010; Duffell & Lawton-Smith, 2015). The three main components of the brain's emotional processing – emotions, feelings, and affects – are rich data sources in coaching due to their interactions with mental and physical responses that regulate our thinking, desire, motivation, behaviour, and relationships.

Pervasive sexual shame across cultures, religions, and communities can profoundly affect the client's sexual identity, desire, attractions, and self-esteem (Litam & Speciale, 2021). For example, in reacting to a shameful incident around sexuality, a client's face might express deep sadness, or they might describe feeling sick in the pit of their stomach. They may share thoughts and affect, such as 'I feel sad, and I think I'd never be a good enough wife, which is humiliating, and I've failed my ibadah (religious duties).' Such emotive language, body expression, thoughts, feelings, and affects require careful handling by coaches to facilitate empowering and lasting change and avoid reinforcing the shame.

Working with Emotion, the Solution Focused Sex Coaching Way

'Feeling talk can sometimes be the best solution talk' (Piercy et al., 2000).

Given the role of sexual shame in sex coaching, it is essential to consider how sex coaches work with emotion, particularly emotional language and its embodiment. This consideration is an essential next step in the SF sex coaching process. Thus, to facilitate this growth, I recommend that sex coaches incorporate SFBT principles and techniques to handle clients' emotions, as proposed by Walker et al. (2022). The following is a summary of these principles in three parts.

Firstly, sex coaches should be comfortable and present when attending to clients' emotional language and avoid shifting swiftly away from their painful emotions. Only when clients feel heard, safe, and supported, i.e. not judged or dismissed, they can begin to access their resources and empowerment.

Secondly, coaches need to pay careful attention to clients' positive and negative emotional language and embodiment. This includes the essential skill of observing clients' non-verbal cues, feelings, and affect. The coach can then create a counterpoint between those negative emotions and problematic talk and the client's positive examples of behaviour, experience, or preferred future.

Thirdly, coaches can reframe their observations into an immersive experience for clients through solution-building language. This transformation is done through slow, steady reflection, repetition, and invitational language skills, using the client's imagery and embodiment to heighten the experience of positive emotion. Furthermore, embodying positive emotion and imagery can inspire the client's own resources to build their preferred outcomes.

Nevertheless, caution must be applied when working with emotions in sex coaching and coaching in general. Coaches must distinguish between therapy and coaching when addressing emotions.

Therapy typically delves into past issues and encourages sharing personal problems and emotions as part of the healing process (Cox, 2016). In contrast, coaching emphasises explicit learning processes. While emotions are not discouraged in coaching, the primary focus remains on the present and the future.

Consequently, sex coaches have to skilfully and actively engage with clients to explore and express their emotions only in the context of their current goals and aspirations (Cremona, 2010). Coaches must always follow the client's lead and move at their pace to align with the objectives, purposes, and ethics of coaching.

In summary, if done carefully, working with emotions can strengthen the coaching process by supporting clients in recognising their resilience and competence when facing challenges and fostering a transformative emotional experience.

Case Vignette – Tini's Story

Tini came to sex coaching to feel more confident with her sexual needs and desire. Tini's goals were common to many Asian women, including Indonesians, that I have seen in my practice. They are typically accomplished mothers and wives in their mid-40s to late-50s and have been married for over twenty years. Inspired by younger counterparts, they seek to deconstruct their internalised sexual shame and lead a more fulfilling and sexual life with their long-time spouse.

Tini: I feel very malu (shameful) to the pit of my stomach for asking my husband for sex. I almost hear my grandma scolding in the background – a good girl must be pious and not have a dirty mind. *(face blushes red, shoulder hunched, breaks eye contact)*

The sex coach applies the first principle: being present to Tini's negative emotional language and embodiment.

Sex coach: *(Pauses, gives an affirming facial expression)* It sounds like you are experiencing such profound malu that you feel sick. That is an uncomfortable feeling to have. *(with a gentle and affirming tone- while being mindful that the dialogue does not expand to 'problem talk')*

Tini:	Umm ... yes, not a nice feeling. *(resumes eye contact with the coach)*
Sex coach:	And you mentioned that all these malu seem to originate from your grandma's beliefs and ideas about what a good girl should be and do? *(in a curious yet gentle tone)*
Tini:	Absolutely! Well spotted ... it's her beliefs and ideas, and these are not mine. *(sighs, smiles, shoulder drops)*

The sex coach applies the second and third principles: continue to observe the positive and negative emotional language and embodiment, followed by solution-building language focusing on Tini's positive emotional language and embodiment, while ensuring that the client's emotions are explored and expressed in the service of their current goals and aspirations. Thus, these combined principles created an immersive experience for Tini to build resources towards the desired outcome.

Sex coach:	I notice that you begin to smile and sigh ... Can I check if that is a sigh of relief? Or?
Tini:	Yes! It is just good to let the sick feeling out! *(smiles, eyes twinkle, shoulders widen)*
Sex coach:	Are we ok to stay in this good feeling for a while Tini? *(Tini nods, sighs)*. Notice that good sensation; where do you most feel that in your body?
Tini:	Interesting, I feel this good feeling in my hips, and now they travel inwards to that pit of the stomach, washing the sickness away.
Sex coach:	*(Pause, allowing Tini to embody the sensation. Seek an exception to build an immersive experience around the positive embodiment)*. Is there a recent moment, even if it's just a second, where you experienced this good feeling?
Tini:	Oh yesterday and not just a second! *(Laughs, eyes light up, looks over her shoulder)* After my belly dancing class with the ladies, oh, I feel good, sexy, and energised!
Sex coach:	*(Teasingly solution-building imagery)* Oh, from your expression, I can imagine that class is fun, sexy, and uplifting! What would be different with your husband if you could bring these feelings from the belly dancing class into your bedroom?
Tini:	*(laughs)* There will be an earthquake, which will wake my grandma up from her grave. That should serve her right. *(winking at me)*

In the following sex coaching sessions, this vignette serves as a building block in creating action plans to be more assertive in her sexual desire towards her husband.

Challenges and Potential Solutions

Be Patient and Attend to Your Own Emotional Well-Being

While the example of Tini demonstrates a positive outcome, be prepared for clients to take multiple sessions to emerge from challenging, negative, and shameful emotions. Thus, as SF sex coaches, our role is to continue to attend, affirm, and be present with these emotions and their embodiment while staying alert to any signs of positive emotion and embodiment. This practice can impact our own emotions too, so it is essential for sex coaches to attend to their personal emotional regulation. This includes strategies such as breathing techniques and mindfulness to promote better emotional regulation in the session and seeking professional supervision.

Avoid Seeking Deeper Meaning and Focus on the Positive

While attending and being present with negative emotions is essential, avoid seeking the deeper meanings – that is the realm of therapy. Instead, hone the skills of recognising positive emotions and their embodiment. Look for positive emotional clues, including sighs of relief, smiles, resuming eye contact, widening shoulders, and relaxed postures. When you highlight and give feedback on these positive signs, check in with the client on the accuracy of your assumptions, and let them be in charge of the experience.

Refer to Specialist Providers When Appropriate

Sexual trauma is another contributing factor to sexual shame (Litam & Speciale, 2021) and may present in the sex coaching environment. However, working with sexual or other trauma and symptoms is outside the scope of sex coaching. As such, sex coaches who are not trained in these specialities should either refer clients out or work closely with appropriate specialist providers.

Conclusion

Working with challenging emotions, including sexual shame driven by religious or cultural norms, is integral to sexuality and sexual health, so sex coaches are encouraged to embrace it. As shown in the vignette, SF coaching seeks exceptions in positive emotional language and its embodiment, which can be tremendously helpful in facilitating clients' sexual empowerment, freedom of expression, and, ultimately, desired sexual outcomes.

References

Britton, P. (2005). *The art of sex coaching: Expanding your practice*. Norton Professional Books.

Cox, E. (2016). Working with emotions in coaching. In T. Bachkirova, G. Spence, & D. Drake (Eds), *The SAGE handbook of coaching* (pp. 272–290). Sage.

Cremona, K. (2010). Coaching and emotions: An exploration of how coaches engage and think about emotion. *Coaching: An International Journal of Theory, Research and Practice, 3*(1), 46–59.

Diamant, J. (2019, April 1). *The countries with the 10 largest Christian populations and the 10 largest Muslim populations.* Pew Research Center. https://www.pewresearch.org/short-reads/2019/04/01/the-countries-with-the-10-largest-christian-populations-and-the-10-largest-muslim-populations/

Duffell, P., & Lawton-Smith, C. (2015). The challenges of working with emotion in coaching. *The Coaching Psychologist, 11*(1), 32–41.

Halim, K. (2021, March 31). *Conversion therapy practices against transgender persons in Indonesia.* Asia Pacific Transgender Network. https://weareaptn.org/resource/conversion-therapy-practices-against-transgender-persons-in-india-indonesia-malaysia-and-sri-lanka/

International Coach Federation (ICF). (2019). ICF core competencies. Accessed 10 July 2023, from: https://coachingfederation.org/app/uploads/2021/07/Updated-ICF-Core-Competencies_English_Brand-Updated.pdf

Litam, S. A., & Speciale, M. (2021). Deconstructing sexual shame: Implications for clinical counselors and counselor educators. *Journal of Counseling Sexology & Sexual Wellness: Research, Practice, and Education, 3*(1), 14–24. 10.34296/03011045

Piercy, F. P., Lipchik, E., & Kiser, D. (2000). Commentary on Miller and de Shazer's article on "Emotions in solution-focused therapy". *Family Process, 39*(1), 25–28.

Riyani, I. (2021). *Islam, women's sexuality and patriarchy in Indonesia: Silent desire.* Routledge.

Walker, C. R., Froerer, A. S., & Gourlay-Fernandez, N. (2022). The value of using emotions in solution focused brief therapy. *Journal of Marital and Family Therapy, 48*(3), 812–826. 10.1111/jmft.12551

Section 6

Coaching with Youths, Families, and Schools

21 Relationship Coaching

Co-constructing Views of Competence

Debbie Hogan

Introduction

Relationship coaching is growing in popularity in Asia and focuses on helping people improve the interpersonal quality of their relationships. The increasing awareness of mental health and well-being has contributed to the popularity of relationship coaching. A key outcome of relationship coaching is enhanced personal growth, improved communication, and positive change in the interpersonal dynamics (Zhou, 2023).

In this chapter, I will share examples from my coaching practice in Asia. I will highlight the use of Solution Focused (SF) coaching using various tools, questions, and processes involved in facilitating client's desired change in three areas of relationship coaching: with couples, youth, and parents. While some might view these as different areas of coaching, the common concerns raised by clients are focused on the quality of the relationship.

SF coaching involves a unique process of co-constructing the client's view of the desired change and highlighting rich details around the preferred future. SF coaching embodies a mindset based on key assumptions regarding the nature of the relationship and the client, as possessing existing capabilities that can be utilised. This often leads to a heightened sense of self-efficacy; hence, we are facilitating the client's alternative view of themselves and their situation. Clients often come in a state of frustration, believing they have tried everything and nothing seems to change, therefore feeling stuck. In SF coaching, our questions tend to raise awareness and create a shift in their perspective. There is a strong emphasis on building 'customership' and desirability for what the client wants different or changed.

Couple Coaching: Co-constructing Views of Competence

Kim and YK were a bi-racial couple in Asia. Feeling in turmoil because their relationship of 4 years was unravelling, their work demands and individual family commitments had led to increased tension. Both attended Ivy League schools abroad and were thrilled that each had landed their dream job. Yet, there was little time to attend to their relationship as they felt pulled in many

DOI: 10.4324/9781003431480-27

different directions. As they started to consider divorce, they sought relation-ship coaching. They shared their story, while blaming each other, and were at their wits' end.

Kim: You can see, things are really bad. We can hardly stand being in the same room.

YK: You got that right.

Coach: I hear sadness and disappointment as you share this. I appreciate you coming. Sounds like a tough time. Suppose at the end of our session you're able to say coming here was worthwhile, what are you hoping for?

The aim for the coach is to acknowledge the difficulty, without getting caught up in the problematic past. Establish the desired outcome from coaching; the presence of what they want, versus the absence of what they don't want. Validate the problem narrative, while containing the blaming and invite the clients to consider what they want instead, making sure both voices are heard.

Kim: If we could talk without yelling … and you not walking out.

YK: If you would stop blaming me for everything, I wouldn't walk out.

Coach: So, what would you start to notice when things are more of what you want?

Kim: If he would actually listen and not leave.

YK: I would stay in the room if she would stop yelling.

Coach: So, what you want is to be able to talk, listen to each other, without blaming.

YK: Yes! That's it.

Coach: Suppose you were able to talk and really listen to each other, what difference would that make?

The coach then explores the interactional difference and impact of doing more of what they want.

Kim: I would feel he cared about me. Listen to me. I don't think he loves me anymore.

YK: I do care about you. It's hard to show it when you're always upset.

Kim: I'm not always upset. I worry about you … about us.

YK: Worried about me. Why??

Kim: Because you work so hard and we don't do what we used to do.

YK: I could say the same thing about you. You work late, too. So why should I come home early?

Kim: I actually think you don't want to be with me anymore.

YK: Of course I want to be with you! I thought you didn't want me anymore.

Exploring the meaning and impact of shifting perceptions as they hear each other helps them to reconnect.

Coach: I'm wondering, what have you heard that surprises you.
YK: I didn't realise she still cared.
Kim: I didn't know he wanted the relationship either.
Coach: What difference is this making now?
YK: I'm surprised ... relieved, actually. I guess I've had my head buried in my work.
Kim: I'm so sad we let it get this far ... I've been so angry at you.

Next the coach explores examples of client competence – times in the past they did more of what they want now. Exploring their success templates: who did what and what difference it made.

Coach: I'm curious about something you said earlier, Kim. It sounds like you want more of what you used to do. What was that?
Kim: Yes, we used to meet after work and eat at our favourite spots. While we studied abroad, we missed those. It's being together and talking about our future. I miss that.
YK: I miss that too ...
Coach: What was important about that?
Kim: It was like we were a team ... sharing ... our lives ... our future ...
Coach: How does that strike you, YK?
YK: Yeah, it was ... it was ... we were in tune ...
Coach: If we continue to explore how to 'stay in tune,' would that be useful?

Using clients' words and metaphors, the coach explores what 'staying in tune' looks like, feels like, and its significance.

When a client repeats a concern, it is important to explore its significance and how they will manage it to support the desired changes. Exploring the influence of culture and context is also important, especially when this theme is raised by the client. In the Asian culture, filial piety is a significant cultural and ethical concept. It relates to the virtue of respect, obedience, and care for one's parents and ancestors. This is a common issue for most Asian couples (Gurusu & Fu, 2020).

Kim: But ... I'm worried if we get off track again. Because the stress and our family stuff is still there ... .
YK: True. I'm not so stressed as you. My family isn't so demanding.
Kim: Well, we both need to spend time with them, right?
Coach: How have you been managing it so far?
Kim: I know we can say here, with you, we want this or that, but will we be able to really do it?

KK: Yeah, we need help on that.
Coach: What would be important to keep aware of so you have the confidence that you can manage this to your satisfaction?
Kim: Yes, I need confidence we can keep all the balls up.
Coach: On a scale of 1–10, '10' means managing it to the best of your ability and '1' is not so good, where are you now? What's working already? What do you want to tweak?

Ending the Couples Coaching

In subsequent sessions, Kim and YK focused on their ability to manage their emotions and stress, how they would support each other in honouring and respecting their families, and what they wanted to continue to develop and grow in their relationship. They talked more about their future and building a family. This was especially relevant, as the eldest son in a Chinese family, YK and Kim felt the pressure from his parents to have children, especially a son. They continued to build trust and confidence in their relationship as they manoeuvred through these challenges.

At the last session, they were very late. They came in flustered. They proceeded to tell me that on the way to my office, they had had a big fight and decided it was over. Since they were close to my office, they decided to pop in to inform me that it was over. They pulled into the parking spot and reminded each other that since they were seeing their coach, the coach was going to ask: 'What's been better? How did you manage that?' When they did that, it totally turned things round. They realised there were a lot of good things in their relationship and when they focused on that, it made a big difference. They knew how to get things back on track. As they shared this with me, they were nudging each other fondly. They proudly reported this was their last session.

Youth Coaching: Proving Them Wrong

Emit, a 16-year-old Indian young man, was referred by his mother to work on his 'bad habits.' His mother described him as lazy, irresponsible, and disrespectful. Emit was not interested in his mother's idea of what he should do. His mother, a single parent, was a high-level executive and was exhausted from managing her 'out of control' son.

Despite all this, Emit came to our session, although sceptical, for good reasons. He had been referred to a lot of other professionals in the past, which he endured to get his mother 'off his back.' While I knew why his mother referred him, I was curious as to why he came. We spent some time talking about his interests. I explained the coaching process and confidentiality. Since there was another stakeholder (his mum), it was necessary to establish the expectations.

Coach: Thank you for letting me get to know you just a bit. I appreciate you coming today even though it wasn't your idea. Would it be useful to talk about your mother's concerns, or are you clear enough?

Emit: I know why she sent me. I don't agree with her. She's always on my back. She's very 'kaypoh.' (Singapore slang, which means 'busy body')

Coach: I'm curious how come you decided to be here, even though it was not your idea.

Emit: I guess if you could get my mum off my back. We don't get along. She tells me all the time that I'm going to end up in prison, or join a gang …

Coach: Sounds rough. But you don't see it that way.

Emit: No! I'm not in a gang. I'm smart enough to not end up in prison.

Coach: So, you know things about yourself that your mum doesn't know?

Emit: Yes! I make good decisions all the time. I do go to school. Sometimes I miss, but I can make it up. I want to prove my mum wrong. She is wrong about me!

Coach: You sound so sure about that. Suppose you did 'prove her wrong.' Would that be something you want to work on during our time together?

Emit: You mean we can do that?

Coach: Sure. These sessions are for you to work on what is important to you.

Emit: Then, yes.

Coach: Great. So, suppose we start today with 'proving your mum wrong.' What do you know about yourself that your mum doesn't get yet?

Emit: Well, she thinks I'm lazy, for one thing. She leaves for work before I'm up, so how does she know I'm lazy. I have afternoon classes, so I don't get up so early. Then I work at a café. That's how I get pocket money. She won't give because I buy cigarettes. But I also buy other things. Then I tell her, I need money for school stuff but she won't give unless I send a letter. She thinks I will gamble. But I never.

Coach: Suppose your mum had superpowers and could listen to you now. What do you suppose she would say?

Emit: She would not believe me.

Coach: And suppose she did this time. What difference do you think it would make?

Emit: Maybe she would think better of me.

Coach: Is this important to you – that she think better of you?

Emit: Actually, yes. She is my mum. She works hard. But she is afraid. Afraid that I turn into my dad.

Coach: Oh, I see! So there is a real concern there.

Emit: Yes, she is worried I turn into my dad. But I don't want. He abandoned me when I was young. He never cared for me. But my mum kept working and got promoted and now she is an executive.

Coach: Sounds like you are proud of her?

Emit: Yes, sometimes.

Coach: So, if we spent time together in 'proving your mum wrong' what are you hoping for?

Emit: That my mum believes in me. Stops worrying. Gets on with her life. She is so stressed that she wants to quit work and focus on me. She feels guilty. I tell her, I'll be ok. Get a life!

Coach: So, you're worried about her too?

Emit: Yes! I think she gave up a lot to take care of me and she has no life except work.

Coach: What do you suppose she would start to notice about you that would give her the idea to start 'backing off' a bit more?

Emit: Maybe I can start being the 'man of the house.' She always says she needs me to be the 'man of the house.'

Coach: Do you know what she means when she says that?

Emit: Be responsible. Respect her. Don't get into trouble. Don't gamble. But I don't gamble. My dad did.

Coach: Suppose you were more responsible and respected her more. What difference would that make?

Emit: I hope she stops worrying.

We used the client's words and explored what mum would notice in him when he is 'responsible' and 'respectful' and the impact that would have on her ability to 'back off.' Emit started to realise that her motives were based on fear and concern for him. Clients often expect the other person to change first. In SF thinking, we explore change mechanism through a different lens. We explore the idea of change happening in the other person when they notice something different in you. Emit caught on to this and it made a difference in tipping the domino in the direction of desired change. He became more sympathetic towards his mum and respecting her, which in turn led to her being more trusting of him.

Emit gave me permission to talk with his mum. This led to coaching sessions with her. Often when coaching youth, we inadvertently coach the parents, or vice versa.

Parent Coaching: Support the Change You Want to See

Ms. T welcomed the opportunity to talk about Emit. She was worried and felt a lot of guilt. Initially, she was focused on solving Emit's behaviour problems. We explored her wishes behind the complaints, which focused on her longings for him to be successful and do well in life.

Coach: Suppose these things happen. What difference will this make for you?

Ms. T: Less worry and free to focus on my own life. Right now I can't, while he is in trouble all the time.

Coach: What changes have you noticed lately that tell you things are improving, even just a little bit?

Ms. T: Actually, things are a bit better. I took leave for a week because I needed to use up leave. I saw a different side to him. He actually gets up and goes to class.

Coach: How did you respond to this new side?

Ms. T: I thought he was goofing off. Then, he took me for lunch and paid for it. I found out he has a job.

Coach: How did you respond to that?

Ms. T: I decided to give him an allowance. Because he doesn't earn much. I was afraid to give him money because he might do gambling. His father did and it was terrible for us.

Coach: How else have you been supporting this new side of Emit?

Ms. T: I feel very happy about it. I just hope he can keep it up.

Coach: What do you know about him that tells you he can keep it up?

Ms. T: I guess I have not been giving him enough credit. I just get so scared that he might join a gang or go to prison.

Coach: Based on what you've noticed lately, what would be different when you 'give him more credit'?

By exploring the interactional connection between 'backing off' and its impact, she noticed the more she 'let go' and trusted him, the more he was responsible and respectful.

Coach: In what other ways have you supported the changes you want?

Ms. T: He told me his grades improved. He was passing his subjects. He will graduate soon.

Coach: That is fantastic. Graduating! Imagine that! How do you plan to celebrate?

Ms. T: Emit told me he wants to be a chef and go to culinary school. It's expensive, but I can manage it. And he has also been saving his money. I'm going to surprise him.

Coach: Really? What do you suppose Emit will say or do when he hears this?

The coach highlights the impact of desired change in the interaction. Ms. T continued to support Emit through this new phase. She started to take care of herself better, joined a gym, and her health improved. Ms. T managed to 'get on with her life.'

The coach met with Ms. T and Emit for a final review session. Both parent and son continued to do well.

Key Takeaways

The SF coaching principles expressed in this chapter include the following:

- Acknowledge the client's problem narrative to support the client's views and perspective, without getting caught up in it. Clients often return to the problem narrative until they sense the coach understands their situation.
- The coach tunes in to the client's readiness to explore alternative possibilities, namely what they want instead.
- Offer a different pathway to change by co-constructing specifics around the hopeful future and desired change. Details of the presence of the desired change open up pathways for exploring the desired change.
- Highlight the interactional view of change management. One does not have to wait for the other person to change first. One can be a catalyst for change by responding differently. Problems within relationships happen interactionally and possibilities for change also happen interactionally.
- SF coaches consistently select the client's words, behaviours, actions, and intentions that support the desired change.
- SF coaches are curious about the client's successful past as resources for present and future success.

References

Gurusu, S., & Fu, L. (2020, October 7). *Exploring filial piety in Asian cultures*. The Epic. https://lhsepic.com/8371/in-depth/exploring-filial-piety-in-asian-cultures/

Zhou, L. (2023, June 20). *The coaching industry market size in 2023*. https://www.luisazhou.com/blog/coaching-industry-market-size

22 Solution Focused Coaching of Teenagers in China

Taking a Friendly Guess

Lawrence Luo and Huajing Yang

Introduction

Coaching teenagers presents a number of challenges. While they may face many issues, they are frequently involuntary clients as their parents make the appointments. In addition, teenagers are often reluctant to open up and talk. A common response to questions is "I don't know" and asking further general questions rarely gets their cooperation, making progress in the coaching session difficult.

This chapter explores using the Solution Focused (SF) coaching model successfully with teenagers who are involuntary clients. The "not knowing" naturally curious stance of the SF coach works well with this cohort of clients who are often wary of sharing. The authors describe how they establish rapport by making a "good-natured guess" and invite the clients to comment on whether or not that guess is correct and illustrate this with case examples. Establishing a game-like communication often has the unexpected effect of relationship building. This lays the foundation for the next step of establishing a contract. Cultural insights into working with teenagers in China are also offered.

Dealing with "I Don't Know"

The most common way to start an SF coaching session is by asking a client what their best hopes for the session are. This is a difficult question and a frequent response is "I don't know." Keeping silent for a few seconds is useful to give the person time to think. Usually the conversation then starts to flow.

However, teenagers can often be reluctant to open up and talk and may continue to sit there or say "I don't know" to further questions. In the book *More than Miracles*, de Shazer et al. (2021, p. 282) describes how to respond to the client saying "I don't know."

We do not repeat the question (unless the client asks us to do so). And we definitely do not comment, nod, or do anything to call attention to ourselves. We have found that it can be helpful to count to six before saying anything else. Doing this without moving, and especially without nodding, is a good

DOI: 10.4324/9781003431480-28

exercise in self-discipline on the part of the therapist, and more important, it typically leads to the client starting to develop an answer. This works particularly well if while waiting you lift up your pen and hold it over your pad as if you're waiting for something to write down. If the client hasn't answered in six seconds we thoughtfully say, "It's a difficult question." Then we relax back into our chairs and give the client another six to ten seconds to think.

Practice is however more complicated than theory. Even after mastering keeping silent and waiting, what happens next often doesn't turn out as we hope. In my experience sometimes no matter what questions we ask, teenagers seem to master the art of keeping silent and waiting far better than we do. Both sides can easily fall into a temporary impasse. Let me share one of my most commonly used methods to move the session forwards – a "next best thing" method, which I call "taking a friendly guess." It's like playing an active guessing game with the client.

The Solution Focused Stance

SF coaching begins with refreshing assumptions: people are healthy, competent, and capable of constructing solutions that improve their lives. Therefore, we assume that a person answering "I don't know" is neither a confrontation against us nor a manifestation of pathology. Instead, we assume the person is answering "I don't know" for an important reason. These reasons may include that they honestly don't know due to lacking previous experience to draw on; the past experience is unbearable to look at, so they are unwilling to know; their mind remains cloudy, so the answer is don't know; or they cannot clearly express what's in their mind, so they are unwilling to speak.

Taking a Friendly Guess

In this case, if keeping silent and waiting for a while does not work, we can try, "taking a friendly guess." This involves offering the client some multiple choice questions or true or false questions. An example of this is outlined below.

Coach: As you don't want to speak up for now, I wondered if I could take a guess? I imagine you're probably facing a number of situations, one is … another is … and possibly there's the third situation … Of course, the possibilities I brought up might not fit what you are facing right now. But I wonder which do you think is the most likely scenario for you?
Client: The second case.
Coach: Could you tell me a little more … .

The coach can also ask clients a yes or no question:

Coach: As you are not speaking up for now, I assume you really don't know how to answer the question.
Client: (keeps silent and nods his head)
Coach: Based on what I've known I'm guessing it's probably a situation of ..., or ... I'm wondering if my guess matches with what you're experiencing.
Client: (keeps silent and shakes his head)
Coach: Oh, it doesn't. Can you tell me in which way my guess doesn't match with what you're experiencing?

When coaching teenagers, the "taking a friendly guess" approach often makes seemingly impossible conversations start to unfold in a fruitful direction. Even if a teenager says few words during the whole coaching session, the dialogue can still go on with his minimal expression, thus at least laying the foundation for further dialogue in the future.

My inspiration for inventing this "taking a friendly guess" comes from Fiske (2012, p. 84), who introduced the story of feeding hope in her book *Hope in Action*. The grandfather who listened to his grandson talking about his despair says, "Your despair is a wolf. This wolf is very powerful. It will kill you and eat your soul. But hope is also a wolf, just as powerful, it will fight the wolf of despair for you." When the grandson asked which wolf will win the fight and which will survive, his grandfather says, "The one that you feed."

"Taking a friendly guess" is a journey of feeding hope to the client. We are playing a mind-reading game with the client, and it is important during this game to pay attention to several points:

1 After saying "I guess," we need to pause and search for a sign from our clients that they're willing to continue this game, whether it's a subtle expression in their eyes or a body gesture before we can continue the conversation.
2 We need to adopt a tentative tone showing that what we are saying is merely a guess. Our attitude conveys that we are doing our best to understand our clients.
3 A well-intentioned guess means that the content of the guess represents a "positive possibility," a desire, dream, goal, resource, etc., which belongs to the person, so even if the person is acting unethically, we assume that the intention behind it is sincere.
4 We need to pay attention to our clients and decide whether to continue, which is based on the client's response. If a client accepts our guess, then we can continue. If they do not, then we can give them the choice to correct us. For example: Oh, my guess is not accurate, what would you like to correct or add?

5 Make sure the topic is something the client is comfortable talking about. For example, I want to make sure that I'm talking about a topic that you're willing to explore.

If these details are ignored, a mere "I guess" statement won't do anything to help the conversation move forwards. Here are some more examples.

Case Examples

Qi is a senior high school student; the head teacher said that he does not study hard or finish his homework, and often sleeps in class. In daily conversations, he reveals that he has no interest in learning and does not like homework or exams. The head teacher recommends him talking to a school coach.

Coach: Hi Qi, so what would be helpful from our session today?
Client: I don't know.
Coach: (keeps silent and waits)
Client: (keeps silent and waits)
Coach: Maybe the class teacher asked you to come, so you are not ready to talk with me.
Client: Nothing to talk about.
Coach: Well, what topics might we talk about that would interest you?
Client: I really don't know.
Coach: Then could I try to make a guess? I will let you decide if it fits your situation, if not, could you please correct me or add to it? (Waiting for feedback to be accepted by the client)
Client: All right.
Coach: Before we started you said you had "exams every day," so I guess tons of homework and frequent exams might be stressful?
Client: (shows noncommittal expression)
Coach: That doesn't seem entirely true. But I think at least, you are not as uninterested in learning as others think.
Client: (shows approval expression)
Coach: Then can I go ahead and guess? (tentative tone)
Client: (shows approval expression)
Coach: I heard from the teacher that you often sleep in class, so you were criticised by the head teacher. In my experience, there are usually several possibilities for sleeping in class. First, I don't understand what the teacher said so it's better to sleep. Second, I didn't have a good rest last night, so I need sleep. Third, I am not interested at all, and listening to what the teacher says makes me feel sleepy. Fourth, there might be other reasons that I didn't bring up. I wonder if for you the answer might be the third one?
Client: Not quite.

Coach: So what else would you want to add or change so that it fits better for you?

Client: (shows non-committal expression)

Coach: I guess that you are not willing to talk at this moment, and that is OK. Can I keep guessing?

Sometimes teenagers reply "I don't know" because they don't have much motivation to share. At this time, if the coach shows understanding and acceptance, and encourages the youth with curiosity, unexpected results can take place.

In the coaching session below with Bing he talked about the upcoming high school physical education exam. In previous training, every time he ran 1000 metres, he followed a friend experienced at keeping up a certain running speed, and when accompanied by his friend, he got full marks. But this time, his friend was not in the same running group so he is worried.

Coach: The friend who runs fast is not in the same group with you. And you are worried there is no one who can lead you to run fast in the new group. What other ideas do you have about what might help you pass the exam?

Client: I don't know.

Coach: I'm a bit curious, has it ever happened to you that you couldn't run with that friend, yet you still ran well on your own?

Client: Yes.

Coach: How did you do it?

Client: I just took my time running, not too fast, not so slow.

Coach: Wow, you did a good job on your own. How did you manage to run not too fast or slow, and still get good grades?

Client: Well, I avoided rushing too hard at the beginning, to save energy. And I avoided running too slow, for it would be very difficult to catch up later. It's better to keep an even-pace.

In another coaching session, Wen said that he was good at socialising, so the coach encouraged Wen to open a conversation by asking him modestly and Wen summed up his skills in making friends.

Coach: How do you make friends?

Client: I don't know. I just did it unconsciously.

Coach: Sounds like you make friends naturally. Well, my friend has a junior high school son, he doesn't know how to make friends but he longs to fit in with his peers, so I especially wanted to ask your advice. In a scene surrounded by unfamiliar peers, how do you get to know them? Do you usually greet each other like: "Hello, I am so-and-so, nice to meet you?"

Client: No, we don't talk like that. That would sound silly. A few days ago our whole grade were mixed up in different classrooms to take exams. After the exam, I just made eye contact with a stranger beside me and said, "This exam is so difficult! I think I blew it." He replied, "Yeah, me, too." And then naturally we started talking.

Cultural Factors Related to Solution Focused Coaching in China

The coaching role is about helping clients explore what they would like to achieve and is not about giving information or advice. However, in Chinese culture, mentoring and providing guidance has a different meaning. A research study conducted by Duan et al. (2014) found that Chinese clients expected their therapists to use directives, specifically at the beginning and the end of relationships. "Start well and end well" (善始善终) is an important value for the Chinese. We see the possibility that appropriate use of directives can also be helpful in coaching as a form of gift-giving for Chinese teenage clients at both the beginning and end of a coaching relationship.

In my coaching experience, I have found that teenagers often expect to get some guidance, for example, from elders whom they respect. Rather than just giving advice, we explore how the SF principles of democracy and respect for youth can be integrated with giving guidance in SF coaching practices. The guidance provided is not mandated, or authoritative, but offered through "leading from one step behind" (Cantwell & Holmes, 1994).

When I coach teenagers and they ask for my opinion or advice I share my thoughts and then ask: "What do you think of it? Which parts of what I said might be useful for you in some way? If it wasn't helpful that's ok, too." In short, as a coach, I see the guidance as an offering, and then I use this to co-create further exploration with them. Using the words "I guess" also gives a kind of guidance.

These ways of offering advice meets not only the cultural needs, but also fits the SF mindset of the client being the expert. We may point out a direction to consider. But what the teenager chooses is up to them.

The SF approach also has many similarities with traditional Chinese cultural values. Postmodern approaches pay more attention to social and cultural factors and what is co-constructed between people, rather than traditional approaches which pay more attention to one's inner experience (McKergow & Korman, 2009). China is a more collectivist society, which values the group over the individual and values things like harmony, duty and interdependence. Therefore, in our coaching dialogue, we tend to use quite a lot of relational questions with Chinese clients and ask how significant others will think, feel, or respond to what they do and what difference it will make to them. This can be done in a way that still keeps the clients' goals in mind but takes into account their cultural context and empowers each client to decide the balance that is important to them.

Final Reflections

When practicing SF coaching with teenage clients in China, the core concepts of "not knowing" and "leading from one step behind" are helpful in creating a relationship of mutual respect, equality, and trust. The coaches' questions asked with curiosity and tentativeness are very different to the condescending, commanding, or spoon feeding communication mode traditionally used in interactions between authorities and teenagers. They help teenagers have the willingness and opportunity to look inward, think independently, and begin to take responsibility for their own future. In this emotionally safe, inclusive, and enlightening coaching process, the teenage client is able to open up their heart, take the initiative to express their true ideas, explore their resources and abilities to deal with problems, and further develop the future they want.

References

Cantwell, P. W., & Holmes, S. N. (1994). Social construction: A paradigm shift for systemic therapy and training. *Australian and New Zealand Journal of Family Therapy, 15*, 17–26.

de Shazer, S., Dolan, Y., Korman, H., Trepper, T., McCollum, E., & Berg, I. K. (2021). *More than miracles: The state of the art of solution-focused brief therapy.* Routledge.

Duan, C., Hill, C., Jiang, G., Hu, B., Lei, Y., Chen, J., & Yu, L. (2014). The use of directives in counseling in China: The counselor perspective. *Counseling Psychology Quarterly, 22*, 442–457.

Fiske, H. (2012). *Hope in action: Solution-focused conversations about suicide.* Routledge.

McKergow, M., & Korman, H. (2009). Inbetween—neither inside nor outside: The radical simplicity of solution-focused brief therapy. *Journal of Systemic Therapies, 28*(2), 34–49.

23 Solution Focused Coaching in Education

Edwin Choy

Introduction

The Solution Focused (SF) approach has wide applications within the school system and education sector. It is a powerful philosophy that fosters a growth mindset using a common set of coaching skills that can be learnt and implemented by management and teachers alike.

My journey in applying SF coaching in the education sector was incidental. I presented an SF coaching workshop for a conference for educators in Singapore to affirm and celebrate the spirit of professional learning amongst teachers. I was then asked if I could package such trainings and offer these more widely for the Academy of Solution Focused Training. I seized this opportunity to apply SF coaching concepts to the education sector.

This chapter will cover how SF concepts are applied in four areas within the school setting. The first is leadership – leaders and middle managers are trained to become SF coaches who then enable teachers to design their best outcomes by leveraging on their strengths. The second is working directly with teachers, inspired by their belief in a child's potential for growth develop skills to enable every pupil to realise the best versions of themselves. The third area is in redefining student discipline to support and empower students to learn new skills for growth. By focusing on positive change, the SF disciplinary approach steers conversations away from offending behaviours towards looking at the outcomes they desire. The final area is working with parents who are crucial stakeholders in a child's learning journey. Parents are engaged in a collaborative way to support their children's journey. Examples and reflections from those receiving the training are shared about the difference the SF coaching approach can make in education.

Solution Focused Coaching in Teacher Renewal Training

My first application of SF Coaching in education was the outcome of a request to develop a personal renewal training for teachers using SF concepts. Many teachers mentioned that developing a growth mindset in students was important. It was thought that it would help students to develop a growth

DOI: 10.4324/9781003431480-29

mindset if teachers also have the same mindset. This was a wonderful opportunity for me to facilitate a session for teachers to do self-coaching.

SF coaching fits very well in a 2-day session where I do group coaching to help them apply the SF strength-based approach for personal renewal. These renewal sessions are entitled 'Growing from Within,' and the teachers are coached to explore the following:

a Using SF thinking by shifting their focus from problems to solutions
b Their strengths, resources, and past successes
c Their best hopes for themselves
d Their growth towards best hopes in small steps.

Positive feedback from those who experienced SF coaching in the Growing from Within sessions included appreciating: becoming aware of their strengths, finding a vision for their lives, getting affirmations from themselves and others, and feeling empowered to take small steps to make positive changes and reach their goals.

Solution Focused Education Through Developing a Coaching Culture

My second application of SF coaching in education came at the invitation of a principal of a school to help in the professional development of his middle managers who were heads of departments. His best hopes were to support them in their growth as leaders. This gave me an opportunity to collaborate with this principal to achieve his best hopes by developing a coaching culture within the school.

The idea behind SF education is to build a coaching culture in a school so that there can be an ecosystem where both students and teachers can thrive. Teachers are the most important layer in a school system. They are expected to educate young students and help them grow in confidence by helping them develop a growth mindset. The aim is that through helping the middle managers to see the teachers as competent and nurture their growth, this in turn supports the teachers to see their students as competent and nurture their growth. This idea is summarised in Figure 23.1. SF coaching is a great fit for enabling this process as it is inherently a language of growth and hope.

Middle Manager as Coach

Teachers spend most of their time helping students learn and grow, and they also need to be supported. It is not uncommon for them to feel stretched as teaching is not the only thing they are doing. They also have many other responsibilities which can weigh them down.

When middle managers or heads of departments learn and develop SF coaching skills this helps them engage the teachers meaningfully in a way that helps them feel supported and grow and these teachers can thrive.

A Solution Focused Thinking School

(An Environment of Positive Education)

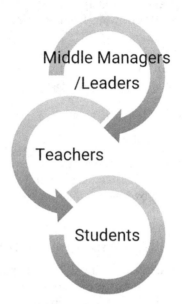

1. See and treat teachers as <u>competent</u>
2. Build an affirming relationship that nurtures <u>growth</u>
3. Develop a growth mindset in teachers through Solution Focused <u>coaching</u>

1. See and treat students as <u>competent</u>
2. Build an affirming relationship that nurtures <u>growth</u>
3. Develop a growth mindset in students through Solution Focused <u>coaching</u>

Figure 23.1 A Solution Focused Thinking School showing how middle managers and leaders support teachers to support students (Edwin Choy, Reproduced with Permission).

Middle managers who engage the teachers they lead with SF coaching help them focus on their strengths, successes, and resources they already have to make progress in their work. Such empowering engagements also help teachers develop a growth mindset that takes away their focus from the problems they are encountering to making small steps towards their best hopes.

For this to happen, middle managers and school leaders needed a more substantial SF coaching training with sufficient supervised practice. They also learned to apply SF coaching in leadership roles like leading change and staff performance review. In leading change, middle managers learnt how to include everyone in the team to co-create a detailed picture of success as their best hopes. They also learnt how to use the scaling tool to help their team assess where they are already at on a scale of 1–10 and then make progress in small steps. In staff performance reviews, the middle managers learnt how to use the scale to help teachers talk about their areas of strength and what they have done well. They also learnt how to talk about their area for progress (instead of weakness) using the scale.

After the training in SF coaching skills, the middle managers are given an assignment to practice coaching with the teachers they lead and we met together for supervision in small groups of four. During these sessions, I would ask them what went well with using the SF coaching approach. They shared that there was a positive atmosphere when asking the teachers to think about their successes. They said that the teachers found it helpful to have discussions that led to a shared vision and were open to sharing both what was already going well and ideas for improvement.

Teacher as Coach

Teachers in SF thinking schools are also trained in basic SF coaching skills so that they can have hopeful conversations with students which in turn help them develop a growth mindset. Some of the basic skills they learnt to use when coaching students are as follows:

a Building on success – highlighting the strengths, successes and resources that students have in them already
b Goal setting – helping students gain clarity on their best hopes for the future they want
c Finding exceptions – helping students focus on moments when they were successful and already growing in the direction of the future they want
d Scaling – helping students envision their growth in small steps.

Reframing School Discipline

Sometime later, I was invited to facilitate an SF coaching training for discipline masters of a group of schools. Their goal was to equip these discipline masters to coach 'problematic students.' The SF mindset is used right from the start in how the training is framed. I used the opportunity to work with discipline masters to reframe the concept of a school discipline committee to that of a student support team.

SF coaching is helpful for educators to deal with student discipline in a positive way by helping students identify exceptions, which are times when the problem does not occur or occurs in less severe ways. Looking at exceptions helps the student to uncover resources and strengths that they can leverage on for making progress. Fundamental in SF coaching are the assumptions that students are experts in their own lives and they have the resources and strengths to find solutions.

The discipline masters in the coaching training went through a mindset shift from seeing students as a problem to be solved to seeing students with a desire to grow and succeed. I then placed them in several groups to team coach them to co-create projects they could implement in their schools that would help them manage discipline issues differently. One of the team's projects had a goal to notice good behaviour in these 'problematic pupils' and report it in a WhatsApp group chat for the discipline committee. Then the various level discipline heads would collaborate to compliment the pupil.

Imagine the positive shock when complimented by several discipline heads in the same week. It was definitely not the 'norm' as they were so used to be being singled out for bad behaviours!

I sent this story to different school principals, vice principals, and school staff developers. One replied to say that they had already been doing something similar. They shared that by noticing and encouraging the pupils when they were doing something good, this led to more good behaviour. Another shared that he had tasked a group of children who had been naughty to do a good deed every day both at home and at school – and this had significantly changed the children's behaviour. They had even learnt to help one another to do more good things. They also had positive feedback from the parents. They said it took time and effort, but it made such a difference to how that child was seen by others and how they saw themselves.

From an invitation to train discipline masters to coach 'problematic' students, it became an opportunity for them to generate useful ideas that transformed discipline at schools.

Parent-Teacher Bonding

Another project I was invited to work on was helping teachers engage parents in an SF way. This was a brilliant idea and aimed to enable teachers to work collaboratively with parents as key stakeholders in the child's education.

In Singapore, some parents have such high expectations of their children's education that they often unfairly place the responsibility on teachers for their children's well-being at school. This often results in unhealthy parent-teacher relationships. However, when teachers are supported by the parents, they find more motivation and joy in giving their best in class. Hence, together with the principal, we co-created this idea of parent-teacher bonding through hopeful SF coaching conversations.

The teachers of these students had already gone through basic SF coaching training. They were familiar with the idea of focusing on strengths, successes and hopeful conversations. We brought the parents of each class together with the class teachers. After ice-breakers and bonding activities, we had the teachers and parents take turns in sharing answers to these SF coaching questions:

1 What has been going well for the students in class (and then at home) since school began?
2 What would tell them, first as teachers, then as parents, that this is a successful academic year for their children?
3 What are the teachers willing to do to help the children be successful in that academic year?
4 What are the parents willing to do to support the teachers in the above goal?

Focusing on what went well, what their best hopes were, and how they contribute to these best hopes for their students and children created a positive atmosphere in class and at home. In one session, both teachers and parents were being coached to be collaborators for the student's success!

The teachers later shared that they had got to know the parents better and it had been a really positive way to start the year which they felt would set things up for better communication during the rest of the year. They said it helped build better parent-teacher relationships as the parents and teachers both had clear shared expectations of the students. It also helped lead to better student-teacher relationships as both could work together to help the pupils feel good and do well in school.

Some of the comments from parents in these bonding sessions using SF coaching questions included that it was helpful to know how well the teachers understood their children, that the communication with the teachers was better as a result, and that they were happy this would contribute to having better learning for their children.

Cultural Reflections

It has been almost 10 years since I began sharing SF coaching concepts in the educational system in Singapore. In Asian society where people are evaluated based on performance and efficiency, it gives me tremendous pleasure to witness the positive reception of educators to the SF approach.

As Hogan (2016) outlines, Asian schools excel academically and the pressure to succeed is often unrelenting. There are pressures from many directions including a focus on excellent academic performance, initiatives from management, and expectations from parents. Teachers often feel squeezed between the expectations of school and parents. Parents feel they have no choice but to place pressure on their children to succeed.

It is counter cultural to notice what is right with a student or fellow teacher and to affirm them. We are used to noticing their mistakes and correcting them as a means to help them improve. We don't consider how people are motivated. It is thought that it is more efficient to tell others exactly how to get things done. However, it is more effective in the long run to invite others to co-create solutions for themselves. It seems from the positive feedback after the trainings that most of the teachers experiencing SF coaching viewed the approach as 'transformational.' This is heart-warming to me.

My observations fit with Hogan (2016) who outlines that there is already much research to show that the SF approach to education is effective in many parts of the world, including Asia as people are finding that a more strengths-based approach has its merits. While there may be some aspects of the SF approach that are countercultural as outlined above, what does fit well is that SF coaching focuses on desired outcomes and taking pragmatic steps forwards. As the SF approach involves creating the preferred future from the client's point of view, it also takes into account goals that fit with

Asian cultural values such as group harmony (e.g. within the classroom or management team) and filial piety.

Conclusion

The SF approach in coaching is not just a 'western' approach. It is an approach that is transferable to educational settings in the Asian cultural context including the highly competitive schools in Singapore.

Reference

Hogan, D. (2016). Introduction to solution focused practice in education in Asia. In D. Hogan, D. Hogan, J. Tuomola, & A. Yeo (Eds), *Solution focused practice in Asia*. Routledge.

Section 7

Health and Wellness Coaching

24   Solution Focused Coaching in Chronic Disease Management in China

Lawrence Luo and Huajing Yang

Introduction

Since the 21st century, with the acceleration of industrialisation, urbanisation, and aging, accompanied by constant changing in lifestyle and environment, people in China and other parts of Asia are more sedentary and obese. The prevalence rate of chronic diseases in the Chinese population has shown an increasing trend. The prevalence rate increased from 12.33% in 2003 to 34.29% in 2018, with an average annual increase of 1.46 percentage points (Zheng et al., 2022, p. 141).

One of the biggest challenges in working with clients with chronic disease management is the "I know it all, but I just can't do it" response. This belief has plagued many clients, whether the issue is dealing with diabetes management, weight loss, or medication adherence. Many clients think they may lack perseverance and sink into self-blame. However, this remorse does not lead to a change in behaviour. This is frustrating for both clients and the professionals that work with them.

This chapter discusses how taking a Solution Focused (SF) coaching approach with these clients can bring about positive change. In the first session, clients often share the story of their struggle. Listening from a non-pathological perspective, this struggle is acknowledged and validated as the client is viewed as doing their best to cope with their challenges. As the clients start to feel accepted and that this is a common and normal struggle, transformation amazingly begins to happen. The coach can then explore what the client's preferred future looks like and help the client move towards life where they can live well and thrive despite their chronic health problem.

The chapter also discusses how the SF approach fits well with Chinese cultural values. Focusing on strengths and resources means the client doesn't have to feel a sense of shame or lose face at having "failed" to follow what medical professionals have advised.

Current Challenge of Chronic Disease Management

The main goal of current health education and health management programmes is reducing risk and inducing behaviour change. This focuses on a logically

DOI: 10.4324/9781003431480-31

oriented change model where professionals present clients with their poor statistics (e.g. BMI, blood sugar, and lipid levels) and health knowledge and then expect them to willingly make the necessary lifestyle changes towards better health. Health management professionals have long hoped that this "scare them and they will change" model would work, but the results have not been satisfactory. When clients don't live up to expectations, professionals wonder if they have neglected some other important information, which should have effectively motivated the client to take action.

Today, there is a need for a new professional in the healthcare system: the action change specialist, also known as a health coach, whose role is to help people make positive changes more effectively. The SF model has unique advantages in health coaching which are described below.

The Epistemology of the Solution Focused Model

Based on the concept of "if it's not broken, don't fix it," we hold the assumption that the client is healthy, capable of change, and willing to change. Our role is to help our clients define their destination, be aware of their resources, and take action for sustainable changes. We have a dynamic view of health care, rather than a static one. For example, even if a person has diabetes, if they are making changes and actively dealing with diabetes through actions, we still consider them as healthy. As a health coach, we believe that clients have the ability to learn, that they know how to make changes, and they are capable of maintaining their own health.

Helping Clients Increase Their Capabilities

Our role is to support clients to reach their desired goals. There are three points we feel are relevant when working with clients who say "I know it all but I just can't do it."

1 Doing what one says is a capability that can be improved.

When our clients are facing the challenge of chronic diseases, supporting them to walk the talk is related to clients' capability. The rationality of the goal is very important and works best when connected to the client's capability. We often say that a good goal is "to jump a bit to reach." In addition, when it comes to walking the talk, it also requires the ability to respond to the unexpected and be flexible, For example, I planned to go outside to exercise, but it rained every day this week, so I didn't exercise at all. On these occasions, whether we have the capability to adjust ourselves becomes the key to putting the words into action. In this sense, doing what one says is a capability that can be enhanced. As a health coach, we can collaborate to support our clients to learn to set a reasonable goal, help them learn to cope with the unexpected, and learn to respond to changes.

2. The mind and body are a unit.

Some clients promise their doctors that they will change, yet don't. Some clients may prepare well, but don't follow through. We found that many of these clients have an adverse physical reaction such as experiencing chest tightness, dizziness, palpitations, or a sense of fear. At that moment they see their only response is to escape. In this situation, we can help clients to face and overcome the physical challenges. We could look for exceptions when they have managed to overcome this physical discomfort, and then explore how they did that and what difference it made.

3. Setbacks are normal.

Many professionals think that if a client agrees to change, then it must be done. Once a client shows a start-and-stop approach to change (such as starting smoking again after giving up), the professional is usually disappointed and puzzled. They then focus on the old problems and give more information about the importance of stopping. The SF coaching approach provides a different focus by exploring examples of successful days when the client managed to keep on track and explores what is important for them in doing something that is very difficult to sustain. These are some useful SF questions in this situation:

- How have you managed to keep on track for these days?
- What difference did it make when you did that?
- What are the good reasons you kept going?
- What will be different when things are just a little bit better?
- As you continue on this path, what would the next thing be that you notice changing?
- What would you like to change even more?
- When is a time you could have given up on your goals but didn't?

Using these ideas helps us move from labelling or blaming the client for not making progress, and instead look at small changes the client has made and how we as health coaches can support them to build on these capabilities.

Maintaining full acceptance of clients and believing that they have the ability to maintain their own health and make continuous improvements helps them increase confidence and hope.

Helping Clients Increase Their Motivation

In addition to supporting clients to improve their capabilities, it can be useful to explore their motivation to change:.

1. Instead of focusing on what we think is best, we explore the client's ideas.

Many health professionals use their own professional knowledge to make decisions that they think are best for the client. This often leads to an impasse as the goals are not shared by the client and the client is blamed for lacking motivation to change. Instead, we ask what the client wants so they are actively involved in making decisions that benefit them, and hence are willing to work on.

2. Focusing on the enjoyment of the process rather than results can lead to a higher sense of self-efficacy.

Some clients enjoy running but give up when the focus is on specific expectations or goals that may be unrealistic and eventually lose the enjoyment of the process. Shifting from a results focus to a process focus can be helpful, by exploring what exercise they enjoy and what makes it enjoyable for them. It can also be helpful to explore a broader picture of the differences it would make for the client when they are able to do the things in their life they enjoy. Descriptions of the presence of those differences can lead to a perceptual change, rather than focusing on what they should do.

Below is an example of a conversation with a client using SF Coaching.

Client Example: Good Reasons for Change

Lin is a family education consultant in her late 30s. She and her husband have been married for many years and she has been trying to get pregnant in recent months. Her test results were good but she worries that her energy levels might not be good enough in the future when she gets pregnant. Her husband expressed his dissatisfaction with her habit of staying up late, hoping that she could adjust her sleep and rest early instead of staying up until midnight.

Coach: What are your best hopes from our session?
Lin: I know I need to go to bed early, but I feel like there's a naughty little girl inside who doesn't want to go to sleep, and the more I know I should go to sleep, the less I want to go to sleep.
Coach: And if our time today lead to something useful for you, what would that be?
Lin: My husband says I will lose my hair if I stay up late. Although I'd like to go to bed early, I think I've solved the problem of losing my hair. I wear a headband every day now and I don't see my hair falling out.
Coach: Sounds like you have arrived at a creative way to manage this. What difference has this made for you?
Lin: Yeah, because even if I go to bed late now, I feel fine the next day,

and I feel quite comfortable playing on my phone to empty my head before going to bed.

Coach: You seem to know what works for you. If our time was worthwhile and you left feeling that it was a good idea to come talk to me, what are you hoping for?

Lin: Well I do really want to have a baby, and know that I need to lay a good foundation for my body to get pregnant by getting a lot of rest so I do really need to make sleep management a priority.

Coach: So what difference would that make when you get more rest?

Lin: I would feel calmer and might be more likely to get pregnant. I think in the future it would also help my baby have a relatively regular routine and he will sleep better.

Coach: So when you focus more on rest what would one step forwards look like?

Lin: I used to go to bed before 22:00 o'clock, but I kept playing with my phone in bed, and I didn't sleep until midnight. So what I'm going to do this time is I'm going to bed at 22:30.

Coach: Wow, you've decided so soon! What might support you as you begin to experiment with this?

Lin: I think I can set an alarm on my phone (start selecting the alarm music).

Coach: Wow, I heard different alarms on your phone. All kinds of beautiful music.

Lin: Yes, if I am going to set an alarm, I should choose music that is very different from the older alarm. It will remind me more effectively.

Coach: You found a way to remind yourself so quickly. I could see your motivation to set up a new sleep routine is very strong.

Lin: I had never thought of using a reminder mechanism before, I used to think that I wanted to go to bed early, but due to the lack of reminder mechanism, I never really took action. I'm looking forward to the new routine tonight!

Coach: How do you hope trying this will make a difference?

Lin: I would feel very excited, very settled, with a better sense of control. I have the ability to adjust my sleep.

Coach: What difference will it make to your husband?

Lin: My husband's eyes would open widely in surprise and delight, and then he would say, "You're amazing. I admire you."

Coach: That sounds really exciting! Now imagine that when finishing our conversation today, you come home, what is the first thing you will do?

Lin: I'll be home around 21:00 this evening. The first thing I would do is to put my phone in the phone storage box in our living room. Then I would have a hot water foot-bath while stewing my Chinese medicine to improve my body condition. Then I would get washed and ready for bed.

This example demonstrates to our clients that we accept them and believe they have good reasons for what they are doing or not doing. This in turn helps them believe in themselves and their ability to change and be willing to explore some next steps towards their goals.

Cultural Factors Relating to Solution Focused Coaching in China

"Walking the talk," also known as suiting action to the word（言行一致）, is regarded as a very important personal quality in Chinese culture and is often used to measure whether a person has high morals. If someone cannot keep their promises, it will not only lead to being judged by others, but very often leads to self-blame, and labelling oneself as a dishonest person.

There is an old Chinese saying that "nine times out of ten, life doesn't work out" (不如意事常八九). The SF approach turns this on its head and explores the exception – the one time things did work out. Using exceptions to explore a client's strengths and capabilities can lead to increased hope and motivation that change is possible. In my experience, it is not the coach who fixes our client's problems, as it is ultimately something our clients decide to do to help themselves. Our role is to accompany clients in the process of taking a pause and exploring what they want for their lives, and then choosing a suitable time to make steps towards this. This process is what I describe in a Chinese saying, "Diseases come on horseback, but go away on foot" (病来如山倒，病去如抽丝). If the client has an epiphany and finds a reason to move forwards, it is really a miracle to celebrate. We are working towards the desired future state the client wants in a way that is right for them.

When we talk about changes, we may be prone to emphasise only the overall results and expect a high degree of changes. Thus, we tend to use proverbs such as "like the sun and moon is brand new by each day and night" (日新月异), "like the sky was turned upside down and the earth was all covered up" (天翻地覆), "from head to toe" (彻头彻尾), to describe the magnitude of the changes. With the nuances of language and cultural influence, we often overestimate our short-term capabilities and underestimate our long-term capabilities. As an SF coach, we help our clients to broaden their horizon by seeing more of the little but important steps they've taken, and all the efforts they've made along the way. There are also a lot of Chinese proverbs advocating how precious and important small steps are, such as "A long journey can be covered only by taking one step at a time"（千里之行始于足下）, "Without accumulating small streams, no river or sea can be formed"（不积小流无以成江海），and "water constantly dripping wears holes in stone"（滴水穿石）.

In all these aspects, the SF mindset is highly compatible with Chinese culture.

Reference

W. Zheng, X. Han, & Y. Lyu (2022). The overall status and population differences of chronic diseases in Chinese population. *Social Science Journal, 2022*(3), 139–149. In Chinese: 郑伟, 韩笑, 吕有吉. 中国人口慢性病的总体状况与群体差异[J]. 社会科学辑刊, 2022, 2022(3): 139–149.

25 Adaptations of Solution Focused Coaching for Podiatry Clinical Practice

The Role of a Clinician-Coach

Marabelle Heng, Helen Banwell, Keran Wei, and Kristin Graham

Introduction

This chapter presents considerations and recommendations of incorporating elements of Solution Focused (SF) coaching in a healthcare setting. In doing so, it identifies how clinicians can move away from less effective traditional didactic education and towards effective collaborative conversations by taking on the role of a clinician-coach. Social and cultural influences will also be discussed.

Didactic Versus Collaborative Health Conversations

Communication is a key component in clinical care, including podiatry practice. Clients communicate their presenting conditions to podiatrists, who then assess and diagnose the conditions. The podiatrist will then communicate their findings, recommend evidence-based management strategies (e.g. rehabilitation exercises, wound dressing regimes, etc.) and any lifestyle changes required (e.g. footwear) to the client. This communication is traditionally delivered in a didactic style. That is, in a 'top-down,' 'one way' manner from the clinician (as the 'expert') to the client (as the 'passive receiver').

Unfortunately, a didactic approach is often ineffective in achieving treatment compliance. For example, direct persuasion to stop smoking and graphic advertisements to warn of potential negative effects have not significantly impacted smoking rates (Erceg-Hurn & Steed, 2011). In fact, such manner of persuasion may make people feel that freedom over their own choices is being threatened, which can elicit hostile motivational reactions known as psychological reactance (Steindl et al., 2015). In contrast, collaborative conversations such as those used in SF coaching have been shown to effectively engage clients in their treatment plans (Heng et al., 2020). This approach is more likely to be successful because it honours the client, who holds critical beliefs on how change takes place relative to their goals.

Coaching in the health industry is defined as 'a partnership with clients to facilitate the achievement of their health-related goals' (Kivela et al., 2014). The principles of SF coaching are applied to healthcare conversations by

DOI: 10.4324/9781003431480-32

(i) adopting a respectful posture through honouring client stories, (ii) tapping on a client's preferences and resources and incorporating them into the treatment plan, and (iii) acknowledging that the conversation is key to change (Lewis & Osborn, 2004).

The effects of collaborative communication in podiatry were recently trialled in Singapore (Heng et al., 2020). The participants, clients living with diabetes, were randomised into two groups. One group was attended to by podiatrists with training specific to collaborative health education ('coaching group'); the other group was attended to by podiatrists without this specialised training (standard practice group). This study found that the coaching group clients fared better for both knowledge retention and positive behaviour changes in relation to foot health and wound management. Further, the study demonstrated the successful adoption of coaching skills by podiatrists.

A Hybrid Between Health Coach and Clinician

In theory, Asian societies, commonly characterised by hierarchical dynamics, may see the health professional as a respected expert and hence view offering input to a treatment plan as disrespectful to them. However, trials in Southeast Asia demonstrate clients' openness and even preference for collaborative discussion with their attending clinician (Heng et al., 2020; Claramita et al., 2013). This may reflect the priority of individual rights and autonomy within the health discussion, over social hierarchy. The uptake of collaboration in these trials could also be attributed to the clinicians' deliberate efforts in initiating partnership. In a collaborative discussion, the medical professional takes on the mindset of a health coach, as opposed to health expert. A health expert holds a superior position of knowledge, whereas a health coach, by function, empowers a client to achieve better health.

SF coaching requires the coach to adopt a 'not knowing' posture – holding silence and providing clients the space to develop solutions through their own strengths and resources. Full adoption of this posture is not possible for the clinician, who is bound by duty and legislation to make diagnoses and recommend evidence-based treatment. A clinician, may however, incorporate the principle of the 'not knowing' stance, by allowing clients space to provide input in the discussion and remaining curious about the clients' personal circumstances.

The conversation between clinician and client reflects the ethics of informed consent: the clinician shares information on treatment options for the client to consider; the client retains the autonomy to raise questions about the treatment options, consider the alignment with their personal healing goals, and even decline or postpone treatment. In addition, a clinician with coaching skills further steers the conversation using appropriate tools, prompts, and guiding questions to facilitate plans to achieve health goals. The cross functions between coach and clinician give rise to the hybrid role:

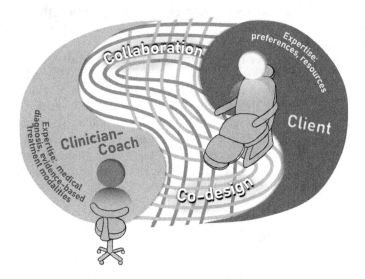

Figure 25.1 Diagrammatic representation of a collaborative discussion between clinician-coach and client. The centre mesh represents coming together to co-create a plan (Ruby Eckermann).

clinician-coach. The client and clinician-coach collaborate to develop a plan tailored to client's circumstances (Figure 25.1).

Tools for a Clinician-Coach

The tools that are needed for podiatrists to be effective clinician-coaches include (i) fostering collaboration with clients, (ii) eliciting motivation for self-care, (iii) eliciting strengths and resources that the clients possess, and (iv) incorporating the clients' personal culture and values when co-designing treatment strategies (Figure 25.2).

Although a clinician-coach may progress stepwise from 'collaborative discussion' to 'co-design strategy' in one session, the conversation may also flow dynamically around the framework.

Collaborative Discussion

A collaborative approach creates the platform for a two-way, harmonious discussion. In contrast to a didactic top-down health education, collaborative and open conversations allow clients to participate and share their perspectives in a conducive environment. Since chronic health conditions and lifestyle choices are intrinsically linked, clients risk feeling judged and uncomfortable when engaging in conversation about their lifestyle. Social stigmatisation by people living with Type II Diabetes has been reported –

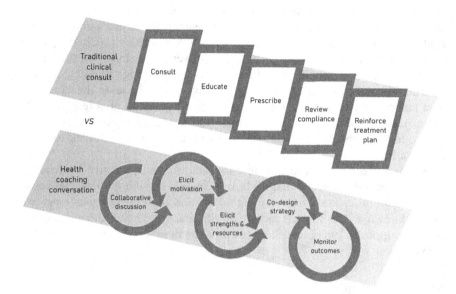

Figure 25.2 Summary of a clinical coaching conversation vis-à-vis a traditional clinical consultation (Ruby Eckermann).

including feeling ashamed or blamed by others for causing their own condition (Browne et al., 2013). Because shame is a poor foundation for behavioural change, fostering collaboration and respect is particularly useful in the management of chronic lifestyle diseases.

The use of open-ended questions is a great tool for gathering information within a collaborative discussion; it yields more information than close-ended questions that tend to elicit short 'yes or no' answers. It is also important for the clinician-coach to summarise the content and reflect it back as it demonstrates that the clients' views were heard and respected. In addition, the practice of reflecting back serves to confirm or clarify information. The clinician-coach gains a clear understanding of the client's perspective, which guides the coaching conversation. This process builds trust and rapport.

In a collaborative medical discussion, the clinician-coach is mindful that beyond the sharing of medical information, it is the client who needs to process the information to suit their circumstances. This might sound like, 'Based on recent research, this medical condition is best treated by ____ (methods, modalities).' followed by checking in with the client, 'Would you like to discuss or explore this further?'

Elicit Intrinsic Motivation

When specific health goals (e.g. healing a chronic open wound) are aligned with broader life goals (e.g. being able to play tennis again), the client's existing motivation is harnessed. A clinician-coach adopts an SF posture of respectful curiosity, to find alignment between treatment goals and personal goals by asking, 'What are some things you would do when ... (e.g. the pain is resolved, the wound is healed etc.)?' Such conversations may reveal that the client values, for example, the ability to walk their dog. Building on this information, the clinician-coach may align this personal goal to the treatment plan and make relevant suggestions to support the health goal (e.g. heal the wound). By working with what matters to the client, clinician-coaches will be able to increase the client's willingness to embrace change and work towards their goals.

Where a client is stuck and unable to visualise goals, creative approaches such as prompting them to imagine how life would be without obstacles could be helpful in momentarily suspending reality and thinking positively instead. This is known as the 'miracle picture' in SF coaching. From there, clinician-coaches support clients in working towards the desired goals through further conversation.

Scaling and Interpretation

Numerical scales are often used by clinicians to understand their client's experience, for example, degree of pain. Similarly, scaling can be used to gauge where client is with respect to their goals. Marking '10' as the future-perfect goal, the clinician-coach asks the client, 'Regarding your motivation for working towards the pain-free life you have just described, on the scale of 0–10, where zero is "I have no desire" and 10 is "the most motivated you could be," where are you at right now?' If the client responds with '3,' the clinician-coach then clarifies with the client, 'What makes it a 3 and not lower?' allowing the client to identify relevant strengths and concerns that contribute to their current state.

Scaling and subsequent prompts unveil the resources and small wins that the client already has under their belt. Strategies can then be developed to progress one step at time (from a '3' to a '4'). This breaks the big goal (perfect score of 10) into small steps. Small goals that are achievable build confidence and positivity.

Elicit Strengths and Resources

A client's resources may include personal strengths, prior knowledge, or previous successful attempts at managing similar problems. Identifying client resources creates an uplifting atmosphere, whereas focusing on what is lacking may trap both client and clinician in cycles of negativity and helplessness. By eliciting strengths and resources, a clinician-coach focuses on the 'half cup full' (i.e. what the client already possesses) (Figure 25.3). With these insights, the clinician-coach nurtures greater readiness by building on a client's resources to take the next step forward.

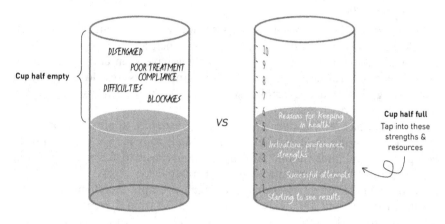

Figure 25.3 'Half cup empty' versus 'half cup full' (Ruby Eckermann).

The scale on the cup represents the scaling question that forms the basis for exploring the client's resources – 'What is in the cup? How did you get to where you are right now?'

Clinician-coaches may invite clients to develop additional skills and know-how, adding to the 'cup-full of resources' (e.g. wound dressing techniques, rehabilitative exercises, etc). In a traditional didactic approach, the clinician jumps straight into the health education and expects the client to comply with advice, simply because it is beneficial for their health. In contrast, a clinician-coach remains mindful of the client's autonomy and engagement in this process by (i) inviting the client into the learning space ('Would you be keen on ... ?') and (ii) seeking permission to share knowledge ('May I show you how ... ?').

Co-design Treatment Plan

Treatment planning should be directed by both the clinician-coach and the client, such that therapeutic suggestions by the clinician-coach are contextualised to factors which influence client choices and decisions, particularly cultural norms. For example, the approach to footwear: juxtaposed against Western habits of keeping shoes on indoors, most Asian cultures discourage wearing outdoor footwear when indoors. If footwear advice by the clinician directly contradicts the client's cultural norms, it will be challenging to persuade clients of change, not to mention disrespectful. Where cultural factors are at play, a co-designed treatment plan is well suited. The clinician-coach could share information on footwear features that support the injured area, while exploring with the client whether and how these could be incorporated into their lifestyle (e.g. duration of use, suitable alternatives, separate indoor sandals, etc).

Monitor Outcome

When monitoring outcomes in a review session, a non-judgemental approach should be maintained. Open-ended questions such as 'How have you been managing?' allow the client to share how they have been coping. To avoid clients feeling scrutinised or judged, clinician-coaches should also refrain from using close-ended questions such as 'Have you been doing ___(plan discussed in previous session)?'

The principles of eliciting strengths and resources apply in monitoring outcomes: focusing on clients' efforts and small wins increases the sense of competence and motivation. Affirmation and positive feelings can build further powerful momentum to engage in treatment.

In pure SF follow-up sessions, the coach prompts the client by asking 'What's been better?' thus kick-starting a conversation driven by positivity and strengths. However, such a practice has limitations in a medical setting as clinicians have a duty of care to monitor the progression of the existing conditions, including deteriorations, and to investigate any new medical presentations. From a clinician's perspective, considering both alleviating and aggravating factors are crucial in clinical reasoning and diagnosis. However, a clinician-coach is mindful that aggravating factors should not be invoked to blame clients for any health deterioration. Where there are concerns about aggravating factors, the clinician-coach invites the client into the discussion and shares information respectfully: 'Could we discuss ... ? I am concerned that _____may be worsening ____ (condition).' The aim is to address gaps in knowledge or blind spots, while maintaining the sense of autonomy, confidence, and competence in the client.

In Table 25.1, we explore further examples of clinical coaching conversations. Notice that the podiatrist does not take on the burden to persuade clients to make changes but maximises the clients' potential by sharing therapeutic information which allows them to make informed decisions about their treatment.

Table 25.1 Examples of podiatry clinical conversations with comments from a health coaching perspective

Topic: Footwear	Comments
Traditional didactic patient education 'Because you have diabetes, you should wear supportive and covered footwear, like running shoes. Wear the footwear both indoors and outdoors.'	☒One-way didactic 'info dump'

(Continued)

Table 25.1 (Continued)

Topic: Footwear	Comments
Clinician-coach approach 'What would you like to work on today?' 'What makes it better?' 'What types of footwear do you have?' Clinician: 'I gather that you have a range of footwear: sandals, slippers, walking shoes and boots. Which one do you use the most and why?' **Scenario A** *Client's response: I like the walking shoes. They are the most comfortable shoes. When I use them, I rarely get any foot pain or skin problems.* Clinician: 'Your walking shoes are designed to support all around the foot, especially around the ankles and arches. That is likely why walking is usually pain-free when you choose this style of footwear.'	Invite participation. Facilitate an open conversation and seek to discover what the client is already doing for that presenting situation. Summarise what the client has said and reflect it back to the client. This builds rapport with the client and demonstrates that you respect their perspectives. Highlight positive points and bring awareness to them. Sometimes, clients are not aware of what they are already doing well. A coach highlights and affirms good practices. The clinician-coach can build on these further by explaining why it works well. This would affirm positive health behaviours and encourage the client to continue doing so.
Scenario B *Client: I usually wear sandals or slippers. They are the most convenient to put on. On the rare occasion, I put on covered shoes, but I don't like them. They cause me pain around my little toe and my feet get really hot and sweaty in them.* Clinician: 'It seems closed-in shoes make your feet feel uncomfortable. Would you like to work together to find something suitable? ... What kind of sandals do you use (use picture aids)?' 'That is a good supportive sandal (that you have chosen) – it has thick supportive straps around the ankle ... May I recommend also looking for something with a heel counter. The sole of the sandal also makes a	Invite/re-invite participation. This is a quick check-in that the client is still on board. If the client declines, respect the choice that have they made. If the client is open to discussion, provide new ideas or recommendations respectfully. In this scenario, the clinician can build on the client's current good practices and further encourage small steps, which are aligned with client preferences, to move them towards their health goals.

Table 25.1 (Continued)

Topic: Footwear	Comments
big difference if you need to walk long distances in them. I would recommend one with a shock-absorptive and supportive sole … . Yes, the sole is similar to that of running shoes, but it's a sandal design nevertheless.'	

Topic: Musculoskeletal exercises	Comments
Traditional patient education and review 'Do these calf and plantar fascia stretches, at least twice a day …' 'Have you been doing your stretches?'	☒ One-way info dump ☒ Close ended question suggests that there is a 'correct' and 'wrong' answer, which may then evoke feelings of being scrutinised or judged.
Clinician-coach approach 'May I show you some exercises that could help alleviate the pain and aid the recovery process?' 'How have you been managing the pain? … What else do you do to manage the heel pain? … How are the exercises going?'	Ask for permission to share/show examples. This respectfully invites them into the learning space. Remember also to invite the client to show back. This builds confidence and mastery in health education. The use of open-ended 'how' questions invite clients to share the strategies they have tried. When monitoring outcomes, use 'how is that going' question instead of 'have you/have you not.'

Topic: Offloading device	Comments
Traditional review of compliance 'Have you been using the offloading boot?'	☒ A closed-ended (yes or no answer) question usually does not invite participation. It also implies there is 'one standard correct answer' and hampers an open, collaborative conversation.
Clinician-coach review 'Could you share with me how you have been managing your wound? … What else do you do to protect your wound?'	The use of open-ended questions allow the sharing of client perspectives in a non-judgemental environment.

Summary

A clinician-coach creates a supportive space for collaboration. Decisions on the implementation and pace of change remain at the client's discretion and are respected by the clinician-coach. When co-designing a treatment plan, consideration of factors that influence the client is paramount. A treatment plan mapped alongside a client's goals and capitalising on available resources is more likely to succeed.

References

Browne, J. L., Ventura, A., Mosely, K., & Speight, J. (2013). 'I call it the blame and shame disease': A qualitative study about perceptions of social stigma surrounding type 2 diabetes. *BMJ Open, 3*(11), e003384. 10.1136/bmjopen-2013-003384

Claramita, M., Nugraheni, M. D., van Dalen, J., & van der Vleuten, C. (2013). Doctor–patient communication in Southeast Asia: A different culture? *Advances in Health Sciences Education, 18,* 15–31. 10.1007/s10459-012-9352-5

Erceg-Hurn, D. M., & Steed, L. G. (2011). Does exposure to cigarette health warnings elicit psychological reactance in smokers? *Journal of Applied Social Psychology, 41*(1), 219–237. 10.1111/j.1559-1816.2010.00710.x

Heng, M. L., Kwan, Y. H., Ilya, N., Ishak, I. A., Jin, P. H., Hogan, D., & Carmody, D. (2020). A collaborative approach in patient education for diabetes foot and wound care: A pragmatic randomised controlled trial. *International Wound Journal, 17*(6), 1678–1686. 10.1111/iwj.13450

Kivelä, K., Elo, S., Kyngäs, H., & Kääriäinen, M. (2014). The effects of health coaching on adult patients with chronic diseases: A systematic review. *Patient Education and Counseling, 97*(2), 147–157. 10.1016/j.pec.2014.07.026

Lewis, T. F., & Osborn, C. J. (2004). Solution-focused counseling and motivational interviewing: A consideration of confluence. *Journal of Counseling & Development, 82*(1), 38–48. 10.1002/j.1556-6678.2004.tb00284.x

Steindl, C., Jonas, E., Sittenthaler, S., Traut-Mattausch, E., & Greenberg, J. (2015). Understanding psychological reactance. New developments and findings. *Zeitschrift für Psychologie, 223*(4), 205–214. 10.1027/2151-2604/a000222

26 Using Solution Focused Coaching in Chronic Pain Management

Jesse Cai

Introduction

The majority of people will experience chronic pain at some time in their lives. Chronic (or persistent) pain, defined as any pain lasting more than 12 weeks in duration, often comes without tissue damage and is often the result of abnormal neural signalling (Lancet, 2021). According to the GlaxoSmithKline Global Pain Index 2017, 85% of Singaporeans experienced head and body pain, with as many as 40% suffering from weekly body pain (Gan, 2017). Bodily pain costs Singapore a staggering $8.4 billion dollars per year – 2% of the city state's annual GDP (Biospectrum Asia, 2017).

Due to the significant impact on their quality of life, these clients often consult with a number of medical professionals to help reduce the pain. As a chiropractor, I work with many clients experiencing chronic pain. In addition to treating their physical symptoms, I also trained as a Solution Focused (SF) coach. I have found the addition of SF coaching helps pain sufferers to cultivate a positive mindset. By focusing on their strengths and emphasising their past successes, I am able to help them increase their self-efficacy. This in itself improves my clients' pain experience. Beyond this, it also encourages them to proactively take part in their own recovery and helps them drive long-term success.

This chapter will highlight how SF coaching can positively impact clients' pain experiences using each step of the OSKAR model of coaching (Jackson & McKergow, 2007).

This chapter will also share how a person's culture can affect many pain-related factors such as how they scale their progress in relation to their pain. The SF approach is respectful of different cultural beliefs and enables the coach to explore what each client wants to be different in their lives and not assume that the pain needs to be talked about or addressed directly, if this is not important to the client.

The Solution Focused Approach

Adopting an SF approach for chronic pain is not intuitive. When people experience pain, the first thing that people want to know is what is wrong.

DOI: 10.4324/9781003431480-33

For those who find out that there is nothing wrong on a physical or tissue level, the question then becomes "What is wrong with me?" As a coach, it is important to acknowledge that the experience of pain is real and has a huge impact on clients' quality of life.

Exploring Outcomes When Living with Chronic Pain

Before I discuss how to approach goal setting for clients with chronic pain, I will share what it may be like to live with chronic pain. This gives better context and insights to help guide your client towards their perfect future. For most people, their pain is never truly constant. The intensity can change from day to day. Even at times when the pain intensity is the same, how the pain affects them can also change. Research has shown that chronic pain not only affects people's physical capabilities but also their mental health, social well-being, work productivity, as well as their overall sense of well-being and life satisfaction (Kawai et al., 2017).

Because experiences of pain can change from day to day, it can be difficult for people living with chronic pain to have clarity about their future. When the pain is better, many things are possible whereas at other times they may be stuck at home unable to walk. The ability to therefore imagine a perfect future can change dramatically based on a person's current state.

With this in mind, the seeming lack of clarity of a client's perfect future is not always because they are unclear of their goals. More often than not, it is because they don't know what their baseline state is or what is reasonable to achieve. For people with chronic pain, setting goals that are realistic and reasonable is important to avoid feelings of hopelessness.

As coaches, most of us also do not have the subject matter expertise to guide our clients to what is a reasonable perfect future either. With this in view, I would encourage you to de-emphasise finding a perfect future for clients who appear to be uncertain. Initially, the work may involve validation of the client's pain and struggles and use of coping questions to explore how they are managing a tough situation.

Noticing how your clients respond to future-oriented questions is important – if they keep moving back to describing their problems it may be important to slow down and explore times when things are even just a little better already that may give clues to what they want more of.

A miracle picture may involve using the phrasing – "Suppose you were living as well as possible despite the chronic pain, what would you be noticing?"

Once your clients start to make progress or gain confidence in managing their own pain situation, you can always revisit the perfect future.

Scaling

One of the basic questions most medical professionals will ask clients is to rate their pain on a scale of 0–10, where 0 is no pain at all and 10 is the worst pain imaginable. This is a validated and reliable scale that is commonly used in clinical practice (Atisook et al., 2021). In the SF approach, we use scales in the opposite direction – that is, 10 is always the positive situation the client wants to move towards.

Just reversing the scale, so 0 is the worst pain possible while 10 is totally pain-free, is not useful for most clients. Their pain may always be there at some level so aiming to be pain-free is unrealistic.

Instead, it can be helpful to use a scale such as "If 10 is you coping as well as possible with your current level of pain and 0 is the opposite, where are you now?" Or "If 10 is living well despite your pain and 0 is the opposite, where are you now?" This is both congruent with SF coaching and respectful of the client's reality where pain is still there.

Another scaling question that I find useful, especially for follow-up sessions, is to ask clients where they are in their recovery. For this scale, 10 will denote a full recovery whereas 0 will denote no progress at all. Satisfaction with progress can also be scaled.

One of the simplest ways of helping clients appreciate their progress is to help them document objective measures of progress, even if there is still pain. This is particularly useful for clients who genuinely struggle to see what has been better. In my clinical practice, I use exercise in conjunction with coaching. When it comes to exercise, improvements can be objectively measured through an increase in strength and managing more technically challenging exercises. Clients sometimes struggle to appreciate this as progress and downplay improvements by suggesting that they are still weak or that their pain levels are still the same. This is why it is very important for SF coaches to help their clients track all signs of their progress and illuminate the improvements they are making.

Helping Clients Find Their Know-How

Another way of eliciting small signs of progress and helping clients become aware of their strengths and existing know-how is asking about their day-to-day experiences in detail, starting from the morning when they wake up, asking for example "What happened next" asking to recount the day so far or the day before so it is fresh in their memory.

There are two things to be mindful of. Firstly, clients may skip to the parts of the day where they remembered experiencing pain. This is a cue to ask about what else they experienced prior to that. Through this, you are trying to demonstrate that despite the challenges of living with chronic pain, they also have pain-free moments. These pain-free periods, however short, are the golden moments in letting them know that there is hope. It is also an opportunity to look for know-how for how they coped when they did experience pain. What helped manage the pain, or get on with the day in spite of the pain?

Secondly, they may move away from that specific day to describe their overall, general experiences. For example, they may share that brushing teeth is usually not painful or sitting at work is usually painful. It is important to direct their attention to that specific day in question to have better clarity of the client's day as a whole and bring attention to the experiences in the day that may have been neglected. If they only talk about general patterns they are already familiar with, they may miss the times that a normally painful activity was pain-free, or that normally they would have struggled with but this time they coped well.

Lastly, I also want to emphasise that pain is a phenomenological experience. In other words, your client's pain is real and what they report as their experiences should always be taken at face value. It is important to acknowledge and empathise with their pain. We do not aim to prove our clients are wrong. Instead, it is about clarifying exceptions – times when things are even a little better, or they coped better, and therefore can identify useful strengths or strategies that they can consciously draw on to help themselves going forwards.

Affirm and Action

Chronic pain affects people both physically and psychologically (Lancet, 2021). Exercise and having quality sleep are examples of health behaviours that can help with chronic pain (Mork et al., 2014). However, it is not always easy for chronic pain sufferers to engage in helpful health behaviours even when they want to and have the necessary information to do so. For example, while exercise is recommended for most, if not all, musculoskeletal pain, it can be painful to perform (Lin et al., 2020). Beyond physical pain, some pain sufferers also avoid exercising or certain movements because of their fear of pain or that these activities will worsen their condition.

Clients may also share that they have no time to exercise or seem that they are making excuses for not exercising. What can be helpful is affirming all the small steps a client has already taken, such as complimenting their awareness that exercise is an important part of their recovery, or that they already have knowledge about what to do.

When it comes to small action steps for chronic pain sufferers, there is nothing too small. Many of my clients struggle to carry out their small action steps. This can cause incredible frustration and lead to unnecessary self-blame. As a coach, it is important to recognise this and explore what could be an even smaller action step. Affirming that there is nothing too small, and exploring all small successes, will lead to a better sense of where they are at and what is a reasonable next small step.

If at any point the client reports the pain to be worse than before or more persistent than before, you would also want to refer them to an appropriate healthcare provider. It is also good practice to confirm that the client has medical approval to start exercising.

Review

I keep my reviews at the end of my coaching sessions simple when working with chronic pain sufferers. Asking what has been helpful from today's session and what the client is taking away (e.g. what they have learnt about themselves or ideas for next steps) can be enough. When clients come back for a second or subsequent session, the normal SF coaching review question is "What has been better since we last met?" When working with chronic pain clients who are really struggling to make even small steps forwards, it can be helpful to change the question slightly to "What has been better since we last met, even just a little bit?"

Cultural Factors Affecting the Experience of Pain

Working with chronic pain clients in Asia is different from working with western clients. Culturally, research has shown that East Asians are more likely to choose the midpoint of a Likert scale compared to Americans (Lee et al., 2002). This is problematic because if a client were to repeatedly choose the midpoint of a scale, it may appear that they are not making progress when they in fact are. Similarly, this phenomenon may also make it difficult to identify when clients are doing poorer than before. When using scaling questions, asking clients for lots of detailed examples of how they got to whatever number they are at on the scale will help circumvent this. With scaling, the actual number is less important than as a tool to gather signs of progress and to give clues to their next small step forwards.

Chronic pain may be seen as normal in some Asian cultures and a large proportion of pain sufferers may not seek help because they view their pain to be harmless or prefer to suffer in silence (Choo, 2017; Lancet, 2023). SF coaching is useful because it allows coaches to explore with clients what is important to them in terms of a useful outcome. We don't assume that they need to focus on or address their pain explicitly. We can work on finding solutions that are congruent to their own value system.

Summary and Conclusions

This chapter has summarised how to use the OSKAR coaching framework with clients with chronic pain and some of the adjustments needed when working with this client group. These include: taking time to validate and acknowledge the reality of their pain, constructing a realistic outcome such as living well despite the pain, scaling progress, looking for exceptions to highlight client's strengths and resources, affirming every small step, and exploring manageable small action steps. The SF approach works well in the

Asian context as it respects what the client sees as important in relation to the outcome, taking their beliefs into account.

References

Atisook, R., Euasobhon, P., Saengsanon, A., & Jensen, M. P. (2021). Validity and utility of four pain intensity measures for use in international research. *Journal of Pain Research, 14*, 1129–1139. 10.2147/JPR.S303305

Biospectrum Asia (2017, June 30). The global pain index – an insightful survey worldwide. *Biospectrum Asia Edition.* Retrieved from: https://www.biospectrumasia. com/news/41/9120/the-global-pain-index-an-insightful-survey-worldwide.html

Choo, F. (2017, June 20). *Suffering from pain costs Singapore more than $8 billion each year: Study.* Straits Times. Retrieved from: https://www.straitstimes.com/singapore/ health/suffering-from-pain-costs-singapore-more-than-8-billion-each-year-study

Gan, E. (2017, September 21). Feeling the pain, a nation searches for relief. *Today Online.* Retrieved from: https://www.todayonline.com/daily-focus/feeling-pain-nation-searches-relief

Jackson P. Z., & McKergow M. (2007). *The solutions focus: Making coaching and change simple* (2nd ed.). Nicholas Brealey.

Kawai, K., Kawai, A. T., Wollan, P., & Yawn, B. P. (2017). Adverse impacts of chronic pain on health-related quality of life, work productivity, depression and anxiety in a community-based study. *Family Practice, 34*(6), 656–661. 10.1093/ fampra/cmx034

Lancet (2021). Rethinking chronic pain [Editorial]. *The Lancet, 397*(10289). 10.1016/ S0140-6736(21)01194-6

Lancet (2023). Chronic pain in Asia: We don't have to endure. *The Lancet Regional Health: Western Pacific, 33*, 1–2.

Lee, J. W., Jones, P. S., Mineyama, Y., & Zhang, X. E. (2002). Cultural differences in responses to a Likert scale. *Research in Nursing & Health, 25*(4), 295–306. 10.1002/ nur.10041

Lin, I., Wiles, L., Waller, R., Goucke, R., Nagree, Y., Gibberd, M., ... Sullivan, P. P. B. (2020). What does best practice care for musculoskeletal pain look like? Eleven consistent recommendations from high-quality clinical practice guidelines: Systematic review. *British Journal of Sports Medicine, 2020* (54), 79–86.

Mork, P. J., Vik, K. L., Moe, B., Lier, R., Bardal, E. M., & Nilsen, T. I. (2014). Sleep problems, exercise and obesity and risk of chronic musculoskeletal pain: The Norwegian HUNT study. *European Journal of Public Health, 24*(6), 924–929. 10.1 093/eurpub/ckt198

Section 8

Faith-Based Coaching

27 Accidental Coaching

Solution Focused Coaching in Ordinary Places

Steven Nicaud

Introduction

Like many of us, the time when I began to learn the Solution Focused (SF) coaching approach and proper life coaching skills was an epiphany.

Although I had been a pastor and counsellor for more than 35 years, I had been reluctant to enter into any kind of life coaching or counselling scenario. I feared not being able to help people. Part of this was because I always looked at myself as a source, an answerer, or a remedy to the dilemmas that people face. Now I realise that I am not the source but simply someone who can help provide a process for them to find their own answers and solutions.

Another thing that affected me was the feeling that I had to come up with those answers to be seen as successful. This was a crushing weight of responsibility that I carried and therefore shunned involvement with talking about people's needs. I have found this to be true for many of my contemporaries. I experienced more comfort behind a lectern or pulpit. Nestled behind my wall against interaction, I could share my perspective and brilliantly make my point, impressing my hearers. It was safe. However, deep inside, I knew I was failing to truly help people.

As I studied SF coaching, it immediately highlighted that we are not solvers of problems but empathetic and compassionate neighbours on the path towards the coachee's idea of resolving their issues. The enlightenment that I received made me feel like I had been let out of a prison cell.

With my newfound freedom, I soon learned that even if I did not have knowledge about the subjects with which the people whom I was speaking with needed help, it did not matter. I facilitated an SF coaching process and watched a quasi-magical transformation of myself in what I felt I could do. My confidence in coaching someone rose to higher heights than it ever had been during the previous decades.

I discovered still more. As I integrated these SF skills and the coaching mindset, they seeped out of me in every interaction with people, not just in professional coaching sessions. This started while telling people about my training in SF coaching and at that moment applied it as an example. Great sessions came from this 'teach what I'm learning' approach.

DOI: 10.4324/9781003431480-35

On the next step of evolution as a coach, I entered an even higher level where I had no intention of coaching anyone but accidentally did so. This is what I call accidental coaching – using my coaching skills in ordinary, everyday conversations.

To date, I have had dozens of these impromptu sessions of serendipitous interactions from which I'll share three to illustrate this experience. I would also like to highlight that, as a professional and ethical coach, I recognise and acknowledge the need to establish a clear coaching agreement and have clarity around the coaching relationship. These are essential understandings and agreements in coaching. I'm also highlighting that unexpected, spontaneous opportunities arise that can become coachable moments and be very powerful.

The Graduation Party

Quite a few of these accidental coaching sessions have occurred at the crossroads of strangers and me when we share a space and time.

As I stood at the bar ordering something to drink, there was loud celebration and happiness in the room. It was the graduation party of a young Chinese man. He was being regaled by friends who seemed to honour him greatly. I had never met any of them.

He approached the counter and ordered his beverage. I made no eye contact, as I am an introvert by nature. I felt him looking at me and reluctantly glanced up, and he raised his eyebrows in salute. I did the same. I sensed his curiosity about me and tried to avoid it.

He said, "Hi! What's your name?" loudly to be heard above the din of revelry in the room.

I replied, "My name is Steven. What's yours?" as I reached to shake his hand.

He asked, "Do you mind if I ask you a question?" He did not wait for my response but just rolled right into the inquiry.

"How do we know what's next? How do we know how to choose what our next thing is?" he blurted out.

I nodded slowly without saying a word, just waiting. I thought to myself that I did not have the energy to get into this after my long, hard day of work. But then, OSKAR coaching questions (Jackson & McKergow, 2007), like a solitary being that lives inside of me, awakened and exited my mouth before I could stop them.

"I'm curious," I said. May I ask you a question? He nodded, waiting for my question. "What are your best hopes for your future?" I asked him, looking deep into his eyes. He responded with his dreams and visions. I encouraged him to dream big and imagine the best-case scenario, even if he didn't do it but it just happened like a miracle. He painted a picture with his hopeful words.

I asked him on a scale from one to ten how close he was to that dream becoming a reality. The game was afoot!

Two hours later, waving his hands to shush his friends who were begging him to return to his own party, he exclaimed, "Leave me alone! Can't you see I'm making life choices here?"

During the time we spent together, he identified 9 or 10 assets he had, and went from a 2 to an 8 on his scale.

We embraced like long-lost brothers, and I encouraged him return to his party.

Over the two hours of conversation, the dialogue was 95% him and 5% me asking the simple question, "What else?"

In the Asian culture, there is an inherent respect for elders, so perhaps the young man was looking for some wise advice from someone his senior who just happened to be there. However, the conversation turned out very differently to what I imagine he expected. Instead of giving any advice or answers, I showed genuine curiosity about what he wanted for his life that defied the normal cultural protocol. We connected as two humans, and he clearly enjoyed the conversation, creating a powerful vision of what he wanted, and what he had already.

The Physiotherapist

I love to exercise, especially swimming. Not just a little, but 50 laps of breaststroke. Swimming is like a small holiday for me, away from the stress of life. When I swim, I am driven by a mission.

This story takes place at a public pool. After a swim, I'm exhausted and like to lie in the sun to catch my breath. I put my noise-reducing headphones in my ears and zone out.

As I was absorbing the rays, there were sudden intermittent shadows over my eyelids. I squinted slightly and standing over me was a middle-aged woman trying to get my attention.

I removed my headphones so that I could hear when I could only see her lips pronouncing. She looked tired and slightly agitated as if she had something to complain about concerning me.

She stood next to me while I was still lying out on the lounge chair by the pool. She began to tell me that she was confused and disappointed in life.

"I need help with my life," she said to me.

I asked, "What's going on?"

She spilled out a long list of problems, which included her partner leaving her and her spiralling drinking problem. I found out she had been a registered physiotherapist for several years. She said the only thing she did well in life was her job and that, in spite of her anxiety and drinking, she never went to work inebriated and was committed.

"I don't know where to turn or where to go to get better," she said. "I am checking into rehab tomorrow. I don't know why I am telling you this," she continued, staring at me, confused about her own forwardness.

I pulled my towel over me, and before I could even sit up, I started asking SF Coaching questions.

"Tonight, as you sleep, before waking up to go to rehab tomorrow, a miracle happened and you found your perfect dream life, what would that look like?" I asked as I moved to a sitting position, and she sat opposite me in the next lounge chair.

She breathed deeply and stared off into the air above and behind me as if she was watching something. I remained silent. After taking a deep breath, a long description of a better life tumbled out of her mouth with many details.

"On a scale from one to ten, how close are you to seeing that dream scenario become reality?" I asked.

She smiled halfway and said, "Maybe a three."

I asked, "Why not a two? What brings you to that number?"

She began to get stronger in her countenance, and many ideas began to percolate out of her, each being interrupted by the next before she could finish each sentence. The ideas were raining on her.

She spoke for close to an hour about what she could do to get better, and all I said during that hour was, "What else?"

I asked again, "Where are you on the scale now?"

She said, "Five! No! Six! No! Wait. I am a seven."

She started to cry, and we stood together. She hugged me and stared into my eyes, saying, "I think you are an angel."

I told her that I was certainly no angel and that everything that just happened came from inside her heart.

About a week later, at the same pool, with the same woman, we met again. "So much has changed!" she exclaimed with enthusiasm.

She shared that the very next day after our initial conversation, she decided she did not need rehab. Moreover, she excitedly shared that she had received a job offer in another city. The new job came with more pay and wonderful benefits at a top hospital.

It is highly unusual in Asia for a woman to approach a man and open up about their life. Yet there was obviously a sense of urgency or importance that overcame the cultural norms. The woman was genuinely seeking help and fortunately, thanks to the SF coaching skills I was equipped with the right questions to help her make a significant difference in her life.

The Ship Broker

I was invited to a restaurant in Singapore by a friend who wanted me to meet one of his colleagues, a ship broker at his firm. As the conversation unfolded, they discussed matters that were completely beyond my comprehension. I felt out of my depth and unable to contribute anything meaningful, so I relied on my newfound friend, OSKAR coaching, to guide me through the interaction.

Wanting to engage the broker in conversation, I started by asking him about positive developments in his work. He responded with concerns about new projects and challenges, using terminology that was unfamiliar to me.

Nevertheless, I persisted with OSKAR's support and asked him to imagine returning to the office after our lunch and discovering that something miraculous had occurred, resolving all his issues.

He took a moment to reflect and then shared his vision of what such a scenario would look like. Although I struggled to grasp the details, I remained present, listening attentively curious about his current proximity to that desired reality, I inquired about his confidence level on a scale from one to ten. He responded, "I'm at about a four."

Surprised by his response, I asked, "Why not a three? What factors contribute to your rating of four?" Encouraged by my repeated prompts of "What else?" he delved into a lengthy explanation, exploring various aspects of his situation. Eventually, he turned to his friend and remarked, "I can see why you spend time with this guy."

This impromptu coaching session taught me that one doesn't need to be a subject matter expert in ship broking to coach a ship broker.

An important cultural value in Asia is that of modesty and humility. It is not the cultural norm to share what you are doing well in an effusive way. The SF approach while focusing on identifying a client's strengths and resources, does so through gentle but persistent questioning, asking only about what a client has done already. We respect wherever they put themselves on the scale, and are not trying to convince them to be higher. Just acknowledging where they are and asking for lots of details about what got them there. Paying attention to how the conversation was resonating and being attentive to cultural cues, there was a moment that opened up that allowed the SF coaching conversation to take root and produce an important yield.

Final Reflections

Accidental SF coaching has become an unexpected and cherished part of my life. It has boosted my confidence and ability to assist others in ways I never thought possible.

In fact, I have come to prefer the spontaneity of accidental coaching over planned and orchestrated sessions. It has shown me that SF principles equip us with skills to become better individuals, friends, and family members. We all have a natural inclination to be helpful, which is one of the reasons I became a minister – I genuinely love helping people. SF coaching has empowered me to fulfil that role more effectively.

As a missionary with awareness about Asian culture and the nuances of transcultural communications, I often have to be very careful about how not to 'step on toes' and become too American in my approach. Although I have become quite adept at this, I find that the SF approach has enhanced my ability to do this. Because of its client-based observational method I have been able to avoid a lot of my past issues of becoming overly western in the way I express my ideas, simply by reason of the fact that the SF approach does not require me to speak much. Therefore, because we listen to the words of the client and respect what is said from their cultural frame of reference, the client is honoured with a comforting space both emotionally and culturally.

So, if you were to ask me, "What's better?" my answer would unequivocally be learning SF coaching has made a powerful and everlasting impact in my life. It was one of the best decisions I ever made.

Reference

Jackson, P. Z., & McKergow, M. (2007). *The solutions focus: Making coaching and change simple* (2nd ed.). Nicholas Brealey.

28   Divine Outcomes

Solution Focused Coaching in Spiritual Contexts

Dennis Welch

Introduction

The Solution Focused (SF) approach is practiced in a multitude of environments – counselling, coaching, education, and medicine. It is employed for health, in the workplace, hobbies, mental well-being, and in the classroom. Beyond the external, physical, emotional, and mental facets of life, SF coaching is also being practiced for spiritual well-being all over Asia. Many ministry leaders in Asia are asking, "How can I use Solution Focused coaching in my ministries?"

SF coaching is being used in spiritual settings of practitioners, through their struggles and in their spiritual growth. It is used with individuals, couples, families, leadership teams, and larger groups. This chapter will explore the practice of SF coaching in ministerial settings and spiritual contexts with examples from practitioners in Asian Christian ministry.

A Couple Wants Something Better

A Christian couple in China seeks help with a struggle within their marriage, seeking to walk a better path together. They engage a leader in their church who has been trained as an SF coach. They begin the session with a prayer, seeking guidance from God. Through this dependence on God and through the masterful questions of the coach, a way forward begins to emerge in the coaching session.

Coaching For Excellence

A teacher at a Cambodian Christian Elementary School has a contracted role to discipline the children as needed, to support the students' growth. The SF coach facilitates a process whereby the teacher can identify and leverage their resources, strengths, skills, positive past experiences, and their faith in God to discover a way forward. Together, they co-create solutions for the teacher to help the children at the school and provide a sense of peace for the client. Examples of SF questions used during the session included the following: "What might you be saying or doing when you are honouring God in your

DOI: 10.4324/9781003431480-36

work?"; "How does your faith in God make a difference in how you go about your work?"; What have you learned that is useful here?"; "When you apply this at the school, what difference will that make?"; "As a Christian educator, in what positive ways might your instruction of the students differ from other educators?"; and "How would those things make a difference to the children?"

A transcript from a session with an individual coaching client in Cambodia shows how the SF questions can be combined with a focus on the spiritual context of the client.

Case Example

Coach: What are your best hopes from our session today?

Veasna: I would like to focus on forgiveness. I know someone who is in a leadership position who has done something wrong to me and others. I'm really wrestling with forgiving him for this behaviour because his response to me when I tried to discuss it with him was arrogance, uncaring, and inflexibility.

Coach: Let's suppose that you forgive him, what difference would that make for you?

Veasna: I'm not sure. I suppose I really have to feel it in my heart. No longer harbouring feelings of anger toward the situation, and my own conscience could feel freer.

Coach: So the anger would be gone, and your conscience would be freer. What might you be feeling instead of anger?

Veasna: I would feel like it was a wrong thing for him to do but we all make mistakes. Even though he did something wrong and won't back down, I need to let it go and move on. I would be at peace about this whole affair. The difficult thing is the point I made about him being a leader. He set a bad example for those who witnessed this chastening of another person. I feel he has a higher responsibility about how he should act. Then, there is the way he responded when I tried to chat with him about it. He was rude, arrogant, uncaring, and unwilling to listen to or consider another point of view. Even if I forgive him for what he did to this man and for the example he gave to the others, as far as I know he still has the same character, and the others still remember.

Coach: So, you would like to have peace about all of that. Forgiveness, a freer conscience and letting go of anger. Is that right?

Veasna: Yes! Absolutely!

Coach: What makes this important to you?

Veasna: Well, God created us to do better than this toward each other. One of His commands to us is for us to forgive one another. It's a big deal to me. God stresses this as a path to peace and love –

something I strongly desire. By not forgiving this guy I'm missing out on those and I'm not being the kind of guy he created me to be. Also, at the end of the day, there is benefit for myself and others if I have a relationship with him.

Coach: What else makes this important to you?

Veasna: I'm also a leader. It burdens my conscience to be this guy who on the one hand did the right thing by addressing this with this leader, yet on the other hand, can't forgive him. It doesn't set the kind of example I want to show others, especially my kids and those I lead.

Coach: I'm curious if you might like to explore how this all connects with your faith.

Veasna: Yes, of course. My belief is that God really wants the best for me. He has given me His teachings to make my life better, especially concerning relationships and how we all interact together. He has given all His children, those who put their trust and faith in Him His Holy Spirit to dwell within them for making these changes in how we see others, interact with others, and help others on life's journey. I know He is ready for me to let go and make this change toward forgiveness.

Coach: Do you mind if I ask you an unusual question?

Veasna: Not at all.

Coach: It might take some imagination. Is that okay?

Veasna: Okay.

Coach: Today, after our session you go about your day in the usual way, doing the usual things. In the evening you go to bed and you fall fast asleep. While you are sleeping, unbeknownst to you a miracle happens. When you wake up, what might be the first small thing you notice to tell you, "Hey, there must have been a miracle?"

Veasna: I don't know. I suppose I would have a clear conscience about this and would be at peace in my heart, but maybe I wouldn't notice this as it should be the norm. Maybe it would occur to me if something reminded me of this issue from before. I think, taking this a step further would be whether to initiate friendly, occasional communications with this guy, perhaps even starting with a letter of forgiveness.

Coach: You might consider contacting this guy. You would feel normal concerning inner peace and a clear conscience. Did I get that correct?

Veasna: Right!

Coach: What difference would all of this make?

Veasna: I think it would make me stronger in spirit. Also, I think I would have set a better example for anyone who knows the situation.

Coach: What might your wife notice?

Veasna: I'd tell her everything ... about the situation which she already knows, about the miracle, and about how I'm feeling. So, she would notice through our discussion of it during early morning coffee time together.

Coach: What difference might this make to her?

Veasna: I think she would honour and respect me more. She knows how much this situation angered me. She also believes what he did to be wrong. Yet, when she knows that I have forgiven him it might somehow be helpful to her.

Coach: What difference would that make for you if she respected and honoured you even more?

Veasna: It would increase her confidence in me as a father and husband, walking in the teachings of Jesus. Of course, that would be great for me too.

Coach: What difference would that make in your relationship with Jesus?

Veasna: I think he would smile on me and think something like, "Well done!" Also, trusting that He played an important role in me forgiving this guy would increase my faith and trust in Him. All good!

Coach: Who else might notice this miracle had happened?

Veasna: Certainly, this guy would notice if I go beyond just forgiving in my heart and reach out to him in some way – if I decide to go that route.

Coach: What difference might this make to him?

Veasna: I don't really know. He has probably long forgotten or ignored that this ever happened. I would hope that my reaching out to him would be well received.

Coach: If you can put your readiness to forgive him on a scale of 1–10 with 1 being not ready at all and 10 being completely ready, where would you be on this scale?

Veasna: 6

Coach: What brings you to a 6?

Veasna: Well, our discussion today has helped. I know the right thing to do is to forgive. I know that is what God wants for me. I know I would be supported in this on all fronts.

Coach: What do you think God wants for you in this situation?

Veasna: That I forgive him and dwell in His peace. He is the judge of these things not me and this guy will answer to Him about it. I'll also answer for my part – forgiveness or not. I know it's important on an emotional and spiritual level, but I haven't gotten there yet. What we've chatted about today has given me some clarity. My faith seems to be an important key here. If I truly trust God's Spirit at work in me, I should expect to be moving closer to forgiveness. Wow! That seems important here. I'm going to need to dwell on that, even pray about that.

Coach: What connection if any do you see between our topic today and prayer?

Veasna: Well, I don't think I've prayed about this much in the last few years. I haven't really talked to God about it. I'm not sure what all that might mean, but I'm sure He is ready to help me through this. When I think about all God, through Jesus has already done for me and yet, He is still willing to do more to help me to overcome this hurdle.

Coach: Might I go with the metaphor of a hurdle a little bit?

Veasna: Sure.

Coach: Okay, so you're on the track, the gun sounded and you took off running. The finish line is ahead, the place where peace and a free conscience dwell. With you is the Spirit of God, ready and waiting to assist you. Within you is all the training you've received from the teachings of Jesus. As you approach the finish line, what might you be considering to make that leap up and over?

Veasna: Prayer. I would pray. Not only that I would make it over, but that I would be doing so for the right motivations as a child of God. I might even need to pause to pray about this.

Coach: What else might help you get over this hurdle and move you up the scale a little?

Veasna: Talking with you today has helped. Thinking about my relationship with God is important too. So, maybe if I work to keep my mind in a more spiritual place I could find that initial push to go up and over.

Coach: Thinking back to that scale, what number is good enough for the coming days or weeks?

Veasna: I guess an 8 would be okay. Something that represented what has to happen in my heart first. If it never goes past that point that might be okay. At least that's how I'm thinking about it today.

Coach: What support if any might you need in this?

Veasna: Really, I think all of that is already available to me in my God and my family.

Coach: That's wonderful we've covered a lot of ground today. Might it be helpful to share what new insights have emerged for you during our discussion today?

Context Matters

Cultural and contextual nuances that must be considered here is that the coach may or may not be of the same background and worldview as the coachee. Working in Asian contexts one must frequently consider "face" or "saving face," a dynamic where one should never embarrass the other. Therefore, this must be considered in crafting powerful questions. For example, note the difference between "What might God think about that?" that could be perceived as containing an element of judgement and "What might God notice?" as a way to explore what changes might be happening for the client. Subtle differences in question-wording can make a significant difference in how the coachee receives the question. Alternatively partnering to ask "how would you like to explore God's role in your life?" allows a client to have control of the coaching process and how much of their faith to bring into the discussion.

Another consideration is language. When the coach, coachee, or both are using a language other than their first or heart language, the words chosen may not translate so well. Words like "miracle," "hope," and others may not have a direct translation or even exist in another language and culture. Therefore, care must be taken to choose alternative words, re-craft the question, or select a different line of questioning that resonates with the client and supports them in moving towards their preferred future.

The wonderful thing about the SF approach is that it is respectful and honouring of a client's frame of reference. By creating a safe and trusting environment and utilising what the coachee brings to the session and focusing on where they want to go, the approach works well no matter the cultural setting or context.

Final Thoughts

With powerful questions and empathetic, attentive listening, coaches pave the road for a better future, walking with the client on the journey. The action steps and changes that are co-created in a coaching session provide strong personal agency for the client to leave the session and begin moving toward their desired outcome.

SF coaching shines brightly for its focus on the solution, not the problem. SF coaching assumptions honour and respect the client as the expert on their own life, its challenges, and celebrations. Furthermore, having those SF assumptions as a part of the coaching mindset of the coach makes the Solution Focused approach a good fit for Christian coaching. Together, within a Christian, SF coaching session, the results of this co-creative process are truly divine outcomes.

Reflection Exercise

We end with some questions to consider what has been useful and how you might use these ideas in your setting.

What are the benefits of employing SF coaching in spiritual contexts that are emerging for you as you read this chapter?

What differences could these examples and concepts make in your coaching?

What sparkling moments shine the strongest?

What would a small step look like for you in taking these ideas forwards?

Section 9

Career Coaching

29 Solution Focused Career Coaching

Through Envisioning the Perfect World

Joyce Wing Tung Tse

Introduction

Over the past 6 years at OMRON, expediting the development of our talents and establishing a robust talent pipeline has become the focal point of our talent strategy. Like many companies, we face the challenge of nurturing a diverse pool of successors for critical positions on both regional and global scales. While we have been successful in attracting exceptional talents who are passionate experts in their respective roles, we continue to grapple with the task of unleashing their full potential, strengthening their mindset, and cultivating their vision for higher leadership positions.

This chapter describes the development of the OMRON APAC Development Centre. It outlines the power of the Solution Focused (SF) approach to career coaching and illustrates the model with examples of how it has helped two talents in the Asia Pacific region gain clarity about what they want for their career. The chapter explains how the company aims to expand this even further, to help more talents to be ready for higher positions, faster and sooner and inspire the next generation, to surpass even their most ambitious dreams.

Development of the OMRON APAC Development Centre

As an effort to develop our talents at OMRON, we have meticulously curated a comprehensive suite of leadership programmes. These programmes aim to facilitate the learning of essential management skills and foster a strategic and growth-oriented leadership mindset in our talents across all job levels, through skill-based training and experiential learning. While this approach has yielded positive outcomes in empowering talents to advance in their careers, the challenge remains as to what more can we do to speed up the career growth of our talents. How can we prepare talents to be ready for higher positions, faster and sooner?

The idea of establishing the OMRON APAC Development Centre came from an observation I had from conversations with our participants in leadership programmes. Most of our participants, even as top talent, do not

DOI: 10.4324/9781003431480-38

have a clear idea of what their career aspirations are. As a result, it is difficult to actively plan what will help move them a step closer to that goal. Some possible reasons for this could be the lack of understanding of the importance of career planning and how to go about doing that or the possible tendency of being less inclined to communicating one's preferences directly and openly, which may be linked to our cultural context (Carteret, 2010). In my personal opinion, talents from an Asian cultural background may tend to shy away from the idea of sharing their goals, or be more hesitant to do so, thinking that being vocal about their career dreams would be frowned upon by others as being overly confident with one's abilities or impractical to achieve.

The aim of the APAC Development Centre is to provide a safe and invigorating space for these talents to reflect deeply on their career. Through a series of coaching conversations that are non-judgemental, encouraging, and free, the focus is on how they would like to work towards their future career aspirations. It is an opportunity for them to consider their preferences, what is important and valuable to them, and how they would like to live their professional lives. The objective is that participating talents will leave the centre with a clear vision of their career goals for the upcoming years, and they will be empowered in their career with a concrete Individual Development Plan to actively work towards achieving those goals. Like drawing a map that points towards a destination, developing talents is a long-term journey that requires time and intentional steps. Through continuous engagement and monitoring of talents, we can also identify suitable development opportunities such as overseas assignments and global projects to further expedite their development. In the long run, the OMRON APAC Development Centre plays a strategic role in changing our development approach from being transactional to being more transformational, proactive and sustainable.

While the objective of the OMRON APAC Development Centre is clear, it can be challenging to materialise. With this in mind, the systematic and process-oriented approach of SF coaching is a good fit in guiding people's exploration of a large topic effectively, helping talents in articulating their thoughts one step at a time. The SF coaching conversation follows a clear process called the OSKAR model (Jackson & McKergow, 2007). This model allows the conversation to place a strong emphasis on finding solutions for the future rather than channelling too much energy into the root causes of a problem and the past. The conversation is positive and forward-looking. For an open topic like career planning, this guided approach is useful in dissecting the subject and helping the talent come to a concrete conclusion step by step.

Starting the initiative small, we piloted two batches of people with a small number of coaching slots for talents from one of our leadership programmes. These participants were provided with a brief description of what to expect from the initiative and what kind of help they would receive if they chose to enrol. We were intentional in choosing an enrolment approach to the initiative as this can only be beneficial if the talent is open and willing to grow in the conversations. The standard duration of a coaching relationship would last for about 6 months.

Setting the Scene

There was a short briefing session with each talent to explain the framework of the coaching process and expected conduct of the coach. One of the most important codes of conduct as an internal career coach is to commit to full confidentiality of the conversation. Our priority is to provide a safe space for the talent to bring their most authentic self to the conversation, without fear that what they share may be made known to their supervisors or the company. Once a mutual agreement is established, the coaching conversation could begin.

Despite the intent of the Development Centre, it is still critical to establish a mutual goal for the coaching session. While most of the talents chose the goal of making plans for their career, there have been times when the talent had a more burning topic to discuss and wanted to keep the topic of career planning for later sessions. Occasionally, talents may go beyond reflecting on their work and move into their personal life, making connections between their career and their life journey so far.

Starting the Coaching Process

The start of the coaching process is usually the toughest. Most talents enter the room for their first coaching conversation with an air of awkwardness, unfamiliar with having conversations focusing solely on themselves, rather than their work tasks or surroundings. Many commented on how strange it felt to have to talk about themselves.

To ease them into the conversation, I would find out more about their current role in the company, their likes, and dislikes about it, their passion, successes, and lessons learned so far. The main objective here was to provide them with time and space for self-reflection on their current position. The belief that every talent comes with existing capabilities and meaningful experiences or "Know-How" in the OSKAR model helps set a positive tone to the conversation, making it easier for talents to kick-start the reflective process without focusing solely on negativity and what they lack. The perspective that everyone is already equipped with "Know-How" that led them to their current successes is particularly helpful in building better self-awareness and confidence to move towards a positive outcome.

In one of my conversations with Melvin, he came to be aware that most of the time, he had taken more of a "go with the flow" approach with his career. For example, he shared how he decided to return to his previous work through his positive working relationship with his ex-boss or took up an offer as internal IT personnel from being an external partner to the company after it was made available to him several times.

This initial step of self-reflection provides a great opportunity to build trust and rapport by listening attentively and allowing moments of silence to happen. Coaching is about giving the talents full control over the conversation and co-creating a space he or she is comfortable with. Melvin's sharing is evidence of how the positive note to the conversation and being comfortable in this personal space allows talents to be free in making cross-references in their life experiences and sharing them readily, even if the enlightenment may be deemed to be socially less desirable.

Envisioning the Future

The next step in the conversation is to have the talent envision their aspiration and establish a career goal with a specific direction, role, and timeline. This is one of the toughest parts of the conversation. Given the practical and humble nature of our talents, they tend to shy away from the idea, fearful that being vocal about their career dreams would be frowned upon by others as being inappropriate, or overly confident with one's abilities.

A very powerful tool in the OSKAR model that I find useful in achieving this objective is the O or Outcome step. This is where we explore the outcome or future perfect that the client wants. One example of a question is, "Suppose you envision yourself in an ideal scenario or perfect world, where would you like to see yourself in your career in the next 5–10 years?" In combination with the self-reflection that has taken place earlier on in the conversation as a practical context, this question encourages the talents to put together a rich image of a desired career outcome that they are passionate about. I ask them what difference it would make when they are at this point in their career – what they would be noticing about themselves, and what it would look and feel like to be in that scenario. We can then use this to explore what they would like more of that transcends a specific role, e.g. confidence, clarity, or feeling empowered. By exploring the details of what they would be noticing when they have more confidence, this means we can both focus on making steps in the short term in their current role, which will help them feel happier overall and prepare them for the larger change in role in the future.

Audrey, a highly reflective talent with a great sense of self-awareness, came to an image of becoming a regional manager in her function in the next 2 years. In sharing this image, she provided a detailed description of what a regional manager would look like, how her current supervisor has inspired her to this aspiration, and why achieving this is important to her, to grow into a more confident person with more personal success.

The open invitation in the question allows talents freedom in their reflection. In my conversation with Melvin, he was candid in sharing many of his observations within the company and the trends in his industry. His image of an ideal career aspiration was a role that has yet to exist in the company. Citing several personal observations of the changes in the industry and the world in recent years, he was certain that it is an essential role for the future. With consideration of his attributes, he was keen to pursue that in the next 10 years. This bold image is a great example of how the future-oriented nature of the question encourages reflection that is borderless and creative. It is always a joy to see the light on the talents' faces when they form a clear image of their best hope for their careers, enlightened by a new possibility.

Action Steps Towards the Future Perfect

At this point, once talents have successfully established their career aspirations, we then build on the image of their career aspirations by identifying important details of these roles such as a clear job description, requirements, and qualifications. Through partnering with the talent we discuss what action steps (the A of the OSKAR model) they might like to try or what they would like to find out more about. This may involve researching the details of the job positions they are interested in. Another good source of information could be by observing the experiences of people who are already in those positions internally or externally. This gives talents a clearer image of the expectations of those positions and what potential development gaps they may need to work on to progress towards the goal.

Another part of the action steps may come from exploring what they would be noticing when there is more of the passion, confidence, or whatever else that they described in the picture of their desired future, even while still in their current role. This allows for hope and motivation for change in the present, alongside preparing for a different role in the future.

Scaling

One of the principles of SF coaching is the emphasis on self-assessment and taking one small step at a time in progressing towards the goal. Talents are asked to rate where they are now on a scale of 1–10. The 10 on the scale is always the positive goal that they are working towards. Talents are encouraged to reflect on how they got to that number, based on their strengths, and their accomplishments so far. With an image of what their current state looks like, talents will then be asked what would a small step closer to their career goal look like. The idea of dissecting a long development journey into one step at a time is powerful in encouraging practical actions to be formed. It helps to ease their anxiety over the need to grow into the 10-point straight away and build their confidence in taking immediate action in this challenging development journey. This makes the development process more realistic, achievable, and less uncertain.

In Audrey's development plan, she identified gaps in strategic thinking and communication skills such as negotiation. She highlighted how having a larger scope of regional exposure, and potentially expanding her responsibilities to specific countries, would be beneficial for her to develop these skills. She also recognised that building her level of confidence would be a catalyst for her overall development.

Final Reflections

The OMRON APAC Development Centre has achieved small successes in facilitating career growth. With these in mind, the long-term vision of the Centre is to develop and engage a substantial pool of talent in Asia where their development is closely monitored, facilitated, and prioritised. Ultimately, through a more proactive approach to development, we will prepare our talents to be ready for higher positions, faster and sooner.

Through the practical and process-oriented approach of SF coaching, we envision cultivating a culture of openness where discussion of preferences and dreams is more acceptable and encouraged, and more talents can be motivated and supported as they pursue their ambitions. Together, we hope to inspire the next generation, encouraging them to surpass even their most ambitious dreams, beyond their wildest imaginations.

References

Carteret, M. (2010, October). *Cultural values of Asian patients and families.* Dimensions of culture. https://www.dimensionsofculture.com/2010/10/cultural-values-of-asian-patients-andfamilies/#:~:text=One%20must%20never%20bring%20dishonor,and%20elders%20is%20critically%20important

Jackson, P. Z., & McKergow, M. (2007). *The solutions focus: Making coaching and change simple* (2nd ed.). Nicholas Brealey.

30   Career Coaching Sessions Using the OSKAR Model

Julie Samuel

Introduction

This chapter will highlight the usefulness of Solution Focused (SF) coaching with clients as a career coach, and specifically how the framework known as the OSKAR model (Jackson & Mckergow, 2007), led to more impactful sessions. This approach facilitated clients having *aha* moments in resolving their workplace challenges, planning their career progression, managing workplace relationships, and improving work performance. It also contributed to clients gaining insights on how to achieve business results and gain new insights on career options.

My clients are mostly based in Asia and their countries of origin include those from Asia, Europe, and America. I have found that in career coaching, the OSKAR model seems to transcend cultural barriers. If and when cultural issues come up, the questions 'What do we need to keep in mind as we discuss this?' or 'What do I need to be aware of that is important to you?' can be used to make sure any important factors from the client's national, organisational, family, or social culture can be included in the session.

I describe what I mean by career coaching and outline the OSKAR model before illustrating this using examples from several different areas of career coaching in the Asian context. My hope is to encourage other career coaches to try the OSKAR model in their career coaching sessions.

What Is Career Coaching?

Career coaching has different aspects including working with an individual to help reach their career goals, help them with their career planning, career changes, and other career-related decisions. Career coaches are often expected to be experts in career planning, resume building, interviewing, and negotiating skills.

The SF approach to career coaching I utilise focuses on exploring how clients can reach their career goals, explore how to overcome their stress points, address corporate team relationship management issues, and help with career-switching.

DOI: 10.4324/9781003431480-39

I do this through exploring clients' strengths, successes, and resources as accessing this important information often leads to breakthrough moments with clients. Most clients are surprised to discover they have the capability and answers within them already.

What Is OSKAR?

The OSKAR model refers to the acronym:

Outcome (O)
Scaling (S)
Know-How (K)
Affirm and **A**ction (A) and
Review (R) as stages in the SF coaching process (Jackson & McKergow, 2007).

The beauty of the OSKAR model is that it does not have to be used in a linear way so S doesn't have to happen after O and the time spent on each area is flexible. The stories below will illustrate these steps in more detail. A table is included at the end of this chapter with examples of questions you can ask.

OSKAR Helps Resolve Workplace Challenges

When faced with an experienced technical project consultant trying to resolve complex project issues that transcended across continents and time zones, neither he nor I initially thought we could find a solution within the hour we had together. We did not share these doubts with each other but just released the brake, engaged the gears, and went with the flow.

In this case, time spent on the O was short as he knew exactly what he wanted as his outcome – how to deliver the project deliverables given the challenges he was facing.

The *aha* moment happened when a question related to his Know-How was asked: 'I'm pretty sure this is not the first time you're facing a challenge in your work. You're a very experienced and senior project consultant. How did you resolve one of your previous more complex project challenges?'

He thought about it for a short while and recalled a challenge he had faced in the past and recounted what he did. He suddenly stopped talking and started writing down step by step what he needed to do to overcome the issue he was currently facing. His facial expression changed from being stressed to being happy. He was surprised that the answer had always been within him and said he now felt confident to execute the plan he had come up with.

Another project director was facing a situation where he had to communicate a very difficult message to his client. Our session was just a few days before his meeting with the stakeholders.

Despite my initial doubts about whether the session could be helpful to him, I stuck with OSKAR. By trusting the process once again we came through successfully. The client was surprised that the answer had always been within him – the K of OSKAR. I asked 'I'm sure this is not the first time you're facing such a situation' to which he answered 'no'. He went on to share a previous occasion. I asked him how what he did then to resolve the issue was related to his current challenge. That's when his *aha* moment happened. He moved from sitting on his chair to leaning forward towards the computer screen (it was an online session) with his hand on his chin and his head tilted upwards. He got his answer.

In both cases, the clients mentioned what they needed to consider in terms of organisational culture as they explored possible ways of resolving their work issues. They talked about needing to be sensitive to team dynamics and the expectations of key individual stakeholders as well as the organisation's management. In this way, they were able to construct a solution that made sense in their cross-cultural context within Asia.

Cultural Reflections

These Asian male clients both worked in industries where women are a minority, especially in leadership roles. While this may have been partly my perception, it seemed as if they wondered how an Asian female coach who had never worked in these industries could possibly partner with them in a coaching conversation on complex issues and find a solution in just one session.

What the OSKAR model succeeded to showcase is that solutions can be achieved in a very short span of time even with complex organisational and cultural issues and hopefully challenge any biases such clients may have towards their coach or coaching.

OSKAR in Career Progression Conversations

During conversations around career progression, clients often know they want something different but can't pinpoint what about their current role makes them uncomfortable enough to toy with the idea of continuing their career with another organisation.

Confidence Gained

When I asked a non-Asian client what made him happy in his previous roles (the K in OSKAR), he went silent. As he recalled them, he sat up (rather than slouching) and tilted his head upwards. As he narrated what made him happy, he realised the role he was in had evolved to something different from what it initially was. Our session helped him to be more confident about his decision to leave his role in one Asian country to enter a new role in an industry he was passionate about located in another Asian country.

Clarity Gained

With another client, our sessions gave her a greater clarity on what her career values are. When exploring the resources available to help her consider where to move to she came up with talking to one mentor about entrepreneurship and another about the area of work she was passionate about. She also decided to ask her friends for job referrals.

As we explored the support she needed to pursue her career goals, she realised that support from her family members was very important. It was a moving conversation as it got deeper and more personal. Through reviewing what was useful to her from our discussion (the R part of the OSKAR model) it enabled her to realise that her career progression was impacted by her family relationships and social culture.

The Asian cultural context this client is in made that conversation with her family more challenging as the area of work she is passionate about is currently not a conventional career route. Our coaching conversation helped her to think about how that conversation could take place in a way that respected both her passion and personal values and her family's concerns. During a follow-up session, she shared that she was able to have a good conversation with her family.

Spiralling Stopped

A client looking to move to another organisation after more than five years in her current organisation said that she would know if she had a useful session together if she felt less ashamed of herself in her current role. She initially focused on her unmet desires and expectations and began to spiral downwards emotionally.

The O part of the OSKAR framework uses questions such as 'What would you like instead?' followed by 'What difference would that make?' and 'Who would notice?'. These questions helped the client define a more positive outcome they can work towards rather than something they are trying to move away from. Exploring the outcome the client wanted stopped her from spiralling further downwards. Instead, she began to move forward.

Hope Gained

When working in an SF way, we pay great attention to language and the assumptions that words and questions contain. One SF tool – the miracle question – asks clients to imagine in detail what their preferred future looks like. When asked this question, one client said '*if* the miracle happens'. I gently interrupted and asked what she would notice '*when* the miracle happens'. The client went silent and became emotional. Then she took a moment to compose herself. When she started talking again she sounded a little more hopeful about her situation. During a follow-up session, the client shared this interruption had shifted her perspective and made her hopeful that it would indeed happen, and she became more engaged in working towards it.

New Option Discovered

Another client wanted to explore his options as he was about to leave his current role. He had previously made a career switch and had been in his current role for about five years. He did not want to return to his old role and had the idea that he would continue with his current role but in a different organisation. However, he was struggling to land suitable roles.

Our sessions revolved around discovering himself, his strengths, motivated skills (those he was both competent in and enjoyed using), career values, and personal values. He said he enjoyed both his previous and current roles. He wasn't sure what options he had for the future.

The turning point was when I asked him to scale his interest in the two roles. When he put a number to them it became clearer that his motivation was more in relation to his first role rather than his second role. Yet he was also clear he did not want to return to this, so felt he was in a dilemma.

He explored roles that would use his motivated skills and where his experience in the industry of his second role would help. He had recently received a job offer that met the right criteria. He also started exploring a third option of setting up his own business while he took time to reskill himself to enter into a new and advancing space.

The OSKAR coaching approach helped this client to discover his strengths and the S part of the model helped him clarify the career direction he wanted to explore.

OSKAR Helps Change Perspective

A client new to coaching came to his first session and repeatedly used these phrases: 'I'm not good enough', 'It's my fault', and 'I messed things up for everybody'.

We started by understanding what 'good enough' meant. I then asked an exception question to access his Know-How: 'When are times you already felt 'good enough'?' He spent some time thinking then said he did in his previous role where he had a strong handle on the projects under his purview. We were then able to continue our conversation from a different perspective.

Another way of accessing Know-How and seeing things from a different perspective can be to ask a client what advice they would give to a friend if they were in a similar situation. This client responded by saying 'there's no way to win this type of situation'; 'It about small wins that amount to something'; 'It's better to do more things than less as the chances of success are higher'.

I reflected these back to the client and asked how they may be useful to him. The client listened intently and then said he wanted to say these statements to himself daily. He wasn't sure if it would work but wanted to try it for a week. I affirmed him (the A of OSKAR) on his decision to try this as an experiment and notice what difference it might make.

When he returned after a week, he appeared calmer. When I asked what had been better since we last met (the R of OSKAR) he said the previous week's exercise of contemplating the truth of his work helped him remember the emotional impact his work has on people. The idea of not being good enough seemed to fade as a result.

In a competitive Asian work culture where individuals seem to need to fight for attention for recognition or promotion quickly, the Know-How part of the OSKAR model seems to be able to change their perspective of 'not being good enough'.

Final Reflections

I learnt over time that it is not necessary to use all the elements of the OSKAR model in every session. When there is more than one session, the review (R) part of the model becomes more prominent. Being curious about what has been better since the previous session allows the client to review progress and what has worked or what they have discovered. Following this exploration, asking what outcome (O) they want from the current session helps them decide whether to continue with the previous goal or start on a new topic. Scaling (S) questions are very versatile and can be used several times during the same session to help give greater clarity over several aspects of the conversation, e.g. motivation, confidence, and progress.

I have found that the questions 'What difference does that make?' and 'Who would notice the difference?' help clients feel more motivated to move forward, as the importance of their goals becomes clearer. Spending a significant amount of time exploring the Know-How (K) part can be very useful to help clients get in touch with all their existing resources and strengths and as shown in the examples above often leads to *aha* moments where they discover they already know what to do.

Asking towards the end of sessions 'what kind of support' they need often starts them to think of the support they would need from their workplace or family or clarify that they feel able to move forward on their own.

A Baby Step Forward

I hope career coaches using other approaches are inspired by the stories in this chapter to experiment with the OSKAR model to see what difference this would make to their practice. For existing SF coaches, who may have been reluctant to try career coaching for fear of not having enough expertise in this area, I hope you will also walk away with some new ideas. Table 30.1 gives examples of questions you can ask.

Table 30.1 SF career coaching questions using the OSKAR framework

Outcome	• If we had a successful session today, what would that look like?
	• What are your best hopes from our session today?
Scaling	• On a scale of one to 10 with 10 being 'very confident' and one being 'not confident', how confident are you that this resume we have worked on together will land you an interview?
	• How confident are you for tomorrow's interview?
	• These questions can be followed by: 'What made you give it that score and not lower?' 'What else?'
	• What would one point higher look like?
Know-How	• How did you land the current role you are in?
	• How did you agree to the best salary you agreed on in the past?
	• What knowledge and skills do you already have? / have you developed in this job? How did you do that?
Affirm and Action	• It looks like you understood the essential elements of a resume! Your revised one has improved including reducing it to X number of pages and removing personal data.
	• I can see a lot of time and effort has been put into this revised version of your resume. How did you do it?
	• Amazing! Your interview skills have improved a lot. You are more confident when answering the questions and you fidget a lot less now!
	• What small step can you take after our discussion today? Something you can do tomorrow or in the next few days?
Review	• What was the most useful part for you in our discussion today?
	• What is your key takeaway from our session today?
	• What has been better since we last met?

Reference

Jackson, P. Z., & McKergow, M. (2007). *The solutions focus: Making coaching and change simple* (2nd ed.). Nicholas Brealey.

Section 10

Novel Applications of Solution Focused Coaching

31 Using Visual Language with Solution Focused Coaching

Chee Seng Cha

Introduction

In this chapter, I will share a case study that demonstrates the transformative power of utilising the Solution Focused (SF) coaching approach together with Chinese idioms and proverbs and the bikablo visualisation technique (bikablo, n.d.) also known as Visual Language in coaching conversation with a client. These resources help to reframe and refocus the conversation from problems to resource discovery to solution, keeping the conversation focused on the surface of the issue, rather than what underlies it. The coaching progressively turned from the state of 'indescribable' to one of 'smooth expression'. The visual notes we co-created brought the client greater clarity of her strength and the possibility of moving on to a new chapter in life, thereby giving her greater hopefulness and an improved quality of life. The case study also shows how visual notes and SF coaching intertwine to enable profound personal growth.

While English as a language medium in coaching conversations facilitates use of metaphorical language, the logograms that make up characters in Asian languages like Chinese, Japanese, and Korean serve a similar function. Many Asian cultures have visual thinking embedded in their core language. This characteristic enables people to 'talk' across language barriers, especially in situations where Chinese-speaking clients often use a mix of Mandarin and other dialects.

Case Study: Leah's Journey

Leah had been in the same job for more than 20 years after graduating from college. When she sought help, she was troubled by work, marriage and family issues, and had been grappling with a sense of stagnation and restlessness in her life. She felt stuck, unable to articulate her desires and goals, and lacked a clear vision for her future.

Leah often felt apologetic for making little progress and slowing down the coaching progress. She frequently used the expressions 难以启齿 (*meaning indescribable*) and 有口难言 (*meaning hard to say*). I assured her that 'slow-moving' is better than 'not-moving' using the Chinese proverb

DOI: 10.4324/9781003431480-41

不怕慢, 只怕站 (*meaning any movement is better than none*) as a way to reframe the coaching progress.

The initial coaching sessions with Leah were challenging as she struggled to put her thoughts and feelings into words. It was as if her emotions were trapped within her, leaving her in a state of indescribable frustration. After a few coaching sessions, Leah still appeared overwhelmed, and discussions repeatedly revolved around the problems at hand.

Recognising the Need for Reframing

One key aim in introducing the bikablo visualisation technique is to facilitate a respectful and sensitive conversation spanning multiple contexts. Leah described her troubles as 家丑不可外扬 (family shame must not be shared with outsiders (idiom)/fig. don't wash your dirty linen in public) and that was why she found it hard to articulate them and responded with 难以启齿 (*meaning indescribable*) and 有口难言 (*meaning hard to say*). Using a different way to communicate with Leah (visually and more abstractly) while respecting her privacy aimed to bypass Leah's verbal barriers and tap into her intuitive and visual thinking. The hope was to make her feel more comfortable and willing to share, thereby helpful in making progress in future coaching sessions.

I introduced her to the bikablo visualisation technique, which involved using a combination of words and simple drawings on a blank piece of paper or canvas (Figure 31.1). This technique aimed to facilitate the externalisation

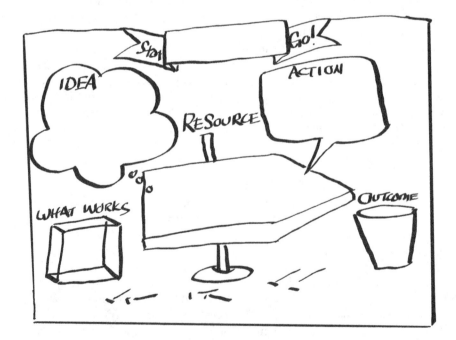

Figure 31.1 Examples of bikablo Icons (Chee Seng Cha).

of Leah's thoughts, allowing her to see and make sense of her inner world visually. At the next meeting with Leah, I introduced her to the bikablo boards, and explained their purpose and the shift in focus they intended to achieve. Visually mapping out the situation, aims to maintain a surface-level perspective allowing exploration of resources and potential solutions without getting entangled in the underlying complexities.

Using the bikablo boards, we mapped out her past and present resources, highlighting both the challenges she faced and the existing resources at her disposal. This visual representation prompted a significant shift in the conversation, as she began to identify potential solutions and resourceful approaches. The bikablo technique acted as a catalyst, enabling us to maintain a productive dialogue focused on positive outcomes rather than getting bogged down by the intricacies of the problems.

Leah was excited about the use of this approach in our subsequent coaching conversations, as she expressed that she had not looked at her life events in such a manner before and felt a sense of relief and excitement.

I also noticed that Leah communicated better in coaching sessions when they were conducted in a mix of Mandarin and Chinese dialects. I encouraged her to express things in her own way. I complimented her for utilising texts from articles, lyrics and books, which I noticed served as great resources in helping Leah express her feelings and thoughts along the coaching journey (Figure 31.2). Leah also cultivated the habit of keeping a journal, documenting her reflections and progress of her personal and professional development.

The literal English translation of this is shown below.

The greatest feature of self-consciousness is

- Control and mastery
- Frame, control, own, follow me
- Listen to own life

> I don't have creativity so I dare not let go
> Those who accuse the pain cannot create
> What is yours?
> Conscious – is mine
> I can create my new world
> Letting go is creating greater
> Start.

Language Reframe

In conjunction with the bikablo visual representation of situations, SF questions and affirmation worked well in Mandarin and Chinese dialects and were used in reframing negative connotations to more positive, future-focused ones.

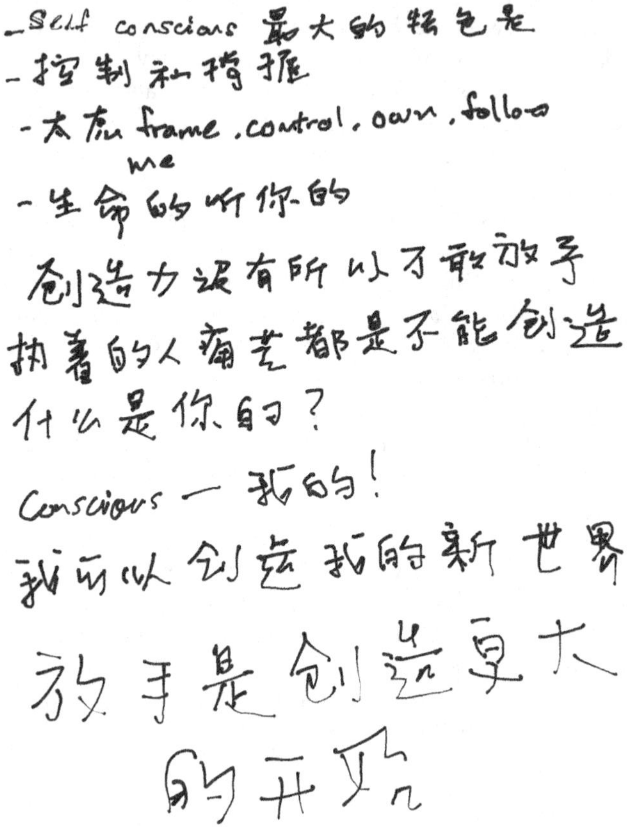

Figure 31.2 Notes Leah wrote in Session 2 (Chee Seng Cha).

Example 1

早知如此，何必当初 (I wished I knew earlier) **reframed to** 从中学习) what have I learnt)

Example 2

寻根究底 (why this happened) **reframed to** 更期待什么 (What do you hope for or want more of)

Example 3

剪不断理还乱 (it not only cannot be settled but also cannot be sorted out) **reframed to** 瞻前顧後 (to look forward and back/to consider prudently)

I complimented her for considering situations with prudence, instead of hesitation or indecisiveness.

The SF questions enabled Leah to change her perspective from 'what is' to 'what will be' and recognised her own efforts in making progress.

Timeline Reframe

Chinese is a high-context language which doesn't have time-related verb tenses (e.g. past, present, or future). Hence, clarifying a situation with Leah to put it in context and the correct timeline is needed. This was done by using the desired future or miracle question such as 'Suppose … ?' (in Mandarin 假设 …) and successful past or resource discovery questions such as 'What did you learn … ?' (in Mandarin 从中学习到 …). These questions contain presuppositions about what will happen and what had happened. In conjunction with visual symbols on the bikablo canvas, such as an arrow pointing to one direction (Figure 31.3), we could agree on which direction is the past or future.

A more organic shape, such as a path from one point to the other point (Figure 31.4), was also used to track progress (another way of scaling) and clarify where Leah wanted to go or stay in the coaching conversation. Whenever Leah decided to stay at one point on the path to explore, instead of feeling a sense of stagnation, she felt the freedom to discover or to move on as she wished. Leah was surprised that she could do this and that she was in control of how she wanted to progress, instead of feeling the need for validation for every step she took. This was also an important milestone where Leah started to sail in the coaching conversation and many actions followed.

Figure 31.3 Desired direction (Chee Seng Cha).

Figure 31.4 Example of a template co-created with Leah for coaching sessions (Chee Seng Cha).

Establishing Clarity Through Visual Notes

In our bikablo co-creation session, I encouraged Leah to kick start the exploration process on her own. Leah sat in front of the blank canvas, uncertain about where to begin. I encouraged her to let go of any judgement or preconceived notion and simply express herself freely. Slowly, she picked up a marker and started making marks on the canvas, doodling lines and shapes that held no immediate meaning.

As Leah continued to explore the canvas, I asked open-ended questions to guide her reflection and encourage deeper self-awareness. I gently probed about her strengths, her passions, and the things that brought her joy. With each question, her strokes on the canvas became more deliberate and purposeful, gradually forming a coherent representation of her thoughts (Figure 31.5).

Figure 31.5 Leah's first attempt to document thoughts on canvas on her own (Chee Seng Cha).

A translation of Figure 31.5 is below:

个案概念化 – case conceptualisation
   收集 – collect
   了解 – learn/understand
   分析 – analyse
   评估 – evaluate
   同理心 – empathy

Discovering Strengths and Possibilities

As Leah's visual notes took shape, patterns emerged, thereby revealing insights that were previously hidden from her conscious awareness. We identified her strengths, passions, and values as they were visually expressed on the canvas.

The process of externalising her thoughts and emotions allowed her to view her life from a new perspective, offering a fresh lens through which she could explore her possibilities.

Together, we delved into her visual creation, exploring the connections between various elements and discussing potential paths she could take in her life. As she connected the dots and made sense of her visual representation, a newfound clarity emerged. Leah began to see herself and her aspirations with a renewed sense of purpose and direction.

Discovering Hidden Gems

As the discussion unfolded, the bikablo boards revealed hidden connections and opportunities that had previously gone unnoticed. The visual aid facilitated a collaborative environment where both Leah and I could effectively brainstorm ideas and build upon each other's insights. By staying on the surface of the issue, we were able to explore uncharted territories, creatively examining resources and alternative perspectives that led to breakthrough solutions. Here are a few examples of actions Leah took as she sailed along the journey:

- Taking the initiative to seek out courses for possible career change.
- Joining multiple support groups to expand her horizon and gather resources for her journey.
- Initiating conversation with family members with clearer intention and expressing how she felt about certain situations. Leah was surprised by her courage to express and how well her conversation with family members turned out.

Embracing Solution Focused Thinking

With the help of the bikablo technique, Leah transitioned from a problem-focused mindset to an SF mindset. By collectively identifying and discussing the resources available at hand, she found herself empowered to explore new possibilities and develop actionable strategies. The visualisation technique acted as a conduit, channelling the collective energy towards resource discovery, encouraging innovative thinking, and fostering a culture of continuous improvement. Here are a few examples of outcomes Leah experienced:

- Even though she did not pursue what she learnt, a new opportunity arose in the company, and she was promoted to a new role. She was also able to implement some of the soft skills she learnt from the course upon taking on her new role.
- Leah made a few good friends from the support groups she joined. She felt supported and learnt from others how sailing through difficult times in life is less scary with friends.

- Leah's relationship with her family members improved. Tapping on family wisdom, Leah felt flowing with the system while being the captain of her own lifeless bothersome. She expressed that it was her choice to sail through the weather or wait it out. She also discovered her own safe zone whenever she felt overwhelmed by situations that she had no control of.

Reflections

Combining visual language with the SF coaching approach can yield several benefits. Firstly, visual aids can help both the coach and the client gain a clearer understanding of the client's current situation. The act of creating and discussing visual representations of the client's challenges and goals enables a deeper exploration of what the client really desires. It helps clients gain insights and perspectives that may have been previously overlooked. Visual aids also provide a tangible reference point that clients can refer back to during the coaching process, helping them stay focused and connected to their goals.

Secondly, visual language encourages creativity and innovation. By introducing visuals into coaching conversations, coaches can tap into the client's right-brain thinking, which is associated with creativity, intuition, and holistic understanding. Visual aids can spark new ideas, alternative perspectives, and innovative solutions. Clients may discover connections and patterns that were not apparent before, leading to breakthrough insights and fresh approaches to their challenges.

Moreover, visual language enhances communication and comprehension. It transcends language barriers and allows for a shared understanding between coach and client. Though words alone may fall short in expressing complex emotions or abstract concepts, visual representations can bridge the gap. Coaches can use metaphors, symbols, or diagrams to capture the essence of the client's experiences and goals, facilitating a deeper connection and empathy.

Chinese culture values balance, moderation, and harmony. We were able to take these concepts into account during the coaching process by exploring what a balanced rather than perfect solution (her words) would look like to make it more relatable and effective for Leah.

Moving Towards a New Chapter

Armed with newfound clarity, Leah embarked on the journey of crafting a new chapter in her life. The visual notes became a tangible reminder of her strengths, values, and aspirations, serving as a compass that guided her decision-making and goal-setting processes. We used SF coaching techniques to focus on her desired outcomes and develop actionable steps towards achieving them.

Over time, Leah's confidence grew, and her once indescribable frustration transformed into a smooth expression of her true self. The visual notes acted as a catalyst, providing her with a tangible representation of her progress and reminding her of her potential. With each coaching session, she gained momentum, building on her strengths and moving closer to the life she envisioned.

In my most recent catch-up with Leah, she expressed that she felt contented and fulfilled in her new chapter of life. She moved into a leadership role shortly after our coaching engagement, and a renewed relationship with a partner and family members. Despite the complexity of Leah's past situations, with the right mindset and tools at the right time, the co-creation journey was a memorable and long-lasting one. Leah continues to flourish and is creating new chapters in her life.

Conclusion

Leah's journey from a state of indescribable frustration to smooth expression exemplifies the power of visual coaching and the bikablo technique in fostering clarity, hopefulness, and improved quality of life. The combination of visual notes and SF coaching enabled Leah to transcend her verbal barriers, explore her strengths, and pave the way for a fulfilling new chapter in her life.

As coaches, we have the unique opportunity to harness the creative potential of our clients, allowing them to visualise their thoughts, emotions, and aspirations. By incorporating visual techniques like bikablo into our coaching practice, we can empower individuals to gain clarity, unlock their hidden strengths, and move forward with confidence and purpose. Leah's story serves as a testament to the transformative power of SF coaching and visual exploration, reminding us of the limitless potential that lies within each individual whom we have the privilege to coach.

Reference

bikablo (n.d.). bikablo homepage. Retrieved on October 10, 2023 from https:// bikablo.com/en/home-page/

32 Solution Focused Graphic Coaching
Unlocking Solutions with Focus and Clarity

Keisuke Taketani

Introduction

Imagination is at the heart of Solution Focused (SF) coaching, providing a transformative opportunity for individuals to "see" situations from different perspectives, "envision" possibilities, and "paint" a vivid picture of potential solutions. It is through this process of envisioning that we tap into the power of visual thinking, as the verbs "see," "envision," and "paint" become intertwined with the coaching journey. While SF coaching already encourages individuals to visualise in their mind's eye and imagine the desired outcome, the integration of visual thinking in coaching can unlock even greater potential. This innovative approach, which I call SF graphic coaching, merges the inherent power of visual thinking with the SF approach, creating a dynamic and impactful coaching experience that harnesses the strength of imagery and visual representation.

To exemplify the power of visual thinking and its ability to enhance understanding, let us consider an infographic entitled "Problem Talk versus Solution Talk" (Figure 32.1). This visual representation captures the essence of SF coaching by juxtaposing the language associated with Solution Focused conversations and problem-focused conversations. By visually displaying the distinctions between these two types of talk, the infographic illustrates how easily complex ideas and principles can be comprehended through visual means. It serves as a compelling testament to the capacity of visual thinking to simplify and clarify concepts, supporting the notion that integrating visual thinking techniques, such as those found in graphic coaching, can exponentially enhance the coaching experience.

In this chapter, we will explore the relationship between SF coaching and visual thinking, diving into the transformative nature of imagination and the power it holds in driving positive change. Drawing on both the principles of SF coaching and the foundations of visual thinking, we will uncover the potential for creating dynamic and impactful coaching experiences that tap into the wellspring of imagination and visually unlock the path to desired solutions.

DOI: 10.4324/9781003431480-42

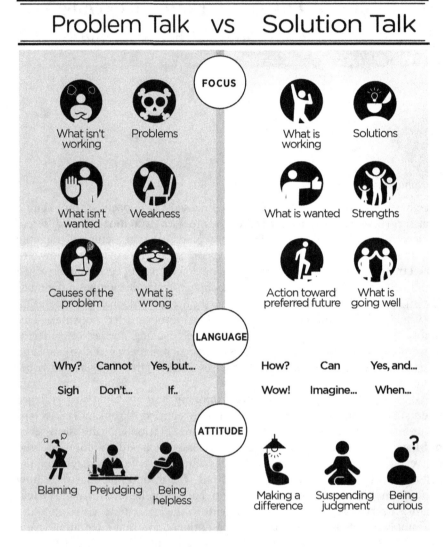

Figure 32.1 Problem talk versus solution talk (Keisuke Taketani).

What Is Solution Focused Graphic Coaching?

A blend of SF coaching and visual thinking, graphic coaching is fundamentally based on the principles and techniques of SF coaching. The process of graphic coaching aligns with the structure of SF coaching sessions. The coach establishes rapport, explores the coachee's goals and desired outcomes, and helps the coachee identify their strengths and resources. However, what sets graphic coaching apart is the incorporation of visual thinking and the use of graphic representation during the coaching session. The coach seeks permission to capture the conversation graphically, and the resulting visuals are shared and discussed in real-time with the coachee. Throughout the session, the coach uses their drawing skills to capture important points, create visual metaphors, and reflect the coachee's thoughts and solutions. The graphics serve as tangible representations that support the coachee's recall, enhance clarity, and facilitate further exploration of possibilities and potential actions.

While graphic coaching offers valuable benefits, it also places an additional burden on the coach. In addition to actively listening to the conversation, observing their body language, and carefully selecting appropriate questions, the coach must also spontaneously capture the conversation through drawings. This requires honed skills in fast drawing and multitasking, as the coach needs to attend to both the coachee's verbal and non-verbal cues while simultaneously creating visual representations. The coach must strike a balance between active engagement and the art of drawing, ensuring that both aspects contribute to the coachee's understanding and progress.

It is crucial to clarify that the graphics produced during a graphic coaching session are not intended to be elaborate or meticulously crafted artworks suitable for display. Rather, they serve as sketch-like representations – a visual extension of the coaching conversation. The emphasis is on capturing key concepts, ideas, and connections as they unfold, fostering comprehension and deepening the coachee's insights. The raw and spontaneous nature of the graphics enables the coachee to engage with the material in real time and actively contribute to the visualisation process.

Benefits of Solution Focused Graphic Coaching

SF graphic coaching offers a range of unique benefits that enhance the coaching experience and support clients in their journey towards solutions (Figure 32.2). This section will explore these benefits and their significance in helping clients gain clarity, express emotions, generate ideas, and foster creativity.

Enhanced Clarity and Solution Visualisation

Visual representations have a remarkable ability to clarify complex concepts and ideas. Compared to verbal explanations alone, visuals provide clients with a tangible and concrete representation of the solution. For example, by asking a client, "What does it look like when you are ...," and visually illustrating the desired state, clients can gain a clearer understanding of their aspirations and visualise the path forward.

Seeing the Big Picture and Making Connections

Graphic coaching enables clients to see the bigger picture and make connections between their current situation and their desired outcome. Through visual

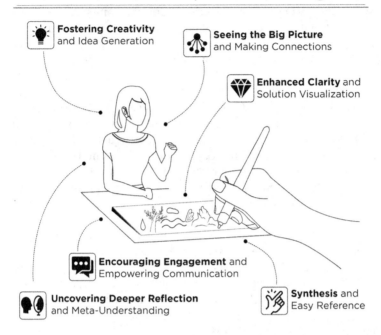

Benefits of Graphic Coaching

Fostering Creativity and Idea Generation

Seeing the Big Picture and Making Connections

Enhanced Clarity and Solution Visualization

Encouraging Engagement and Empowering Communication

Uncovering Deeper Reflection and Meta-Understanding

Synthesis and Easy Reference

Figure 32.2 Benefits of graphic coaching (Keisuke Taketani).

aids, clients can identify patterns, interdependencies, and potential obstacles. By visually mapping the journey from the present to the future, clients gain a holistic perspective that empowers them to navigate their path with increased awareness and intentionality.

Encouraging Engagement and Empowering Communication

Clients often grapple with the challenge of expressing their thoughts and emotions verbally. While this is a common experience across various cultural backgrounds, it is particularly applicable to Asian culture, where indirect and ambiguous communication styles are frequently encountered. The utilisation of visual thinking techniques offers a safe space for clients to externalise their thoughts, emotions, and ideas, fostering deeper exploration and understanding. Visuals have the unique ability to act as a shared language that transcends cultural nuances, especially in group settings with diverse cultural backgrounds. By harnessing the power of visuals, graphic coaching empowers clients to surmount communication challenges, enabling them to express themselves more clearly and participate in collaborative discussions aimed at achieving their coaching goals.

Uncovering Deeper Reflection and Meta-Understanding

The use of visuals in graphic coaching allows coaches to ask questions that might be difficult to articulate without visual aids. By pointing to specific elements in the drawing, coaches can explore relationships, emotions, paths, and uncertainties. Meta-questions, such as reflecting on the reflection itself, become accessible through the visual representation, enabling clients to dive deeper into their thoughts and gain new insights.

Fostering Creativity and Idea Generation

Graphic coaching taps into the creative potential of clients by engaging different parts of the brain. By leaving empty spaces and inviting clients to fill them, the coach creates opportunities for clients to generate more ideas and explore diverse perspectives. The blank canvas becomes a catalyst for creativity, encouraging clients to think beyond conventional solutions and unleash their imagination.

Synthesis and Easy Reference

One of the remarkable benefits of graphic coaching is the ability to summarise the coaching session in a single page. This visual synthesis provides clients with an easy reference point to recall the conversation and grasp the key outcomes. The visual representation serves as a vivid and tangible reminder of the coaching journey, enabling clients to maintain focus and continuity as they progress towards their desired solutions.

Application of Graphic Coaching

Graphic coaching, particularly in the SF context, is a relatively new field of practice, and much of it is learned through hands-on experience. Drawing from my background as a graphic facilitator and visualisation practitioner, I have gained insights that can guide those interested in applying graphic coaching ideas themselves. Here are a few practical tips based on my experience.

Coachee's Perspective

Seek confirmation from the coachee regarding the visuals you create. Recognise that drawing is subjective, and that the coach's interpretation may be reflected in the drawings. Ask the coachee if the visuals accurately capture the conversation, and be open to their suggestions for any necessary changes. To maintain neutrality, opt for simple and neutral images rather than animated characters. The purpose of visuals is to serve as a methodology for helping the coachee unlock their potential. Strive to draw like a Zen master, employing simplicity, profundity, mindfulness, and equilibrium.

Selective Drawing

Apply the same principle of SF coaching, that is, focus on drawing solutions rather than problems, and what the coachee wants rather than does not want.

Allocate more space and colours to capture the details of the solutions when the coachee discusses them. By consciously highlighting solutions, you reinforce the client's focus on the desired outcome.

Embrace Empty Space

Leave empty space on the canvas to encourage clients to fill it with their ideas. This white space serves as a source of creativity, allowing for additional insights and possibilities to emerge during the coaching session.

Erasable Materials

Select materials that are easily erasable. For digital drawings, a tablet with erasing capabilities can be a convenient option. For old-school drawings, start with a pencil and, once confirmed, add lines and colours using brush pens.

Remember it is not necessary to be a skilled artist or illustrator to practice graphic coaching effectively. Recognise that during coaching sessions, time is limited, and the focus should be on the power of the visuals to help clients clarify and focus on the solution. The quality of the drawings lies in their ability to facilitate the coachee's understanding and engagement, rather than their artistic beauty.

Case Studies

Here are three case studies to describe the practical application of graphic coaching, the power of visual thinking, and its impact on client engagement, solution generation, and overall coaching effectiveness.

Case Study 1: Mike

Mike, a Singaporean, relocated to Bangkok for a 6-month emerging leadership programme in a multinational enterprise. While facing the pressure to perform within a limited timeframe, he was also dealing with various personal and professional challenges. During the coaching session, a visual representation was created, with the left side of the drawing reflecting Mike's current situation, portraying a slightly crumpled and messy appearance. Mike realised that this actually mirrored his current reality, with many things happening at once. A dotted portrait (centre bottom) was added to symbolise it. As the coaching session continued, Mike described his desired state of emotional well-being and acknowledged his own strengths. Yet, the middle part of the drawing remained empty. I asked what if there was a stairway as a metaphor for achieving Mike's goals. However, Mike expressed uncertainty about the stairway, suggesting that it could be a downward slope instead. This conversation opened up a new perspective, leading to the ideation of confidence-building steps, such as writing positive notes, starting therapy, and engaging in more exercise (Figure 32.3).

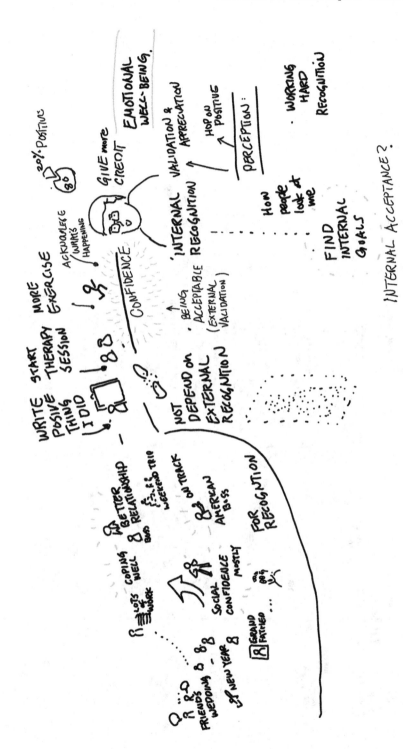

Figure 32.3 Summary of Mike's coaching session (Keisuke Taketani).

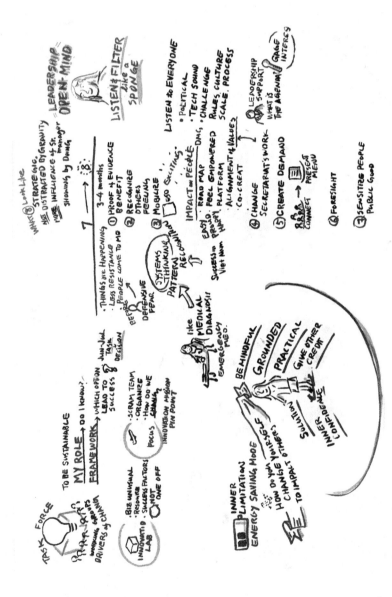

Figure 32.4 Summary of Grace's coaching session (Keisuke Taketani).

Case Study 2: Grace

Grace is a German executive in an international organisation with decades of experience in Asia. While her intellectual agility helped tackle day-to-day work, graphic coaching proved to be beneficial in providing her with clarity and focus for the long term and seeing the big picture. Grace identified openness, active listening, and filtering as key qualities from the conversation. Visualisation also served as a means to capture the multitude of ideas Grace generated. When asked the miracle question, Grace's actionable ideas flowed continuously. While coaches often take notes on paper, using visuals offered an alternative method to capture and share these ideas effectively (Figure 32.4).

Case Study 3: Aroon

Aroon embarked on his first overseas assignment in the Philippines, facing the challenges of cultural differences from his home country, Thailand, and being the only male member in his team. He desired to develop meaningful relationships with his teammates and gain a better understanding of himself and others. Visuals played a significant role in his coaching sessions, particularly when exploring the question of what it would look like when a miracle happened and he engages with his team with smooth and meaningful conversations. Aroon visualised specific situations, such as having lunch together, and posed specific questions in his mind. During this process, he delved deeper into his imagination and considered the possibility of everyone conversing in Tagalog, a language he didn't understand. This realisation prompted Aroon to recognise the need for courage in asking for translation or tuning in to the vibrational aspects of the conversation, even when he couldn't fully comprehend the words being spoken in the local language. By using visual representations, Aroon was able to explore complex concepts, such as the dynamics of team interactions and language barriers. Visuals provided a tangible means to deepen his understanding and generate actionable insights. Additionally, visuals helped Aroon capture and summarise key points, allowing for easy reference and reflection on his coaching session (Figure 32.5).

Conclusion

My journey in practicing graphic coaching within an Asian context has been an insightful exploration of bridging the art of visual thinking and the SF approach with the subtleties of Asian culture. The concept of "striving to draw like a Zen master" naturally emerged as I engaged with individuals from Asia and those navigating this diverse landscape. My aspiration is to seamlessly infuse elements of Asian culture into the artistic style, composition, and symbolism, creating a harmonious blend with the SF approach.

Figure 32.5 Summary of Aroon's session (Keisuke Taketani).

Yet, Asia's cultural diversity adds depth to this endeavour, where a single visual representation may hold different meanings for different people. For instance, the sleek bullet train signifies speed, comfort, and safety in Japan, but it may not resonate with those coming from rural villages in Vietnam where bicycles and motorcycles are the norm. Thus, it remains paramount to collaborate with clients to determine culturally relevant visual representations.

Furthermore, I've grown to appreciate that graphic coaching isn't confined solely to individual sessions but extends its power to group settings. In diverse, multicultural groups, some individuals may hesitate to voice their thoughts verbally. It is particularly applicable to Asian cultures, where indirect and ambiguous communication styles are frequently encountered. In such scenarios, the visual medium provides a shared space for active engagement, fostering a common visual language that transcends linguistic and cultural barriers.

Looking ahead, the potential for graphic coaching to enhance the practice of SF coaching is immensely exciting. I'm eager to explore the use of visual metaphors as a dynamic approach that widens the spectrum of knowing. Additionally, empowering clients to draw and reflect on themselves, rather than relying solely on the coach's drawings, offers new opportunities for growth and self-expression. By skilfully intertwining words and visuals, SF graphic coaching holds the potential to enhance the effectiveness of SF coaching, rendering it even more adaptable and influential in diverse cultural and professional contexts.

33 How Solution Focused Sales Conversations Empower Buyers

Benny Tan

Introduction

Why is a chapter about selling in a book about coaching? After all, the two practices seem to be in conflict with each other. One is more altruistic, and the other is centred on personal gains. There are differences, but both have more in common than many think. In this chapter, we'll explore the powerful effects of Solution Focused (SF) coaching in sales conversations.

If you're a sales leader or professional, you will see how this approach could increase your credibility and productivity with clients. If you're a non-sales focused coach, I will share how this approach could help you and your client reach common objectives in non-coaching situations.

The Challenges of Buying and Selling

Retail and consumer shopping have always been straightforward. Buying is now much easier, thanks to the digital economy accelerated by COVID-19. Online shopping significantly reduced the need to interact with human sellers.

Corporate buying is different. Business buyers don't shop on a whim. They seek solutions to address change that could influence or affect the entire organisation., They look towards solution providers and their sales professionals for answers.

Despite the ease of information today, buying decisions are not getting easier. Addressing change remains complex and difficult to manage. Gartner, a leading research company, reports "Customers' struggle to change decreases their ability to buy" (2020).

For many business buyers, conversations and interactions with sales professionals often disappoint, leaving them more confused and sometimes lead to ineffective decisions.

If you're a sales professional, you've probably had your share of rejections and resistance from buyers.

As a business owner, corporate buyer and a sales professional myself, I've experienced challenges on both ends of the process. I've also experienced

DOI: 10.4324/9781003431480-43

significant satisfaction from assisting my clients and collaborating with sales professionals who serve as trusted advisors.

The difference for me lies in having an SF sales conversation.

My Journey with the Solution Focused Approach

I'm a Sales Performance and Management Consultant with 35 years in corporate B2B sales, performance consulting, training, and coaching in Asia. I founded and created the Dealxpert™ Sales System and I help clients improve sales and capabilities. I have worked with multinational clients across various industries including engineering, services and technology.

In early 2023, I decided to pursue a formal accreditation programme in coaching to earn credentials for my practice in sales coaching, learn if I was doing it effectively and develop my coaching skills further.

I selected an SF coaching course by The Academy of Solution Focused Training in Singapore run by Debbie and Dave Hogan. I've known them for many years, so, deciding was easy. I wanted to learn from someone I trusted and who personified characteristics of great coaches.

The course was a revelation as I saw parallels between the SF coaching philosophy and genuine professional selling. Customer centricity, powerful questions and deep collaboration towards solutions, and leveraging existing know-how were some examples that excited me.

The SF approach is not only a powerful coaching philosophy but also has real world application in sales.

Even if you're not in sales or sales coaching, interactions with clients often veer into sales territory. These moments demand your expertise and engagement, distinguishing them from pure coaching sessions. Possessing this knowledge equips you to navigate such conversations when the need arises.

Below I explore the similarities and differences between coaching and selling, and then focus on the use of SF coaching in sales conversations.

Selling Versus Coaching: Conflict or Synergy?

The International Coaching Federation (ICF, n.d.) defines coaching as "partnering with clients in a thought-provoking and creative process that inspires them to maximise their personal and professional potential".

Coaching is inherently altruistic, focused on helping coachees achieve their goals. The coach expects no personal benefit apart from a sense of fulfilment of making a difference to the coachee. While it's undeniably a business, the act of selling isn't done while coaching. A coach's expertise lies in coaching, not selling.

Sales professionals, on the other hand, are tasked to generate revenue. Their prowess is in selling, their primary job role. Unfortunately, the perception of selling and salespeople, are often skewed, tainted by encounters with unscrupulous sellers. Yet, genuine sales professionalism aims for mutual benefits.

I define selling as "the art and science of managing and influencing perception and behaviour leading to buying decisions". It is a pursuit of mutual benefits. A sales transaction is the reward for successfully helping buyers address change.

The second part of ICF's coaching definition states, "The process of coaching often unlocks previously untapped sources of imagination, productivity and leadership" (ICF, n.d.). This is critical in an SF sales conversation.

Incorporating coaching principles in sales conversations isn't a manipulative sales tactic or an attempt to embellish the sales profession. It's an imperative for the sales profession for these reasons:

1 Both coaching and selling seek to help clients find solutions.
2 Both cater to clients seeking to navigate and adapt to change.
3 Sellers and coaches are change agents to facilitate that process.

Selling and coaching are both rooted in the success of their clients gauged by their fulfilment. Embracing the SF approach in sales dialogues ensures precise understanding and effective collaboration.

The State of Selling Today

To succeed, sales professionals need effective sales methodologies or frameworks that promote successful behaviours during the sales process.

Most have shifted from pushy and manipulative sales tactics to a client-centric consultative and solution selling approach.

"Solution Selling" refers to a seller-driven approach to package products and services as solutions to a client's complex needs instead of pitching products and features, otherwise known as "box pushing". This is particularly true in B2B deals where sales cycles are long, involve multiple stakeholders, and the sales value is high.

The rapid pace of technology has lowered entry barriers to creating new products and services resulting in breakneck innovation and relentless product evolution. Selling is now more challenging as sellers need to keep up with market knowledge and the customer's business, and familiarity with their own products.

A critical success factor in sales methodologies lies in carrying out effective sales conversations to uncover needs, address buyers' pain and convey compelling value propositions.

To my knowledge, no one has incorporated coaching philosophies and practice in their sales methodology. This is a missed opportunity that when realised, can deliver outstanding rewards.

Adding SF coaching in sales dialogues expedites solution identification. Whether or not the solution involves the seller or their products, such dialogues empower buyers, granting them a sense of ownership. It fosters better comprehension of needs while allowing sellers to refine their focus and re-prioritise.

It's a paradigm shift from seller-driven solutions towards a collaborative process, where the buyer's vision takes precedence. Here, the sales professional leverages strategic questioning to draw out the buyer's vision of possible solutions.

The end results are empowered and involved clients collaborating with sellers towards achieving their goals. This leads to a stronger, more transparent business relationship based on mutual respect and shared interests.

The Importance of Solution Ownership

The concept of ownership is pivotal in both coaching and sales. When clients are actively involved in shaping a solution, they naturally feel a greater sense of ownership, commitment, and satisfaction. This principle holds true for coaching outcomes or business solutions. A client engaged in the solution-building process, is more likely to feel invested in the outcome, leading to better long-term results and relationships.

For example, a home renovation is a complex project requiring significant time and money for an outcome you'll live with for years. You would never hand complete control to an interior designer with no input. You're involved in every step from design to colours to material to furnishing and budget. They may provide the resources, expertise, advice, workmanship and material, but it's YOUR vision they're building.

Sales conversations often break down when the seller is focused on selling or pushing their products. They miss out on an opportunity to empower buyers to take ownership, relying on their ability to persuade through other means.

Pre-requisites for Successful Sales Conversations

While coaching and selling share numerous parallels, a key distinction lies in domain expertise. Coaches often adopt a non-directive approach, guiding clients to find their own solutions. Sellers, however, must weave their domain expertise into the conversation, offering insights and advise to help clients make informed decisions. Expertise combined with an SF approach, revolutionises the sales conversation, turning it into a collaborative, value-driven discussion.

G4PS™ in Action

I developed a framework called *Filling the G4PS*™ (a play on the word GAPS) and then later added SF coaching questions to the process.

G4PS™ is an acronym for Goals, Position, Priority, Possibilities, Plan, and Solution, each an essential milestone in the conversation. Many sellers glaze over goals to hastily propose solutions, missing the chance to build a compelling business case. G4PS™ ensures crucial information milestones aren't missed.

It promotes joint exploration of possible solutions while clarifying needs and envisioning the ideal outcome. With deliberate and insightful questions, it minimises assumptions (the "not knowing" equation of SF), leverages client's know-how and fosters a strong sense of ownership.

As my expertise lies in sales performance, most of my conversations are centred around this topic primarily with senior executives of sales organisations including CEOs, Senior VPs, and Heads of Sales.

Below shows the *G4PS*™ process in action during a sales conversation when combined with SF questions with one such executive

Case Example

Dennis Ang was a new Regional Head for an industrial tech company in Southeast Asia. He was tasked to lift the business from stagnation to grow and maintain a 15–20% annual growth. Dennis just wanted a training as his team hadn't had any formal sales training for many years. My experience suggested the need and solution was more complex than that.

1 **Goals**: In coaching and selling, it is essential to first understand the client's goals. What do they want to accomplish, improve or manage, and what does success look like for them. Some useful SF questions included:

   • What aspects of sales performance do you want to address: people, process, culture, skills or something different?
   • How come this is important for you?
   • What would be a successful outcome for you for your and the team?
   • What would be some small indicators that you were on the way to that?

2 **Position**: This gauges where the client is compared to his goals,. Dennis wanted his team to improve customer engagement through better communication and presentation skills. He also wanted a sales methodology to meet the growth targets.

   The scaling tool charts the progress in the direction of the desired change and questions included:

   • Where are your team today in their progress?
   • On a scale of 1–10, with 10 representing your highest level of customer engagement you need to perform well and "0" representing no skill, where are they now?
   • How did they manage to get to that point on the scale?
   • What else is working?
   • How would you notice things moving 1 point higher on the scale?

3 **Priority**: Dennis had his long list of items to cover so we prioritised these using questions like "What area of improvement takes precedence? What's most important now? What are your top 3 priorities for this project?"

Differentiating between urgent and important items provided additional context to prioritise.

We prioritised sales process, customer engagement, and communication for immediate development.

4 **Possibilities**: This milestone explores other solution possibilities and is one of the most empowering parts of the process. Dennis initially came to me with a solution in mind. It would've been easy to say, "Ok, let's do a 3-day training focused on the 3 priorities we discussed" and send a proposal.

Instead, we expanded and further explored possibilities in three areas – the training programme, sales execution, and subsequent competency development.

- Apart from the training, what else do you think your team needs to reach the desired state?
- How can we help the team internalise what they learned?
- What do you think a future development programme will look like?
- What are your ideas as to how to go about this?
- You mentioned coaching? When do you think that would be most useful?

We expanded the scope from training to include coaching and implementing a new sales system. It is in this milestone that the seller's expertise and insights are introduced. Exploring their vision and ideas often leads to more possibilities and a sense of ownership for the outcome.

5 **Plan** and **Solution**. Once there was enough clarity on goals, priorities and possibilities ... this milestone was about articulating what the solution looks like, and developing a detailed plan including timeline and deliverables.

Dennis wanted to be involved from conducting an assessment to what goes into the training and coaching to justify this investment to his head office and this conversation helped him greatly.

The solution comprised of a tailored training programme that was highly interactive with role plays, a sales software to use and coaching to reinforce.

G4PS™ isn't a one-time exercise. It's a conversation that can occur many times through the course of a project.

Impact on the Client

The programme was well received by the sales teams and there was an openness to further development. Some of the team members have seen much improved customer engagement and attended 1 to 1 coaching to further sharpen their skills.

Cultural Reflections

When reflecting on the impact of culture on my work, the SF approach seems to work very well in the Asian cultural context. The use of the client's language is important, for example picking up on particular words that are meaningful to them and clarifying these if needed to check both the buyer and seller are on the same page.

In Asia the concept of hierarchy is also important. There is the cultural tendency to refer to the wiser expert for advice, in this case the seller's knowledge of their products. So a pre-requisite to be able to have an SF sales conversation lies in first establishing the seller's credibility and subject matter expertise.

As in all sales conversations, the 80/20 rule of 80% listening and 20% questioning / talking applies. The SF approach sees the client as the expert in their context and situation so many questions are needed for the seller to find what the client wants, where they are already and their next steps forwards in order to guide the conversation towards providing a solution tailored to their context. However, in Asia, clients do not want to be interrogated. Sometimes, they just want answers so finding a balance must be considered in the dialogue. Expertise and advice may need to be introduced earlier but contextualised to allow more clarification through coaching questions.

One of the most powerful tools of active listening in this case is in pausing and waiting until the client replies – giving them time to reflect.

Conclusion

Incorporating SF coaching principles into sales conversations is a transformative approach that empowers customers to gain clarity about their needs and envision potential solutions and outcomes.

It minimises friction, fosters trust, and opens the doors to enhanced collaboration and ownership. It's a customer centric philosophy that redefines sales as a problem-solving journey, where selling means solving.

Sellers may be experts of their products, but buyers are experts of their problems. An SF sales conversation is a powerful bridge that empowers buyers to make better buying decisions and enable sellers to deliver the best solutions.

References

Gartner (2020, August 4). 5 ways the future of B2B buying will rewrite the rules of effective selling. *Gartner*. Retrieved from: https://www.gartner.com/en/documents/3988440

International Coaching Federation (n.d.). About ICF. *International Coaching Federation*. Retrieved on 29 November 2023 from: www.coachingfederation.org/about

34 Solution Focused Coaching for Incarcerated Fathers

Edwin Choy

Introduction

This chapter outlines a Solution Focused group coaching programme used in the Singapore Prison Service to help incarcerated fathers move from a sense of shame about their past mistakes to build a life of hope for their preferred future.

This chapter outlines what is covered in the coaching group which is called I CAN CHANGE, such as constructing best hopes in many areas of their lives, scaling where they are already and creating next small steps forwards. The positive impact on the fathers and their families is described and cultural reflections on using this model within the Asian context are offered.

Background

The focus on rebuilding family relationships has been found to be effective in reducing recidivism for the incarcerated (Farmer, 2017). The I CAN Fathering course developed by Dr Ken Canfield (Centre for Fathering, n.d.) is a training course for fathers and we at the Centre for Fathering Singapore have been running this fathering training for the Singapore Prison Service since 2013. In 2022, I had the opportunity of redesigning our prison fathering training and I incorporated Solution Focused group coaching into the new design.

Now by incorporating Solution Focused coaching tools, these incarcerated fathers are building a life of hope for their preferred futures. This new redesigned Solution Focused fathering training is called "I CAN CHANGE"; CHANGE is the new acronym (see below) for the best hopes of this new course.

I CAN **CHANGE** is a training and coaching programme that empowers a struggling incarcerated father to begin his transformation to be a thriving father. This training leverages evidenced-based Solution Focused coaching and pioneering fathering research (Canfield, 2006) to help an incarcerated father to:

DOI: 10.4324/9781003431480-44

- Connect with his family
- Hope for a new future
- Aware of his strengths, success and resources
- Nurture his children
- Grow in small steps towards his new future
- Equip himself with new skills for growth.

Outline of the Sessions in the I CAN CHANGE Coaching Programme

The first session involves helping the fathers adopt a new growth mindset, one that stops focusing on past mistakes and begins focusing on future possibilities. The fathers were told at the outset that there were no bad people in the group but only good men who had made bad choices in the past. Instead, they could begin making better choices for a different future. They were then coached to explore what they wanted for their life in the future in the areas of family, work, and habits or choices.

Each father then shares their reflection. It's a glimpse of a possible new future! Everyone celebrates with a round of applause after each sharing.

The second session involves strengthening their marriage as a foundation of lasting change. We had already met up with the wives outside prison to share what their husbands will be learning. They each answered the question: "What are your best hopes for your husband and your marriage?" There is already a hopeful anticipation that something different and better is coming.

In this second session, we bring the wives into the prison for a session where they are coached to have hopeful conversations about their marriage. There were 5 marriage builder communication exercises in this 3-hour session. For each communication exercise, the couple is coached to take turns to ask their spouse Solution Focused questions which requires a response. Below is an example of a second session.

Round 1:
Husband to ask wife:

- What has been most difficult for you since we were separated?
- How did you manage to cope even though it was that difficult?

Response by husband to wife:

- I am sorry that … .
- I am impressed that …

The above is repeated with the wife asking the same questions.

The couples are coached to have such conversations both ways using Solution Focused questions such as:

- Where are we on the scale of 1–10 in our marriage if 10 is the best?
- How come we are at that number and not lower?
- What is going well despite our current situation?
- What are my best hopes for my marriage in the future?
- What difference will each of these hopes make?
- What can we do now even during incarceration that can help our marriage move up one small step on the scale?

The last communication exercise helps the couple nurture their marriage by having each list five qualities they love about their spouse and take turns in sharing with each other. This is followed by an affirmation exercise where each couple takes turns to express, in front of all the couples, what they each appreciate and love about each other. It's a celebration of their love that is hopeful and they conclude the affirmation with a warm loving hug. They are asked to share by filling in the following statements:

My dear _____,

Thank you for ... .
What I appreciate you most is ...
My best hope for us in our marriage is ... .

And I promise to ... .
I love you my dear _____. (Then give your spouse a loving hug)

Your Love,

We met with the fathers on a weekly basis. The first question they are asked to think about is: "What went well for you since we last met?" In answering this question, the fathers shared with us that the marriage builder segment in the previous week was one of the best things that happened for them. Not only were they able to spend 3 hours with their wives sitting side by side as a couple, but they also had conversations that gave meaning to their relationships.

In the third session, the fathers are coached to have a more hopeful perception of self, that is more than the labels given to them at this stage of their incarceration. They are coached to reflect on and share each of the following exercises:

a My Positive Beliefs
b I Can Be a Good Dad
c I Can Learn Life Skills
d The Real Me: six qualities I possess, four things I still have, two persons I know.

In addition, they also explore and share individually what difference each of the above will make for them.

At the end of each session, they learnt and sang the fathering theme song "The Heart of a Father." The goal is to present this song as a group of incarcerated fathers to their families. When they become more familiar with the song, they are given the responsibility of choreographing the song with meaningful actions. It will be their ideas and their creativity to convey their love for their children through their singing and actions during the grand finale.

Over the next few weeks, they learnt new skills through the I CAN CHANGE fathering training. They learnt how to connect with their children as fathers by being involved, consistent, nurturing and aware of their children. In the nurturing segment, they are coached to manage their anger better by noticing how they can be calm. They are coached to map their anger and also what they have done that helped them to calm down (Figure 34.1).

Each father then shares how they usually calm down from their anger based on their anger map. They are then coached to reflect on and share their responses to the following Solution Focused questions:

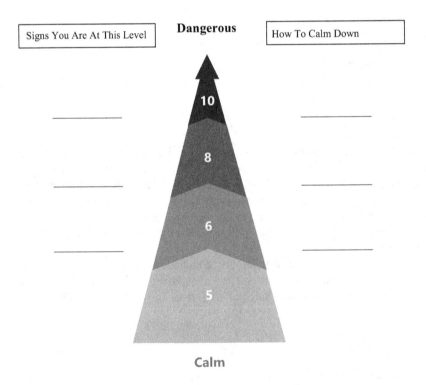

Figure 34.1 Reflection exercise: Anger map.

(Edwin Choy, Reproduced with permission from the Centre for Fathering Singapore).

- Write down a time when you managed to be calm instead of letting your anger go out of control.
- How did you manage to be calm? What was different then?

The nurturing session ends with them preparing words of affirmation for their children to be expressed personally during the grand finale which is the last open visit session for the family.

In the ninth week, the fathers are coached to envision their new future. They start by reflecting on their best hopes for their marriage, the relationship with their children, their career and health when life is at its best after they are out of incarceration. They also reflected on how these best hopes will be helpful to them. As with all the reflections they are coached to do, each father then shares what they wrote in their best hopes.

They are then coached to envision in greater detail what success would look like for each category (children, career, marriage and health) and plot where they are now on a scale of 1–10 where 10 is the best (Figure 34.2).

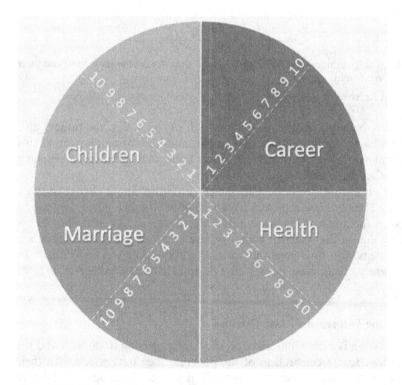

Figure 34.2 Scaling best hopes exercise.

(Edwin Choy, Reproduced with permission from the Centre for Fathering Singapore).

I Can Change (Solution Focused Change)

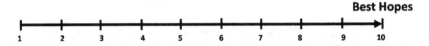

Best Hopes

1   2   3   4   5   6   7   8   9   10

I Can Change My Marriage		
Your Scale Now:	Small Steps:	Best Hopes: 10
What is going on well?	What's My Next Small Steps	My Best Hopes in my Marriage

Figure 34.3 Table summarising best hopes, where they are on the scale now and their next small steps.

(Edwin Choy, Reproduced with permission from the Centre for Fathering Singapore).

Once they have placed themselves on each of the scales, the fathers also reflect on what is going well at that number, and how come they are at this number and not lower. This increases their hope and optimism in reaching the future they have envisioned.

At the 10th session, the fathers are coached to think about change in small steps. They already have a picture of what life will be like when they are at their best in the areas of marriage, fathering, career and health. They know where they are on the scale for each of these areas currently. They now are coached to envision tiny steps they can take even while in incarceration to make progress. They then gather all this information together in a table (Figure 34.3).

Impact on the Fathers and Their Families

The 11th session is a culmination of all they are preparing to do with and for their families. It is a celebration of the progress they have made with their families since they began the programme. It is also the final open visit where the whole family including children are invited to attend. We designed family bonding activities so that these fathers can have a memorable time bonding with their children. After the bonding activities, they had 15 minutes of uninterrupted time to spend as a family.

After that, each father says the affirmation they have prepared earlier to their children in front of all the families. Each time a father affirms his child/children, everyone applauds in celebration.

For the grand finale, the fathers stood in front of their families ready to present the song they had choreographed – The Heart of a Father. Some children ran to their fathers who were singing. They prepared well and yet when they finally had to present, some fathers could not sing as they were overcome with emotion, as were some of the family members. Parting was difficult that day. From being separated and lacking in connection, these fathers now experienced how much they wanted to be with their families. It was this desire to reconnect with their families that motivated the fathers to make lasting changes. Some of them had tried to give up a substance habit but had not succeeded; however, when they thought of a child that needed them, they felt genuinely motivated to stop using. Even the mothers supported each other despite having met only through this programme.

The final session involves only the fathers and is called "Celebrating What's Right with You." When asked what went well since the last session, the fathers could not stop talking about the open visit when their families visited them for a planned family bonding event. They even suggested that the children should stand with them when the fathers sing the fathering theme song. The music and lyrics moved them and they found a powerful way to express the bond they never experienced before since coming into incarceration.

This is a time for them to celebrate their successes – the changes that took place in relation to each of their best hopes however small, the better relationships with wife and children, and the hope of a different future. This final session ends with a ceremony where the certificate of completion is awarded. Each father is given a certificate that belongs to someone else and walks up to that person, hands over the certificate, and congratulates the recipient; those watching applaud. This goes on until each father has both given and received a certificate.

One of the inmates, Joe, contacted me a few months after his release. We met up and I was so impressed by the progress he has made. He became closer to his two boys and even set up a renovation business for himself. I asked him to write a testimonial on the "I Can Change" programme for this chapter and this is what he wrote:

In the 'I Can Change' programme, I learnt that I must not focus on past mistakes. I can make choices that will have a better future. Most of all, I have learnt how important it is to have a strong bond with my family. Rebuilding lost bonding with our children is not easy. We as their father need to have more patience and understanding to let them trust us again.

I was gone when they were young. When I came back, they were all grown. Still, they are hungry for the love and concern of a dad. Now my bonding with my children is deeper than before. I am determined to be the best father for my boys.

Cultural Reflections

As I reflect on how the Solution Focused coaching approach has been helpful in this Asian context, I am amazed once again how the principles transcend cultures. As outlined in You (1997), Confucianism emphasises what is expected in our behaviour towards others. This leads to values such as the concept of honour, reverence for others, harmony, proper order in society, an awareness of what others do for us and what we should do for others. Failing this leads to shame and disconnection in relationships. The behaviour that led to incarceration brings shame to the family and fathers feel like they have lost their authority as fathers and rights as husbands. Instead, the Solution Focused approach helped them see that they are not defined by past mistakes and having a vision of a preferred future is not only possible but achievable in small steps. One father told us that through this programme, we have had "returned the responsibility of fathering back to us which was taken away when we were incarcerated."

Instead of shame, they experienced hope in their relationships. The Solution Focused group coaching focuses on what is still going well, what they love about their spouse and children, and how they can make different choices towards a better future.

References

Canfield, K. R. (2006). *The heart of a father: How you can become a dad of destiny*. Northfield Publishing.

Centre for Fathering (n.d.). I CAN fathering workshop. Retrieved on 5 December 2023 from: https://fathers.com.sg/programs/father/

Farmer, M. S. (2017). *Importance of strengthening prisoners' family ties to prevent reoffending and reduce intergenerational crime*. Ministry of Justice, UK. Retrieved from https://www.gov.uk/government/publications/importance-of-strengthening-prisoners-family-ties-to-prevent-reoffending-and-reduce-intergenerational-crime

You, Y. G. (1997). Shame and guilt mechanisms in East Asian culture. *Journal of Pastoral Care, 51*(1), 57–64.

Section 11

Final Reflections

35 The Difference That Makes a Difference

Reflections on Solution Focused Coaching in Asia

Debbie Hogan, Jane Tuomola, and Sukanya Wignaraja

Introduction

In this concluding chapter, we reflect on how Solution Focused (SF) coaching has evolved and discuss the wider impact of SF practice in Asia. In the conversation that follows, we discuss the application of SF practice in a culturally diverse context and share what motivated the editors and authors involved in this project. We end with some reflection questions for the reader to think how they will use what they have learned from this book in their own work setting.

Cultural Context

We each shared ideas about how the SF approach takes into account a client's cultural context.

Sukanya: SF practice is a way of working that remains respectful to the individual. In terms of cultural sensitivities, it's an effective way of working, whether with individuals or with groups or with organisations as a whole. SF practice, intrinsically, takes into account the many factors that influence identity and culture.

Debbie: Exactly, SF practice lends itself to being aware of the particular characteristics of the person or organisation you're involved with; it highlights the uniqueness about their identities, their culture, and their community. And we remain aware of all of those factors that influence what happens.

Jane: I agree it's all about the client's preferred future from their frame of reference. When I, as a British person, came to Singapore, I wanted to work respectfully in this cultural context because many things are different. And I found SF practice allows me to help people to bring in the balance of different factors that are meaningful to them. It might be that somebody's family culture that is much more important to explore, national culture is not even a part of the conversation, but the questions allow the client

DOI: 10.4324/9781003431480-46

to bring in what is important to them in the way that it's important to them.

Debbie: That reminds me of how I would see Insoo respond when people in training workshops would explore or ask about the impact of Asian American or Western culture. She maintained that what was more interesting and relevant for her was the individual culture which that person represented, and not necessarily their culture of origin or their country of origin; it was about the uniqueness of that individual. Even within families of one culture, there are unique cultural elements within that family, within that person and that's what we pay attention to.

Sukanya: Yes, exactly. So even when we talk about Asian culture here, it is still about the uniqueness of the individual and that is the mindset that SF coaches have. We pay attention to those very details, and we allow for that space for clients to remain true to who they are. That is what sets SF practice apart.

Debbie: Also, the way we now live and interact globally, we intersect and impact each other, constantly. For example, Singaporean culture is an amalgamation of many different cultures and peoples. So again, we're very interested and curious about that person's culture. Everybody is influenced and impacted by everyone and everything now. SF practice helps us key in on the unique factors of that one person.

Jane: What was interesting for me is that for some authors culture is a theme throughout the chapter, but for others, it isn't. One of the chapters has a metaphor about being a fish in water; i.e. when you're in the same culture as your clients, you don't necessarily see what you're doing as culturally sensitive, because you both have a shared understanding of the context so it can be hard to step back and reflect on this. So it was really interesting, almost a dichotomy of some people who said well, SF coaching just lends itself really well in this context so I am not aware of doing anything different. And other people commented in detail on specific cultural nuances and how they bring that into their work.

Applying Solution Focused Practice in Diverse Settings

From the reflections on culture, we moved on to consider how this book illustrates the use of SF coaching in a wide variety of settings.

Debbie: When we thought about the different sections in the book, and how to represent certain common themes, we realised that coaches nowadays are working across a truly diverse spectrum. Our chapters include more established areas of coaching such as executive and leadership coaching, internal coaching within organisations, team coaching, and life coaching. We also have chapters on newer applications of coaching, such as working with youth, health and wellness coaching, spiritual coaching, and sales coaching. Others, exciting areas that we had hoped to include were working with LGBTQI communities, and newer fields like financial coaching, but sadly some authors we invited were not able to contribute. The coaches demonstrated great ingenuity in finding ways of making SF coaching practice fit with their specific areas.

What Motivated People

As the conversation progressed, we reflected on what kept us and the authors motivated and focused on completing this book.

Debbie: When I think about the authors we invited to take part in this book, I realise there was a common element: a belief and passion about this project. Many could have dropped out but they stayed because they wanted to share their work and their story. This in itself intrigued me because as editors, we too had many reasons why we might have abandoned this book project: illness, trauma, experiences that would have derailed anyone. However, there's something important about wanting to share the story of how SF coaching makes a difference that kept us all going.

Jane: That's why I've loved being an editor because it is about bringing people's voices to the world that otherwise would not be heard. Most of the contributors are not in a setting where they would be writing about and publishing their work. And yet, they are doing amazingly inspiring work in such diverse areas and that's what kept me going. It is extraordinary when you consider that we all began from the same Level 1 SF coach training and yet, people have gone in such different directions. They have really made SF coaching practice their own. What I like about the book is that there are so many unique voices, completely different areas of practice, and different ways of using SF coaching. But SF remains at the heart of what they do. There's a commonality across the book and yet, everybody's got their unique flavour of how they've presented it. It's a huge testament to everybody's hard work and perseverance to keep going to shape it up into that final story.

Sukanya: I think that's the remarkable thing about the contributors; these are practitioners at different levels and in different fields and we have such rich diversity in the writing; the quality is really excellent. For many of them, this has also meant going outside of their comfort zones to produce something that will be lasting in its influence.

The Solution Focused Rumour

Debbie: Our first book, *Solution Focused Practice in Asia* (Hogan et al., 2016), was published 8 years ago. At that time, people were getting engaged with SF practice and being curious about it. The chapters in the current volume demonstrate a maturity and depth of understanding and a strong belief in SF practice as applied in coaching. A whole body of work has been developed, and they're paying that forward because it's changing not just them and how they work, but the organisations and the people that they work with and their families. It's a ripple effect. It's about the human stories that resonate with people and how all this makes a difference. This is what this book highlights.

Jane: I initially came to SF practice as a clinical psychologist so I learned Solution Focused Brief Therapy first with individuals or couples. Using SF Coaching broadens the impact beyond the individual - as this book shows it can work with groups and teams and even lead to organisational change with hundreds of people. The ripple effect created means there is an ongoing impact on the individuals, the team, the wider organisation and even families and wider network outside of work. For me, that's the big takeaway; SF coaching is so much more than an individual conversation with one person. The impact is inspiring.

Debbie: In his endorsement of our first book, *Solution Focused Practice in Asia* (Hogan et al., 2016), Harry Korman talked about Asia being infected with the SF virus. He quoted personal communication from Steve de Shazer who had said to him that 'Solution focus is a slow virus. Sometimes someone tells me that they heard about this stuff 10 years ago, didn't like it, thought it was oversimplistic and now it has eaten itself into their practice in such a way that they can't stop doing it.'

I believe that SF practice is now more than a rumour in Singapore; it has gained currency because people are hearing about it from those they trust. They could pick up any book, but it's about the people who are the carriers of the message. I think that makes a difference.

Jane: Debbie, the Academy of Solution Focused Training has been training coaches for 20 years in Asia. What's it like for you when you look back over the years and at where we are now?

Debbie: I've been reflecting on that because this is our 20th year. I would always describe myself as a little fish in a big pond and I would tell people I was very lonely in this big pond. What amazes me is that the pond is now so crowded that I can no longer call it that; I might describe it as an ocean. What has happened here in Singapore and spread across Asia is the very vastness of that ocean. There are thousands of practitioners – who knows what will flow from their work and interest. I'm struck by the natural growth and development of something that is bigger than any one of us. It's a mission or a cause. We are all in this because it is about people development. And I am in awe because I'm now a small fish in a vast ocean.

Debbie: I'm curious also, Jane and Sukanya, to hear your thoughts because you've been involved in it for almost from the beginning. What are your thoughts on where it's all headed?

Jane: When I first got to Singapore, coming from a completely different cultural context in the UK, I wanted to be culturally sensitive in the work that I did. I would go to therapy training courses and would ask how this worked in Asia, and what was the same or different. People would seem baffled by my questions. Culture wasn't really on the same radar then that it is now. Since then books on many different therapeutic approaches in the Asian context have been written. I like that people are aware and respect that we need to take culture into consideration and that with this project, we are adding to this. I love the Thai phrase 'Same same but different.' For me it sums up our book. You can read every chapter and see that most of what is written about would work anywhere in the world. Yet there are some particular nuances to pay attention to, depending on where you are. And for me, being part of that journey of putting this on the map of expanding the application of SF coaching is important.

Sukanya: I also came to SF practice as a therapist 15 years ago. And what I find truly remarkable is how this way of working is so easily transferable from therapy to coaching. This is what sets SF practice apart from so many other modalities. And our book highlights this isomorphic quality of SF practice across many different areas. It's a seamless transition. It's extraordinary when you see it happening; whether in life coaching, in organisations, or working with young people. It's the same set of principles and beliefs and the mindset of the coach.

Debbie: As you spoke, the word that came to my mind is isomorphic. I agree that it's one of the most unique things about SF practice. It has to do with how we think about change mechanism and our influence. It is not simply a technique.

Hopes for Our Readers

Concluding our reflections, we took a moment to think about our hopes for how this book impacts our readers.

Jane: There are areas where I have both professional and personal expertise, but I've never done career coaching for example. Reading those chapters made me realise how many similarities there are and made me believe that I could do this also. So that is my hope for our readers that they understand this way of seeing the world and the change process can be applied in many sectors where you do not need to have expert subject knowledge. I am hoping our readers are inspired to bring SF coaching to new areas. Also, for example, those coming from a healthcare background who may not want to become fully trained coaches could be inspired by reading how using SF coaching tools in their medical settings could benefit their clients.

Debbie: It defies the belief that one must be a subject matter expert in order to be able to work in any kind of arena. SF practice teaches us that we bring expertise in a different way, and we can work in a variety of settings that may be new to us, because the focus is not on being an expert of that landscape, but it's two people coming together and really working collaboratively to bring about the desired changes, or to bring about the vision of the other person. So, it's less about expertise in content and in material, but more about how you work well together and inspire others.

Sukanya: My best hope is that it opens up possibilities for them. I think that's also what SF is about. It opens your mind to new possibilities, new ways of thinking. And I think with this book we are offering our readers exactly that: the opportunity to think differently.

Debbie: Compared to a laborious, problem-solving, problem-focused, energy-zapping paradigm, I notice that when people catch a little glimpse of the difference that SF coaching offers, there's almost a spark or a smile or raised eyebrows as if to say, that's interesting … tell me more. And that's my hope, to inspire people to learn a little bit more and be curious about interacting with some of these ideas to see what difference it makes, because we hope that it's a difference that makes a difference.

Sukanya: That's a really good catch phrase. The difference that makes a difference.

Reflections and Next Steps for the Reader

We end this chapter with some questions for our readers to reflect on.

What inspired you from reading this book?
What difference might it make for your work?
What are your wow moments/realisations?
How might you take these ideas forward in your work?
What is your next small step to build on what you have learned?

Reference

Hogan, D., Hogan, D., Tuomola, J., & Yeo, A. (2016). *Solution focused practice in Asia*. Routledge.

Index

Note: *Italicised* and **bold** page numbers refer to figures and tables.

242–243; possibilities 247–248;
strengths 247–248; timeline reframe
245, *245*, *246*
VUCA (volatility, uncertainty,
complexity, ambiguity) 116

Walker, C. R. 154
Watanabe, T. 85
Wisdom of the Geese 110–113

Wittgenstein, L. 15, 17
wrapping up the session 8

Yeo, A. 112
You, Y. G. 276
youth coaching 12, 164–166

Zheng, W. 185
Zhou, L. 161

Printed in the United States
by Baker & Taylor Publisher Services